BURTON

Other books by Penny Junor
Diana Princess of Wales
Margaret Thatcher
Babyware

BURTON

THE MAN BEHIND THE MYTH

PENNY JUNOR

SIDGWICK & JACKSON
LONDON

First published in Great Britain in 1985 by Sidgwick & Jackson Limited

Copyright © 1985 Penny Junor

ISBN 0-283-99104-6

Printed in Great Britain by
The Garden City Press Limited, Letchworth, Hertfordshire
for Sidgwick & Jackson Limited
1 Tavistock Chambers, Bloomsbury Way
London WC1A 2SG

Contents

List of Plates

Richard Burton as a young man (*Camera Press*)
The cast of *Youth at the Helm* (*Robert Hardy*)
The Druid's Rest (*John Vickers*)
Emlyn Williams and Richard (*Emlyn Williams*)
Filming *The Last Days of Dolwyn* (*Emlyn Williams*)
Richard and Sybil (*John Topham Picture Library*)
The Boy with a Cart (*Popperfoto*)
A Phoenix Too Frequent (*Christopher Fry*)
Richard with Dic Bach (*BBC Hulton Picture Library*)
In the Miners Arms (*BBC Hulton Picture Library*)
Richard in Pontrhydyfen (*BBC Hulton Picture Library*)
Burton as Hamlet, 1953 (*Robert Hardy*)
Burton with Claire Bloom (*John Topham Picture Library*)
Burton as Sir Toby Belch (*Robert Hardy*)
Burton in *King John* (*Robert Hardy*)
Burton with Zena Walker in *Henry V* (*Angus McBean*)
Burton with Rosemary Harris in *Othello* (*Angus McBean*)
Richard and Sybil (*Rex Features*)
Richard reading (*Camera Press: photo Tom Blau*)
Richard in Celigny (*Camera Press: photo Bob Penn*)
Burton as Jimmy Porter (*Camera Press*)
Richard alone (*Rex Features*)
Burton as Mark Antony (*Camera Press: photo Bob Penn*)
Richard with Sybil and Kate (*John Topham Picture Library*)
Richard with Elizabeth Taylor (*Sheran Hornby*)
Burton in Gielgud's *Hamlet* (*Rex Features*)

Acknowledgments

This book could never have been written without the kindness and generosity of so many people who gave up time to talk to me about Richard Burton, and their friendships and experiences with him. I am deeply grateful to them all, and in particular to Lady Baker, Christopher Fry, Sir John Gielgud, Robert Hardy, Sheran Hornby and Emlyn Williams, all of whom were pestered more than most, and to Frank Hauser for kind permission to copy his letter from Richard.

Also to Dennis Bowden-Williams and Arthur Colburn who introduced me to so many people in Port Talbot and made my visit to South Wales such a treat.

Special thanks also to my family and children, and to Jack in particular, who, for the first four months of his life, had to compete with a word processor for my attention.

Very many thanks also to Margaret Willes, who pulled the manuscript into shape. One could not hope for a better editor. I am lastly grateful to Diana Korchein for her help in researching the pictures for this book.

Of the many books I have read and referred to on the subject, the following were particularly helpful and my thanks to their authors and publishers:

Richard Burton by Fergus Cashin (W.H. Allen, 1982)
Richard Burton by Paul Ferris (Weidenfeld & Nicolson, 1981)
The Street where I live by Alan Jay Lerner (W. W. Norton & Company, 1978)
John Gielgud directs Richard Burton in Hamlet by Richard Sterne (Heinemann, 1968)

To Jack, who else?

The author and publisher wish to thank the following for permission to quote:

J.M. Dent & Sons Limited, *Under Milk Wood* by Dylan Thomas
The *Sunday Telegraph*, review of the film *Cleopatra* by Philip Oakes
The Washington Post, editorial entitled *Slings and Arrows*
New York Herald Tribune, review of *Hamlet* by Walter Kerr
William Heinemann Limited, *Meeting Mrs Jenkins* and *A Christmas Story* by
   Richard Burton
Newsweek Inc, review of *Hamlet*
David Lewin, interview in the *Sunday Mirror*

1

Boy from the Valleys

Richard Burton was in his element. He had a captive audience, a drink in hand, and he was warming to his theme. Suddenly the actor Robert Hardy broke the spell. He was an old friend, and well used to his stories. 'Come off it Richard,' he said, 'that's not what happened.'

Burton rounded on him with sudden fury. 'Never forget,' he boomed, 'we are the myth makers.'

Myths abounded, and those he did not create from his own experiences, he borrowed from others. He used friends' stories, friends' experiences, even friends' relatives, and wove them into his own past.

Sunbathing aboard the Burtons' yacht off Naples, while his host gave an interview to a journalist from *Cosmopolitan*, Stanley Baker heard Richard tell a story about his father, a one-legged miner.

'That's not your father,' said Baker indignantly, 'that's my father.'

'What does it matter whose father it is?' said Burton and went on with the interview.

He never did see how it could have mattered, or why his friend was so upset.

Throughout his life, from his humble beginnings in Wales to his latter days as superstar, Richard Burton's regard for the truth, and his ability to face up to the reality of life, were very slight. The truth was never as palatable as fantasy, fact never as much fun as fiction. And so he entertained. Even as a child he entertained; he had a remarkable ability to hold people's attention, and make them believe everything he told them, to wring every emotion possible from them. What it took to make them react, what story he told, was neither here nor there. The fact that they should laugh, gasp, recoil or even cry, was all that mattered.

And although he will be remembered for many things: for his voice – that deep, rich Welsh; for his magnetism; for his much publicized marriages; for his affairs, perhaps; and even for his drinking; those people who knew him well will remember him for his stories. They were outrageous, hilarious, and frequently repetitive, but they were a way of life, and whether he had an audience of two or two thousand he had a compulsion to hold court, and people were entranced.

There was one story in particular that he never tired of telling. It was the day of the Grand National and in Pontrhydyfen his old grandfather, whose only means of getting about was in a wheelchair, had backed the winner. So, Grandfather, with his winnings in his hand, was wheeled off by his son down the hill to the village pub where they had a mighty celebration. At closing time, both men in good voice, they had set off for home, Richard's father laboriously pushing the chair back up the hill again. As he reached the house, he let go of the chair for a second to open up the front gate, but when he turned round to push it through, he saw the chair careering back down the hill with Grandfather egging it on with cries of 'Come on Black Sambo, come on Black Sambo,' until he was silenced by a brick wall at the bottom. 'And you wouldn't have known him!' Richard would finish triumphantly.

It was told as a funny story, but behind the laughter lay the roots of a deeper and darker side to Richard Burton, and a fear which was to remain with him throughout his life. To understand this, indeed to understand anything about the man, one must go back to the coal-mining valleys of South Wales where he was born; valleys filled with song and poetry and beer. Men worked hard, drank hard and played hard, and boys grew up in the expectation of a lifetime in the dark, dusty pits.

Richard was not born Richard Burton; the name came later. He was born Richard Walter Jenkins, on 10 November 1925, a miner's son, the twelfth child. His birthplace was the small village of Pontrhydyfen, a thriving community in those days before the surrounding pits were closed, four miles up the valley from the industrial seaside town of Port Talbot. His father, affectionately known as Dic Bach (Little Dick), for he stood not much more than five feet high, had lived there all his life. A good-looking man, he had a finely sculpted face, high cheekbones and wide eyes, which Richard inherited. He had worked the coal-face for many years, and was something of a character in the village, known to everyone as a bit of a rascal who drank too much, partied too much and told a good tale over a dozen pints in the Miners Arms.

It was generally agreed that his wife Edith, who, like many of the womenfolk, did not drink and was a good chapel-going soul, had a difficult time with her husband. The old folk in the village still speak of her with great admiration. She was a small pretty woman, with deep-set eyes and fair curly hair; a woman who was always cheerful, always coped, who ran a clean house and looked after her brood well, but who was driven into the ground with the sheer exhaustion of childbirth and child-rearing. In addition to the cooking, cleaning, scrubbing, darning and washing for her own family, she took in laundry for other people to supplement the family income. It was no secret that a fair proportion of Dic Bach's wages from the pit found their way each week into the till of the Miners Arms and into those of other favoured hostelries around.

Writing a portrait of Christmas in the 1920s for the *Daily Mail* many years later, Richard introduced more than a hint of the real Dic Bach:

The man stood in the doorway of the clean, bare, poor kitchen. He was short, muscularly obese, swaying, moustachioed, smiling with the inanity of those who know they have sinned, and with absolute knowledge that whatever he did, short of homicide, suicide, infanticide, genocide or rape, he would be forgiven.

For a God in whom he did not believe had given him wit and intelligence, a rough masculine beauty, and charm. And the greatest of these three shall always be the last, and he had buffooned himself out of a multitude of insane predicaments, blackmailed and bullied and beguiled black impasses into nonchalant muscle-bound struts down sunlit cols.

Anyway, there he stood, having crashed open the kitchen door, and looked with great and immensely drunken benevolence at his large family – the beautiful mother, the tot, the toddlers, the elder boys, the eldest girl, ranging in age from thirteen down to the tot.

He smiled hugely and sang as he hugely smiled that they should 'forgive and forget all the troubles we've met. . .'.

The assembled family, having waited in agony for days for him to come home with the pay, tried desperately, warned by their mother beforehand, to look stricken or helpless or pitiful or reproachful or contemptuous or sorrowed or sorrowing or downright bloody nasty.

But the great smile, the black twinkling eyes, the unforgetful voice were hard to withstand, and slowly the faces began to break. . . .

The wage packet had gone forever, poured down his throat, and it would be a black Christmas.

The man had had yet one more of his legendary earth-tremoring benders, and on this one he must have found his bed in chicken coops for the feathered evidence was still about him.

Life in the mining communities of South Wales in the 1920s was tough and there were black Christmases. Children grew up in the knowledge that when their schooldays came to an end, they would follow in their parents' footsteps: daughters would find good husbands and bear them babies; sons would follow their fathers down the pits. The alternative was the steel works or the tin plate works in Port Talbot. The number of miners' children that moved out of the area or out of the industry was small, and few even dreamed of it. The mines were man's work, and the boys of the Rhondda Valley were nothing if not real men.

As Richard later wrote in *A Christmas Story*, for all young boys at that time:

the ambition for the walk of the miners in corduroy trousers, with yorks under the knees to stop the loose coal running down into your boots and the rats from running up inside your trousers and biting your belly (or worse), and the lamp in the cap on the head, and the bandy, muscle-bound strut of the lords of the coalface. There was the ambition to be one of those blue-scarred boys at the street corner on Saturday night with a half a crown in the pocket and, secure in numbers, whistle at the girls who lived in the residential area. The doctor's, the lawyer's, the headmaster's daughter.

But whatever the hardships, whatever the deprivations, the mining community looked after itself. No family went hungry, and no family went cold. There were families in the valleys with children who had no shoes to wear, in the desperately poor communities like the Goitre, a couple of miles away, but not in Pontrhydyfen. The women worked around the clock, the men spilled into the pubs on their way home of an evening – and consuming fifteen pints after a full shift underground was not uncommon (nor enough to incapacitate them). The old men, whose working days underground were over, sat around on chairs in the streets telling stories; and the children roamed the hills, taunted their elders, teased the opposite sex. Everyone's entertainment, for young and old, was largely self-made.

The one exception was the Chapel. The puritan influence of the Chapel ran far and deep but, despite the strict teachings, the Baptist faith brought music and poetry flooding into the hills, and into the hearts and souls of every man, woman and child living in them. Chapel was not a solemn place. Chapel was a meeting place, a social get-together, where the minister had to call for silence before he could begin, and where the first dramatic chords on the organ gave the cue for what everyone in the congregation had been waiting for: the chance to sing; and to sing, not like self-conscious Anglicans, afraid of the sound of their own voices, but loudly and lustily.

Non-believers were few and far between, and many a non-believer went to Chapel in any case just for the singing. Richard's father, however, didn't believe in God, and didn't go to chapel. As Richard later said of him, 'He didn't believe in anything, least of all himself.'

Dic Bach Jenkins and his wife, Edith Thomas, were married on Christmas Eve, 1900. He was twenty-four, and already mining, like his father before him; she was just seventeen and, although she had been born in Swansea, her family had moved to the Avan Valley, where her father worked in the copper works. By the time she married, Edith was working as a barmaid in the Miners Arms in Pontrhydyfen.

Children arrived fast and furiously. The eldest, Thomas, was born in 1901, next came Cecilia in 1905, Ifor in 1906, William in 1911, David in 1914, Verdun in 1916, Hilda in 1918, Catherine in 1921, Edith in 1922, and two daughters between Ifor and William who had died in infancy. So, by the time Richard appeared in 1925, his mother had given birth to twelve children. Richard was born at home, in No. 2 Dan-y-bont, a house the family had moved to a few months earlier, that still stands in the shadow of the vast viaduct sweeping into the village from Port Talbot. It is a stretch of that winding road known as the Bends between Pontrhydyfen and Port Talbot, which Richard later came to describe as the most beautiful he had encountered in all the world.

By all accounts Edith's twelfth child doted on his mother. Like many a toddler he followed her everywhere and was utterly distraught if she left his sight for a moment. But the relationship was short-lived. In October 1927, two weeks before Richard's second birthday, his mother gave birth to her thirteenth and last child, another boy, called Graham, and a few days later died from complications arising from the birth.

The family was suddenly deprived of its core; and none felt the loss and the dramatic change that Edith's death brought about more than Richard. Dic Bach, never a responsible man at the best of times, was unable to cope with the two youngest boys, and so they were taken under the wing of the elder members of the family. Graham, the baby, went to live with Tom, the first born, now twenty-six, a miner, married, and living in Cwmavon, a couple of miles down the valley. Richard was taken off to live with his eldest sister, twenty-two-year-old Cecilia, and her husband Elfed James, also a coalminer, in Taibach, a district of Port Talbot. They had no children of their own at the time so, from a house bustling with the noise of four brothers and three sisters still under one roof, two-year-old Richie, as everyone called him, had to adjust to a very different life with a mother substitute half the age of the one he had lost. Cecilia says that, despite his earlier passion for his mother, once he had come to live in Port Talbot, he never cried for her, and never mentioned her name again.

Cecilia was a striking looking young woman, capable and down-to-earth like her mother, with great patience and warmth. She adored her little brother, and became the total mother substitute, although Richard never called her such. She was Cis or Cissie to him, her husband was Elfed, and there was never any confusion in his mind as to their relationship. But in every other respect he was brought up as their own child.

When Richard first arrived in Port Talbot he spoke no English, only Welsh. Cis and Elfed were then sharing a house in Caradoc Street with Elfed's sister, Margaret Dummer and her family, and, although he soon learned to speak English too, Richard never forgot his Welsh, and in fact spoke Welsh to Mrs Dummer, whom he knew as Aunty, until the day she died.

The Dummers had one child at that time, a son called Dillwyn, almost the same age as Richie, and the two grew up like brothers. For six years the two families lived together, and the two boys were never separated. If one was ill, the other would share his bed to try to catch the disease too. They shared a pair of roller skates, shared a bicycle, and shared dozens of relatives. Elfed's parents and assorted aunts and uncles were all living within a stone's throw and were, in fact, distantly related to the Jenkinses of Pontrhydyfen. Cis and Elfed's maternal grandmothers had been sisters. And so, in moving away from his immediate clan up the valley, Richard was in no way a lost soul in a sea of strangers. He was, moreover, a frequent visitor to the assorted Jenkins households back home, and family from Pontrhydyfen likewise came to call from time to time on the James family to catch up on gossip of a Sunday afternoon.

The driving force in the Dummer family was Mrs Dummer senior, 'Grandma' to both Dillwyn and Richard, who lived in the next door house in Caradoc Street, and was an omnipresent figure in everyone's lives. She was a devout Chapel-goer and a strict disciplinarian, and the children lived in awe of her. Dillwyn's father gave Dillwyn a good hiding often enough, and Elfed would mete out the same to Richie if they were caught misbehaving, but Grandma Dummer's punishments were worse. If she found they had been telling lies, she would hold their hands on the hot iron grate of the fire.

The small coal fire in the front room was the only source of heat in those little terraced houses in Caradoc Street. A big steel kettle sat constantly on the hob, bread was baked in the oven below, and the families took it in turns to stand up to warm their backsides. In winter it was bitterly cold, even in the room with the fire; the bedrooms were like ice-boxes, and condensation frequently ran down the inside of the window panes. In later life Richard would talk about the misery of being cold, as he was as a child, and if there was one thing he did with his wealth, it was to make certain that he was never cold like that again.

The one commodity that was in plentiful supply was coal, which came from the local mine and was delivered, a ton at a time, by horse and cart. It would be dumped in a pile outside the front doors of the houses, and it would then be down to the children and their friends to carry the coal in buckets through the house, along the narrow little hall and out the back into the yard where it was stored. It was hard work, and the boys ended up black from head to toe, but were never paid for the job.

Another job that fell to Richard was scrubbing potatoes for his Aunty Edith – Edith Evans, Elfed's married sister, who kept a fish and chip shop nearby. He would sit out in the backyard, chattering away, surrounded by pounds of potatoes and buckets full of water, and his payment at the end of it all was a good helping of chips wrapped up in the daily paper. He was a great talker even then, and he used to tell Edith that when he grew up he was going to be a preacher, a writer or an actor. He was a good-looking little boy, with dark tousled hair, bright blue eyes, and a dimple in his chin which made him look disarmingly angelic. And he knew how to charm his elders.

The family didn't have much money, but everyone ate well. They lived on simple fare: sausages, faggots, pies, cheap cuts of meat, and nothing was wasted. Today's boiled hock of ham would go into tomorrow's pea soup. What meat they had was bulked out with plenty of boiled potatoes and bread, or turned into a thick filling broth like Cawl, a traditional Welsh dish made out of lamb chops, with leeks and other vegetables. Another traditional dish was Lava Bread, not a bread at all, but a dish made from seaweed, and a distinctly acquired taste. Richard called it 'Colliers' Caviar' and, although in later life he could and did eat the genuine article frequently, he always secretly preferred Lava Bread; just as, for all the exotic food he ate in the top restaurants throughout the world, he loved nothing quite so much as sausages and mash or tripe and onions.

Tea and Sop was the usual breakfast fare; again, a concoction that turned cheap ingredients into a filling, warming and nutritious meal. It was made with bread, condensed milk, and tea, all mixed together into a kind of porridge. Bread was a staple, to be dunked into the gravy to make a meal go further; while between meals children would go out into the street to play clutching great hunks of bread with jam and occasionally butter on them too.

There was not much money, and once Cissie and Elfed had moved into their own house, No. 27 Caradoc Street at the end of the row, they took in a lodger to help make ends meet. The lodger was called Elliot, who in time took the house next door and turned it into a small grocery and sweet shop. It was Mr Elliot's son, Tommy, that Richard later wrote about in his account of Christmas:

There was the breathless guessing at what Santa Claus would bring. Would it be a farm with pigs in a sty, and ducks on a metal pond, and five-barred gates, and metal trees, and Kentucky fences, and a horse or two, and several cows, and a tiny bucket and a milk-maid, and a farmhouse complete with red-faced farmer and wife in the window? And a chimney on top? Pray God it wasn't Tommy Elliot's farm, which I'd played with for two years and which I feared – from glances and whispers that I'd caught between my sister and Mrs Elliot – was going to be cleaned up and bought for me for Christmas. It would be shameful to have a secondhand present. Everybody would know. It must be, if a farm at all, a spanking-new one, gleaming with fresh paint, with not a sign of the leaden base showing through.

He did not, as it happened, get either a new farm or Tommy Elliot's farm that Christmas. His present was a niece, Cissie's first child. With the coming of their own children, Elfed and Cecilia's funds were even more stretched than before. Yet, despite the hardship, Cissie was always cheerful and never remotely resentful at having to provide for her brother. Elfed was a generous soul too, and although Richie exasperated him frequently, and earned the back of his hand on countless occasions, he brought him up as his own, and provided him with as much as he could afford. They ran a clean, God-fearing home. Neither of them drank, both attended Chapel regularly, and they were generally liked and respected by everyone who knew them.

There was no electric lighting in the houses in Caradoc Street in those days, and not one inside lavatory the entire length of the row. The houses were lit by gas lamps. Baths were taken in a tin tub, filled with hot water boiled up on the stove. The closest any household came to carpet was coarse coconut matting; most families, the Dummers and the Jameses included, covered the flagstone floors with sand which they carried home from the beach, and swept out daily. It served the dual purpose of making the floors warm while keeping them clean.

The street was divided into three distinct sections: lower, middle and upper, and each section had a separate gang of children who roamed together and fought the opposition at every available opportunity. Richie, like Dillwyn, belonged to the gang in upper Caradoc Street, by virtue of the fact that their houses were at the top end of the street. There were no houses opposite the Jameses at that time, although an entire row was later built. No. 27 overlooked a steep open hillside, down which the children used to slide on tin trays in the winter time, scramble over, and camp out on in summer. Nowadays the whole place is changed. The M4 motorway runs straight through the heart of Port Talbot, set high above the town on tall concrete pillars, and the hillside, after which the district was commonly known as The Side, where Richie Jenkins and his gang roamed is now cut off from Taibach. The only compensation is that London, once a twelve-hour marathon by car, is now barely four hours away.

In the 1920s and 30s London might have been a foreign land. It was certainly not a place that any child from Caradoc Street thought about, far less visited. Life was very insular. Holidays were outings organized by the Chapel to resorts further along the coast, when everyone packed into a coach in the early morning and returned home again, tired, tousled and salty, at the end of the day. No one had cars; if they wanted to go anywhere, they walked. The sight of men walking four miles or more to the pits at either end of the day was not unusual. It was the only way to get to work; and, indeed, the sound of wooden clogs on the streets was a familiar noise to wake up to, and one that heralded the return of the menfolk in the evening.

There was, of course, a railway that ran through Port Talbot, but not many people from Caradoc Street travelled on it; not as fare-paying passengers anyway. The children used to get a ride occasionally. The tracks ran past Cissie's house at the end of the row, and Richie and Dillwyn and their friends would jump over the fence, and if they knew the engine driver they would get a free trip down to the docks, where they swam in the summer time, or went fishing.

For the people in Taibach the railway was another source of employment for a lucky few. The signalman, sitting up in the old wooden signal box day after day, vigilantly waiting to let the trains safely through, used regularly to cut the children's hair – including Richie Jenkins'. The road to the signal box, and the station itself, ran alongside the churchyard, and many were the times, at four or five in the morning, when the engine drivers and firemen would be walking to clock on for work, and would be scared half to death when their hats were mysteriously lifted from their heads by little boys with poles, hiding behind the wall to the graveyard. They in turn would scare themselves half to death, tripping over tombstones as they made good their escape in the pitch dark.

When he was five years old, Richard began school at Eastern Infants in The Side, the nearest primary school, just round the corner from Elfed's house, attended by all the children from the neighbourhood. At the age of eight girls and boys were split up, and the boys packed off to the boys' school, a short walk down the road from the infant block. The classes were vast by modern standards: fifty children to a class was not unusual, but discipline was infinitely better. While children indulged in all manner of devilish pranks out of school, and were duly beaten were they discovered, they grew up with a very healthy respect for adults in authority, induced partially, no doubt, by the *mores* of the Chapel, and, quite simply, the fashion of the time.

Thus, while by the age of eight Richie Jenkins may have been an accomplished smoker, and have acquired something of a taste for beer, he had also learned to read quite fluently, and had fallen under the spell of a master, the first of two who were to shape the course of his life. Meredith Jones, who taught the scholarship class at the boys' school, was 'quick-thinking and quick-talking', as Richard later described him, 'to the point of brilliance. He was all electricity, sparkling and flashing: his pyrotechnical arguments would occasionally short-circuit but they were never out of power.' He was a powerful personality, remembered vividly in Taibach today. A dedicated and inspired teacher, he had two abiding passions: rugby football and English, and passed his love of both on to Richard. It was he who founded the Taibach Youth Club where Richie, at fifteen, acquired his first real taste for the stage. It was he who turned Richard's skill with a ball, crudely learned on the street, into a recognizable game. And it was he who coached the eager eleven-year-old through his scholarship exam and so on to the Port Talbot Secondary School; and, four years later, paved the way for Richard to be re-admitted to the school.

The 'Sec' was one of two grammar schools in Port Talbot at that time. The 'County' was the other, and there was great rivalry between the two; they referred to one another as 'County Bulldogs', and 'Secondary Cabbages'. As a 'Secondary Cabbage' Richard encountered the second schoolmaster who was to play a major role in his life.

The young Richard Jenkins was always a bright boy, but never a swot. He was as much of a trouble-maker as anyone, although by comparison with today's standards, the trouble children made was mild. Mild or not, however, he was never keen to own up to anything. Dillwyn was usually the one who took the blame for joint escapades that misfired, because from a very tender age the young Jenkins could adeptly lie his way out of any situation. As Dillwyn who twinkles to this day like a naughty eight-year-old, says:

> Richie was an actor all his life. He'd always say 'Dillwyn did it, Grandma', and I'd have it.
>
> There used to be a man who lived in a big house called Mr Church, and he had a belt with a great buckle four inches thick that he used to hammer us with if he caught us misbehaving. Just for fun we'd go and bang on his door; then we'd start running, and sometimes he'd be waiting for us round the corner, and wallop us with his belt. Then I'd go home and my father would say, 'What's the matter with your ear then?', and I'd say, 'Oh, I walked into a wall.' If I had told him what really happened, I'd have had a good hiding. But then Richie would come in and say, 'Ah, Mr Church hit him today,' and I'd get another hammering.

It was not often they were caught red-handed, but on one occasion there was no passing the buck. Most of the children in the street spent Saturday afternoons at the local cinema, known to all and sundry as the Cach, or shithouse, built in the 1930s when the magic world of talking movies arrived. Previously children had spent their Saturday afternoons watching slide shows at the Gibeon Chapel, which everyone knew as the 'Magic Lantern'. It had been the scene of a famous riot in the 1920s, when one half of the congregation turned on the other half brandishing umbrellas, and beat their fellow-worshippers with such violence that the police had to be called to restore order. The outcome was that a second chapel was built across the road so that the two factions could continue to worship without fear for their lives.

The Cach was built between the two chapels, and seeing a film there was the high spot of the weekend. The cinema was run by an old boy called Bertie Roberts who did his best to keep order. He evidently saw it as his role to keep the insect life at bay too. He could be seen at a Saturday matinee frantically striding up and down the aisles administering a liberal dose of insecticide with a large spray gun. (He said it was perfume, but they knew it was insecticide.) Another of his tasks was to stop children leaving in the middle of a film, because light from outside flooded in whenever the door was opened and disturbed everyone else. So he would bar the exit with a great stick, and if the film happened to be a love story, which Richard and Dillwyn, like most of the little boys, loathed, there was no escape.

Admission was twopence in those days, and the two boys usually had to cadge the money from their parents, plus a few extra pennies, if they were lucky, officially to be spent on sweets from Katie David's little corner shop. The one day when no cadging was required was when Dillwyn's baby sister was born (at home in the upstairs room, as most babies were in that part of the world), and the family wanted him out of the house for a while. That day there was no shortage of pennies for the shop.

Only Richard and Dillwyn didn't normally spend their money on lemon sherbets or lollipops like the other children. They bought cigarettes – five Woodbine in a pack for three ha'pence, and a box of matches, which they would get through during the course of the film, puffing away in the back of the stalls. Needless to say, both boys would have been skinned alive if their parents had ever discovered. So, if they happened to have any cigarettes left over when the time came to go, they grudgingly threw the remainder over the wooden bridge so that no one was ever the wiser.

13

One night, however, rather than throw the last precious Woodbine away, they decided to smoke it on the way home. But they had already jettisoned their matches. 'Never mind,' said Richie, then all of eight years old, 'there's a chap coming up there; go and ask him for a light.' So Dillwyn duly did as he was told. 'Got a light, mister?' he asked as the figure loomed up to him in the darkness.

'I've got a light, yes,' said a horribly familiar voice; and his father delivered the first good hiding that Dillwyn ever remembers having for something that he (rather than Richard) had actually done.

Their smoking days had got off to an inauspicious start. Dillwyn's grandfather was a pipe smoker and had a rack of pipes, which the boys were often asked to take to the old man. One day they pinched one which still had the remains of some tobacco in it, and stole away up the hill to a large rock in Mrs Moss's field above the houses, where they had pitched a tent. And there they began on the dregs of the pipe, until they could no longer see each other for the smoke. Both boys staggered back home that day a lurid shade of green.

It wasn't only Grandpa Dummer's pipe that turned them green. One of their favourite pastimes was to go to visit Tom Francis, a strange old boy who kept pigs for Mrs Thomas, and who lived rough in a shed next to the animals. He ate what the pigs ate, brewed foul-tasting tea in old tin cans, and made his own tobacco from dry leaves and herbs. But the boys loved sitting around talking to Tom Francis, drinking his filthy tea, and would spend hours with him. Once when Tom went off to feed his pigs, Richard and Dillwyn pinched some of his leaves, rolled them up in ordinary paper, lit up, and simultaneously turned green.

They acquired a taste for beer, on the other hand, with no ill effects whatsoever. They would frequently be sent off to the pub round the corner to buy some beer or some cider for their parents, usually taking a jug which the barmaid would fill up for them to carry home. And not all of it went home. Or they would go to the window of the off-licence, the Jug and Bottle, and Richard, putting on the deepest voice he could muster, would ask for a flagon. Sometimes he would be lucky, sometimes he would be sent packing.

If the two boys were going to be caught out, the day of reckoning, once the Dummers and the Jameses were living in separate houses, would always be a Sunday. The families would get together and compare notes, and this was when Richard and Dillwyn's accounts of what had happened during the week didn't always tally. If they didn't, the boys would be taken quietly aside by their fathers – Elfed in Richard's case – and punished; not so much for having done the deed, whatever it was, but for having lied about it. The result was that Richard learned to be even more adept in the art of pulling the wool over everyone's eyes.

Old Grandma Dummer, for instance, never knew that the reason Richie was so keen to play hymns on her piano was because he was playing the piano in the pub in the evenings, and she was the only person he knew with a piano on which he could practise. And although he wasn't playing 'Onward Christian Soldiers' in the pub, practising hymns and improving his touch was better than not practising at all.

Although Richard had won a scholarship to the 'Sec', during the course of his four years in the school, he channelled most of his energy into sport: rugby, and, to a lesser extent, cricket. He also auditioned for the school plays, not so much because he had a burning ambition to be an actor, but because the people in the play were generally regarded as a cut above the rest, and he liked, even then, to be the centre of attention.

This is how he first encountered Philip Burton, the school's senior English master, who was known for the work he had produced for radio, and for a theatre company that he ran locally; therefore quite an impressive figure in the pupils' eyes. But if Richard was impressed by Burton, Burton was not noticeably impressed by Richard; and the first time he auditioned for a part in a play, he failed to be chosen. It was in Richard's fourth year, in January 1941, aged fifteen, when he finally came to be chosen for the small part of Mr Vanhatten in a production of *The Apple Cart* by George Bernard Shaw. Setting foot on the boards for the first time in his life was not an earth-shattering occasion, and he was not singled out as a 'natural'; but given that Mr Vanhatten was an American, and that Richard spoke with a heavy and unmistakable Welsh accent, which no amount of long 'a's could disguise, it was not surprising.

At much the same time his teachers at the 'Sec' were drawing the conclusion that Richard Jenkins was not going to be a 'natural' scholar either. It was wartime, Cis and Elfed now had two daughters to clothe and feed, and Elfed realized that instead of wasting time in a classroom, getting nowhere very special, Richard could be out at work, bringing in an extra wage to help the household.

Elfed's young brother-in-law had been a handful as a small boy, but now that he was an adolescent he was increasingly difficult to handle. He was spending money quite openly on cigarettes and beer, borrowing from Cis's housekeeping allowance to take girls to a dance or to the pub, then being unable to pay her back. He was turning into a rough, tough, miner's son, and he and Elfed began to clash. There were family rows. Cis would try to protect her brother, but it made matters worse. The School Certificate Examination was looming up in June; she wanted him to stay on long enough at least to take that. Elfed wanted him to leave straight away. His father could pull strings in the local Co-operative Stores to get him fixed up with a job, at a time when jobs were hard enough to come by. And so it was done. Richard stayed at school until the end of the spring term, and in April he hung up his school cap, and went to work. He had no qualifications, and seemed set for life as an unremarkable nine-to-five employee in Port Talbot.

By chance, however, this was the very time when Richard's former scholarship class teacher from Eastern Boys, Meredith Jones, was embarking on a revolutionary scheme to open a youth club in Taibach. His partner in the venture was the local county councillor, Alderman Llewellyn Heycock, who had managed to prise funds for the club from the Glamorgan Education Authority. The man he recruited to take charge of drama at the club was Leo Lloyd; and it was these three men who first inspired Richard to better himself, to aim for something higher in life than employment at the Co-op, and who, each in their own way, gave him the means.

Before these men came along, there had been nothing for young people in Taibach. There was the Cach, a snooker hall, and plenty of pubs, of course, but nowhere for them to belong, nowhere they could meet their friends, have a go at new activities, be introduced to new ideas, discover the Arts, look further than their own stunted horizons. As Meredith Jones frequently used to proclaim in Welsh, 'My members are not cultured and refined – yet – but they're "here" and they're "alive".'

The 'club house' was the Eastern Elementary School, a condemned building with a leaking roof and dim gas lighting, inadequately warmed by coal fires. It was wartime, equipment and facilities were in short supply, but they made do. Richard, Trevor George, and Gerwyn Williams (who afterwards became a Welsh Rugby International) even managed to have boxing contests with the club's one and only pair of boxing gloves shared between them. They opened a canteen – despite rationing – with a little unofficial help from the American Forces stationed nearby at Margam Castle. And a lot of time and energy was spent in the dusty roof timbers, mending the blinds which had to be drawn over the skylight during the blackout each night.

The first time the club held a 'parents' evening', their first public performance, the lights failed and, while everyone sat waiting for the fire service to come and rig up some temporary lighting, Richard and Trevor George leapt onto the stage and entertained the audience with their impersonations of Hitler and Mussolini, scantily lit with a torch and a couple of candles.

Leo Lloyd had cast Richard as the lead in his first dramatic production, the part of the Convict in *The Bishop's Candlesticks*, which was to be done in mime. It was a one-act play adapted from Victor Hugo's *Les Misérables*. Rehearsals had gone well and the first night was looming close, when Leo asked Meredith what he had in mind for a stage. Meredith, who could be put off by nothing, paused for a second's thought, and said, 'We've got some tables and blackboards and we can use the desks.' Thus, with some bricks shoring up the blackboards to compensate for the slope of the desk tops, a stage was rigged up. What they hadn't allowed for in this cunning construction, however, was the weight of the actors pounding about; the first performance was scarcely under way when movement from above started to work the bricks loose, which in turn sent the blackboards springing up in the actors' faces. As quick as a flash, Tommy Lane forsook his debut as one of the Gendarmes and, grabbing some other hefty recruits, disappeared underneath the stage. Putting their hands on their knees, they took the weight of the blackboards, and the actors striding about on top, on their backs. And the show went on.

This was the show, in fact, which first made Richard think of acting as a possible career. He had taken the job that Elfed's father had

17

managed to arrange for him, and was working as an outfitter's apprentice in the men's clothing department at the Co-op. He hated it. For a miner's son in a tough mining community, a rugby player, a boxer, it was the ultimate indignity; and Richard responded accordingly. He grew belligerent and resentful. He was not much good at the job: taking a couple of hours over a local delivery, for example; chatting to friends and relatives who came into the shop; or forgetting to take the wartime clothing coupons from customers; so that his employers were beginning to reconsider their wisdom in taking him on. At home he became more and more fractious, smoking, drinking in pubs (although still under age) with rough town lads. The one benefit derived from his months in the Co-op was a knowledge of how to fold a suit professionally. In later years, if ever he saw anyone folding a suit any other way, he would show them how it was done. In every other respect the ten months he spent behind a shop counter, folding bills and money into a little tin canister that shot across the ceiling to the accounts department, were entirely wasted.

Ten months was all he spent there, however. The three men at the youth club were working together to give him a new future. Whenever Richard was asked in later years what were the most far-reaching influences of his life, or what made him opt for a stage career, he would always cite these three men:

Meredith Jones with his breath-taking effrontery and his eloquent and dazzling generalisations, hurled and swept me into the ambition to be something other than a thirty-bob-a-week outfitter's apprentice.

The Alderman, the County Councillor, the Chairman of the Glamorgan Education Committee, provided the means. Llewellyn Heycock used his wide powers to have me re-admitted to the Grammar School after ten months' absence – in those days, and perhaps these, an unprecedented act.

Leo Lloyd, eyes gleaming, monastically devoted to his job – it is difficult for me to realise it was all done during his spare time – focussed the ambition. He persuaded me that acting was infinitely fascinating. He taught me the fundamentals of the job: to stand and move and talk on the stage with confidence. He taught me unsparingly and I learned quickly. He taught me discipline and he taught me, by influence, and from his own devotion to the craft, that 'reality' can be greater on the stage than off. He taught me the power of the spoken word and the rudiments of its use. He channelled my discontent and made me want to be an actor.

It didn't happen overnight. But by August 1941, Richard had a firm notion that he was going to go somewhere in life; and recognized that the route via which any boy of no means could leave the valleys was education. His new-found ambition was enormous. The rough, tough, wild fifteen-year-old, looking and behaving far older than his years, holding his own with the working young men of the town, had to don a school cap and go back to school. The humiliation was something Richard never forgot. It was one of the hardest things he ever did in his life.

It had taken some persuading on the part of both Meredith and Llewellyn for Port Talbot Secondary School to accept him. His ten months in the Co-op had done his reputation no good at all, and, while his old headmaster knew that there was potential in the young Jenkins, he also knew that four years in the school the first time around had done little to bring it out. He was unhappy about taking him on again, but the school governors were persuaded – Llewellyn Heycock was, after all, Chairman of Glamorgan Education Committee and had some clout in such matters. Meredith, as one of the finest teachers at the Eastern School, was also someone whose judgment commanded respect.

There was one further voice of assent. In April 1941, Philip H. Burton, the English teacher from the 'Sec', became commanding officer of the newly-founded local cadet force, No. 499 Port Talbot Squadron of the Air Training Corps. Meredith Jones, who was always one of the first to offer his services in working with young people, became a flight officer and coached the squadron rugby team. He brought a lot of his youth club members into the squadron, Richard amongst them. Since he could no longer play rugby at school, this was an ideal opportunity to carry on with the sport; in addition there were weekly drill evenings at the squadron headquarters in the County School, where he learnt the rudiments of airforce training.

Thus when Llewellyn Heycock was working on the Secondary School governors to try to secure re-admission for R.W. Jenkins, Meredith was able to enlist Philip Burton as an ally. Philip had cast

Richard in a radio play he wrote about the ATC, called *Venture, Adventure* (the Corps' motto), and agreed with Meredith that, although he was prone to being somewhat wild and unruly, he had potential. He promised his flight officer that he would keep an eye on the boy when he returned to the school, to ensure that he did not become a bad influence on the other pupils.

Philip Burton was a bachelor of thirty-eight; a rather solitary man, who had been a schoolmaster all his life, teaching first mathematics, then English, yet who nurtured a love of the theatre, and devoted all his spare time to it. He was somewhat eccentric, lived in lodgings run by a lady called 'Ma' Smith, and, although extremely well read and very highly thought of by his colleagues, he was always regarded as something of an odd fish. His accent was almost pure English, with just a touch of Welsh about the vowels, which was seen as a bit of an affectation for a miner's son from the mining town of Mountain Ash, not twenty miles away.

This was not entirely fair since both his parents were English immigrants. Philip had been born to them late in life and, like a lot of elderly parents who have young children, they brought him up in a somewhat precious atmosphere, forbidding him the pleasures and rough and tumble of street life that had so filled Richard's childhood. English was his only tongue and, although he learned Welsh at school, he never learned the colloquial language that the other children spoke, so he was never easily accepted as one of them. A further difference separated him from his peers: religion. His parents were Anglican, while the vast majority of the community were Methodist Chapel-goers. In an age when most of the activities in the community arose from the Chapel, this was a serious handicap.

When Philip was just fourteen his father was killed in a mining accident, and thereafter he was brought up by his mother, who had none of the intellectual agility of her son. Nevertheless, she was devoted to the boy and eager to see him do well. And well he did. After school in Mountain Ash he went on to the University of Wales at Cardiff, where he won a double honours degree in pure mathematics and history: In 1925, at the age of twenty, he took up a teaching post at the Port Talbot Secondary School.

His time at university, when he spent a lot of time in the theatres in Cardiff, had only served to convince him that English was the subject he really enjoyed, and in particular its application in the theatre. But the theatre was not the sort of work a miner's son with a mother to support could take on. It was far too precarious. Teaching was a safe and a respectable profession, and although Philip Burton later switched from teaching maths to English, it was to be many, many years before he made the break from teaching altogether, and went to work full-time for the BBC in Cardiff.

Burton never married, nor had girlfriends worth noting. His lonely childhood had turned him into a very private person. He kept himself to himself. What is certain, however, is that having no children of his own through whom he could try to live his thwarted ambition, he sought out potential candidates from the boys he taught.

One such protégé was a boy called Owen Jones, who, thanks to Philip Burton's grooming, had won an open scholarship to the Royal Academy of Dramatic Art, one of the leading drama schools in London. From there he had gone on to play Shakespeare at the Old Vic, with a very promising career ahead of him, until it was interrupted by the war. He was subsequently injured during service in the RAF, and died in 1943.

The fact that Philip Burton had taken this working-class Glamorganshire schoolboy under his wing with such fabulous results was common knowledge by the time Richard was reinstalled at the 'Sec'. There had been others, too, that he had singled out and promised great things to, but whose parents had intervened. Not only was the English teacher the local celebrity, as indeed he had been when Richard was first in the school; he was now a potential passport out of the valleys.

Richard Jenkins was quick to see the opportunity and to take advantage of it. He made a play for the teacher's attention. He had an engaging personality, and he knew how to use his charms. He went out of his way to make certain that Philip Burton noticed him. He would stay behind after class to ask questions about work, to discuss a piece of poetry or a passage from Shakespeare. He wangled the rota by which senior boys and masters took turns in firewatching duty, so that the two of them were on patrol in the school the same night, and could talk. On one occasion he told the older man that he cherished a secret ambition to be an actor. Could the teacher perhaps give him a few hints? On another he confided that life at home was difficult; that his mother was dead, he lived with his sister, and did not get on with her husband. Little by little he sowed the seeds which he knew might bear fruit.

Philip Burton took the bait. Richard had all the makings of a successful protégé. As Philip said later, 'I was fascinated by him. I thought he had incredible potential and great need.' And so, one day, he invited Richard to go home for tea with him after school, thus beginning a unique relationship. They would sit over tea day after day in 'Ma' Smith's front room, with books spread out on the table before them, as the teacher began the awesome job of rounding off the edges of his raw recruit and preparing him for a worthwhile future.

The future he saw for Richard – the future he would have liked for himself – was as a classical stage actor, and there was no way any company would take on someone who spoke as Richard did. The voice was strong, but the accent could have been cut with a knife; and it was no easy task to change it. There were not many 'standard' English voices around, after all, for Richard to copy, and he later said that these sessions with Philip Burton had made up 'the most painful and hard-working period of my entire life'. The voice was not all. He had to learn breathing, delivery and movement, and many other skills that an actor needs for his trade. At the same time there was the more immediate hurdle of the School Certificate examinations looming up at the end of the year, so still more time had to be found for school work.

Not many months after these sessions had begun, a room fell vacant at 'Ma' Smith's house. She took in several lodgers, and early in 1943 one of them was called up for military service. Believing that Richard was unhappy at home, which was not strictly accurate, but the impression, nevertheless, that his protégé had quite deliberately given him, Philip Burton suggested that Richard might like to move into the house. Richard was delighted by the idea. Burton went to talk to Cissie and Elfed about taking the boy into his care, and the matter was resolved.

Although such an arrangement may sound strange today, the circumstances in which it arose, in the light of the poverty and uncertainty in which they were all living in Port Talbot in 1943, made it less bizarre at the time. Philip Burton was a professional man and, as such, highly respectable. Cissie and Elfed were awed and grateful that someone of Philip Burton's standing should take such an interest in Richie and be prepared to offer him such a chance in life. They were also quite relieved to be free of the extra person to feed, clothe and generally provide for. No sooner had Elfed managed to get Richard out of the classroom to do a little bread-winning, than he had been back behind a school desk again, cadging money from his sister for beer and cigarettes, and placing a considerable strain on their meagre income.

So, in March 1943, Richard moved out of No. 27 Caradoc Street and went to live in the vacant room at 'Ma' Smith's. He was delighted with his achievement. The coaching continued, school continued, and activities at the Air Training Corps continued, and Richard basked in the kudos of having being singled out by the great Philip H. Burton. He was on his way. But if he thought it was going to be an easy route, he was mistaken. His patron proved a hard task-master – pedantic, didactic, precise – and demanded as much from his pupil.

Burton cast Richard in two plays he was producing that year, *Glorious Gallows*, performed at the school, and *Youth at the Helm*, an ATC production to raise money for the Corps. Private rehearsals went on until late at night in the front room, as Burton worked to extract perfection. If it was not one of these plays, it would be Shakespeare; long passages, heroic monologues, that Richard would have to deliver time and again.

Although there was a lot of work to do on his voice, which the teacher described as 'raspy and uncontrolled, with no range', there was nothing he could teach him about poetry. Richard had a natural feel for it, as many of the Welsh have. The chapels are full of music and poetry, and he had grown up with a profound and lasting love of both which gave him endless pleasure throughout his life. He had an instinctive flair for language too, and in this period of intensive coaching and study he inherited Philip Burton's passion for Shake-speare.

As Richard's final year at the 'Sec' drew towards its end, and the cramming for the School Certificate eased off with the exams taken, Philip Burton turned his mind to the future. What next for his protégé? The theatre was the ultimate goal, but first, university. Having been there himself, he was convinced that, no matter what one wanted to do in life, there was no substitute for a university educa-

tion, no social equalizer quite like a degree, and the more prestigious the university, the better. There was no question in his mind
that Richard had the ability to get there, as the results of his School
Certificate exams confirmed. He had passed in seven subjects, to
'matriculation' standard, which meant that, provided he could find
a university that would offer him a place, he would be assured
entry. The only difficulty would be paying for it. Unless Richard
won a scholarship, the fees would have to come out of Burton's
own pocket; there was no way the Jenkinses or the Jameses would
be able to find the funds; and, although he earned a little extra with
his occasional broadcasting, it was wartime and Burton was not a
rich man.

But while the war brought few enough advantages, it did provide
Richard Jenkins with one that coloured his entire life. Towards the
end of the war the RAF was running a recruiting scheme for would-
be young airmen, offering a short university course at Oxford or
Cambridge to likely candidates. Most of them were recruited from
the Air Training Corps squadrons based around the country and, as
commanding officer of 499 Squadron, Philip Burton was in a
strong position to choose which candidates were put forward.

It was a unique opportunity. If Philip Burton could have chosen a
university for his protégé from all the universities in Britain, he
would have chosen one of these two – the ones that he would have
liked to have attended himself. And here was the chance, not only of
going to university, but of being paid to do so. It was an oportu-
nity that could not be missed and could not be wasted. Academically,
there was no problem; socially, there was. For all his new-found
polish, on paper Richard Jenkins was still a working-class coalminer's son and in 1943 class barriers were still a force to be
reckoned with. There was very little social mobility, and Richard's
humble background would not impress an RAF selection board. If,
on the other hand, he were the son of a schoolmaster. . . .

Philip Burton put forward the idea of adopting Richard, giving
him his name, and turning their current situation into a legal and
permanent father-son arrangement. Richard was quick to see the
advantages. He was keen to secure a place at university whatever
the cost, and the cost of giving up his surname seemed negligible.
Jenkins was a very common name in the valleys anyway; it was no
hardship to lose it, whereas Burton had distinction.

This time it was necessary to get Dic Bach's approval, because in the eyes of the law he was still his son's legal guardian. Nothing had been drawn up to give Elfed that status, despite the fact that he had brought up his brother-in-law as his own son, and paid for his upkeep out of his own pocket, for the past sixteen years. Yet, appropriately the matter was first raised with Cis and Elfed, and they agreed, as did the rest of the family after a little misgiving in some quarters, that it was for the best.

By a quirk of fate, however, Philip Burton was twenty-one days too young to be able to adopt Richard. The legal minimum between adoptive parent and child was twenty-one years, and he fell just short of it. The only alternative option was for him to make Richard his ward, binding only while the boy was a minor (at that time until the age of twenty-one). The legal document subsequently drawn up, nevertheless, gave Richard the schoolmaster's surname, and was to all intents and purposes an agreement of adoption. It gave Philip Burton uncontrolled custody of Richard, and the obligation to clothe, feed and educate him. In return his ward would 'absolutely renounce and abandon the use of the surname of the parent and shall bear and use the surname of the adopter and shall be held out to the world and in all respects treated as if he were in fact the child of the adopter'.

Philip Burton organized all this without ever meeting Dic Bach. He never went up to Pontrhydyfen to talk it through with the old miner. Someone else took him the document to sign. He was an amiable man; he loved his son and he was pleased if he was doing well, but he didn't have much real interest in his life. Dic Bach was wrapped up in his own world, his pet whippets and his drinking companions. The theatre was as alien to him as Mars, and talk of university equally meaningless.

Thus on 17 December 1943, a month after his eighteenth birthday, Richard Jenkins took on a new name, the name that was going to take him out of the Rhondda Valley, away from the pits and the poverty, and to Oxford University.

2

The Perfect Part

In August 1943, while Oxford was still to Richard just a city of dreaming spires, and he was awaiting the results of his School Certificate exams to come through, a small advertisement in the local paper caught Philip Burton's eye. Emlyn Williams, it said, was seeking Welsh actors and actresses, including 'a Welsh boy actor', for a new play he had written, due to open in London in the autumn. The play was a comedy, *The Druid's Rest*, and was being produced by H.M. Tennent, one of the big West End theatre managements. It was the chance of a lifetime.

Burton wrote off straightaway putting Richard's name forward. He was the boy's schoolmaster, he explained, and had directed him in a number of amateur productions, in which his pupil had shown great promise. In due course he had a reply inviting Richard to audition in Cardiff. Richard and Philip arrived together, and found the place alive with hopeful applicants and ambitious parents eager to put their offspring on the stage. In charge of weeding out the possibles from the no-hopers was a young woman called Daphne Rye, casting director for H.M. Tennent; and it was she who first spotted talent in the pock-marked face of seventeen-year-old Richard Jenkins.

He looked slightly spivvish at that time. He wore his dark curly hair slicked-down, and his adolescent body was ungainly. But his face looked as if it had been sculpted, with high cheek-bones, a perfect mouth, and eyes that held the attention of anyone they fixed upon.

Once Daphne Rye had whittled the numbers down, Emlyn Williams interviewed the remaining candidates one evening in the Sandringham Hotel. After a dismal procession of 'no-goods', Emlyn remembers Philip Burton coming into the room and introducing himself as the schoolmaster who had written in about his pupil. He beckoned to Richard, who stepped forward to meet the playwright, and fixed him with wide blue eyes. He was a remarkably striking boy, despite the bad skin, and well aware how attractive people found him – both men and women. Emlyn was instantly impressed. 'A boy of seventeen, of startling beauty and quiet intelligence. He looked – as very special human beings tend to look at that age – he looked . . . imperishable.'

He started to chat to Richard and ask him what he had done in the theatre; and to Emlyn's everlasting delight, in an accent as thick as the Margam Hills, Richard explained that he had just finished playing Professor Higgins (the professor of linguistics who sets out to teach a Cockney flowergirl to speak perfect English) in G.B. Shaw's *Pygmalion*.

Fortunately *The Druid's Rest* was set in Wales, so the strong Welsh accent was a positive asset, and Richard was given a part. He was told to report to the Haymarket Theatre in London for rehearsals in October; the play was to begin touring the provinces in November and come into the West End two months later. Richard went home to 'Ma' Smith's that night feeling fifteen feet tall. He was on his way.

Another boy who went home from those auditions in Cardiff with a future secured was a fifteen-year-old called Stanley Baker, who had also been chosen for a part in *The Druid's Rest*. Coincidentally, he too was a miner's son who had been taken under the wing of a kindly schoolmaster in much the same way as Richard; and, indeed, Emlyn Williams had also been the beneficiary of a schoolteacher's patronage. Both Richard and Stanley were somewhat daunted by London initially, both away from home for the first time, both very green and very Welsh, and they were drawn to one another, to a friendship which, despite the occasional falling-out, lasted for the rest of their lives.

Emlyn was well pleased in his choice of Richard. He noticed from the very first rehearsal that Burton had a quality on stage which was very rare: an ability to draw attention to himself by not claiming it; by being very still. Offstage, he was a little reserved, obviously conscious of his accent and of the need to work on it, but he was never shy. He could hold his own quite adequately with the rest of the company and was not cowed by their seniority. On one occasion, as Richard was walking away from rehearsals with a book in his hand, Emlyn asked what he was reading. 'Dylan Thomas,' he replied. 'He is a great poet'; and suddenly he stood still and began to recite, 'They shall have stars at elbow and foot . . .' in a rich, deep voice that echoed into the darkness of Upper St Martin's Lane.

When rehearsals were over, the company set off on tour. By this time the greenness had departed, and Richard and Stanley, with no real adult supervision, were living fast and loose, sharing digs together in the various cities they played to, drinking too much, and pursuing girls with mixed success. One morning Richard came boasting to Stanley about his conquest of their landlady. 'I've had her,' he said. 'Last night I had her in front of the fire, and in the middle I felt as though my feet were on fire and I thought I must be in hell. Then I realized that I was too close to the fire and my socks were burning.' Stanley, just sixteen to Richard's eighteen, was mightily impressed, and believed the story implicitly for twenty years or more until Burton finally admitted he had made it up.

In Nottingham he was talking to a group of young miners in the pub. One of the group was a teenager from Derbyshire called John Dexter, who was interested in the theatre; he later became a director and worked on several occasions with Burton. John said he was about to go off and do military service. 'Tell them you're a homosexual,' advised Richard, evidently expert in means of dodging the draft. 'Tell them you've got V.D.'

Yet, back in Port Talbot, his own papers for admission to the armed forces were complete, and he was only too pleased to have been accepted. Richard Burton, as he now was, would be expected to enroll at Exeter College, Oxford, in April 1944 for a six-month course, combining English, which was the subject he had chosen to read, with intensive RAF training. There would be no academic qualification at the end of it, merely the hope that the recruits would return to the university after the war and take a degree in the proper way.

It was a strange time to be at Oxford. Because of the war, those people who would have gone to university soon after school had gone into the services instead, so the vast majority of the student population was much older than the normal undergraduate. The exceptions were those students on service short courses, like Richard, or young servicemen who had been invalided out. Nevertheless, in 1944 Oxford was still a bastion of the middle and upper classes: the public school fraternity, who talked alike, thought alike and came from similar privileged backgrounds; and when Burton arrived in the place he might have been a foreigner. He had precious little in common with any of them. He also had precious little time for any of them. He referred to them as 'toffs' and, at least in the early days while he found his feet, sought the company of other ex-grammar school students, particularly those whose accent resembled his own. He even found someone from his own town, a girl called Bunny Evans, with whom he spent a lot of time in the early days.

But it was not long before he found his feet, and thence his way to the hub of dramatic activity in the university. By good fortune his tutor was Nevill Coghill, a Fellow in English Literature, director of OUDS, the Oxford University Dramatic Society, and a man already much respected for his work in the theatre. Coghill took a great shine to the young Burton, both as a person and as an actor. He later said of his career, 'I have had only two men of genius to teach – W.H. Auden and Richard Burton. When they happen one cannot mistake them.'

Richard's handsome masculinity was not lost on his fellow students. He was a magnet for both men and women, and would hold groups spell-bound in any one of the pubs in the city, while he told stories of home, of his hard-drinking, coal-hewing family, his exotic ancestors whose origins changed with every telling; or he recited Shakespeare. Shakespeare was his passion and he knew many passages by heart; and respected anyone else who did. It was this common interest that forged a friendship with one of the greatest 'toffs' on the course, Tim Hardy, who later became the actor Robert Hardy, and remained a close friend throughout his life.

They were both at a meeting of the newly-founded Experimental Theatre Club in Oxford. Thirty or forty people were crammed into a little room and were arguing the toss about who was going to direct the forthcoming production of *The Dark Beneath the Skin*. Various names were put forward by a series of speakers, fresh from the playing fields of Eton, when a sudden scraping of furniture stilled the room, and an alien figure rose to his feet from behind an upright piano in the corner – dark, pock-marked, rough. 'If you want this play directed properly,' he said in a deep, developed voice that had everyone frozen to their chairs, 'I'll get you the best director in the country.' Then after a suitably dramatic pause, he added, 'My father', and sat down.

'Who is this father of yours who's so marvellous?' asked Tim Hardy a little later in the day as they pored over a navigation map. 'Has one heard of his name?'

'He's not my father,' replied Richard, 'he's my adoptive father. My father's a Welsh miner.'

Immediately fascinated by each other, they talked on, and Tim told Richard that he was going to be an actor.

'What do you know about Shakespeare?' Richard asked.

'That's my subject,' said Tim, 'and when I come back after the war, I will major in it.'

'Any thoughts about *Henry IV Parts 1 and 2*?'

'They're just the greatest plays ever written,' said Tim.

'Right!' exclaimed Richard, and the friendship was sealed.

It was a rare alliance. Richard didn't have many friends at Oxford. He was always the centre of attention at a party, always someone that other people wanted to be with, but not many of them were allowed to get close. He performed for them: he told stories, he sang Welsh songs, he drank daring amounts of beer, he wooed women with extravagant poetry, and never ever left a group without some shocking or humorous exit line.

His drinking capacity was well known in the university. It was a means of staking his claim in an alien environment, and it became something of a challenge to his fellow undergraduates, none of whom could even begin to hold the same amount without becoming drunk. Beer appeared to have no adverse effect on Richard whatsoever. So, on one occasion someone spiked his pint with a generous measure of clean wood alcohol from the laboratories. The effect was devastating. He rocked on his feet, his eyes glazed over, and he fell head over heels down a steep flight of stairs, landing heavily on the base of his neck at the bottom. This misguided student prank, aggravated by various blows received on the rugby field, was the beginning of a back problem which gave him pain with increasing severity for the rest of his life.

Financially Richard was able to keep pace with his companions at Oxford. No one had very much money to spend but, having earned a little from the theatre already, he was better off than some. Tim Hardy one day asked if he might borrow a hundred pounds from him to go to Paris for the weekend. He obliged, but gave Tim the money in twenty £5 cheques. In case he did not spend it all, explained his friend, he would find uncashed cheques easier to pay back.

Nevill Coghill staged one major production with OUDS each year, and in 1944 it was Shakespeare's *Measure for Measure*, which was already fully cast when Burton approached his tutor for a part. Coghill would have liked to use the newcomer, ideally as Angelo, but having already given the part to someone else, found it impossible to change. He did suggest, however, that Richard understudy the character, which would at least get him in to rehearsals, and if the lead went off sick or there were any other problems, he would have a chance to play.

Richard attended the rehearsals assiduously and, as luck would have it, the undergraduate he was understudying did go sick, so frequently in the course of the run-up to the opening that he had to pull out of the production altogether, and left the way free for Richard, who stepped, word perfect, into his shoes. He gave a performance of Angelo that was seen by a number of impresarios up from London, and talked about by succeeding members of OUDS for years to come.

He played the part with extraordinary power. As always, he was rather wooden and bow-legged in the way he moved. Never a graceful actor, he constantly gave the impression of looking for some mark on the stage where he should be to deliver the lines. Having assumed his position, however, he then spoke with astonishing passion and fire, which transfixed his audience. *Measure for Measure* was staged in the quadrangle of one of the colleges, and in the course of an impassioned speech, Burton clawed the stone arcade at one corner of the quad with such force that the soft Oxfordshire stone crumbled under his fingers, and a piece of it fell into his eye. This was obviously very painful, and the eye wept profusely, streaking the make-up on his face, but he played on without faltering.

Burton was the envy of all his fellow recruits. Not only did

Coghill get permission from the commandant of the University Air Squadron for him to be released from a good deal of RAF drill training, he also secured permission for him to grow his hair long for the part, while the rest of the boys were subjected to a weekly 'short back and sides' whether they liked it or not.

Richard was in no doubt by this time that the stage was where his career lay, but he did not like his friends to think he was taking it too seriously. He always felt it would diminish his intellectual standing. When he first met John Dexter at Nottingham, he had said that acting was all very well, but he was going to university, that was the important thing. Now that he was at university, he would say, 'I want to be able to turn it on and off like a tap.'

He told one friend that he thought Tim Hardy would be a better actor than he ever would, yet for some reason he considered him ill-suited for the theatre, and saw it as his mission to dissuade him. He invited Tim down to Wales one weekend. Philip Burton, he said, wanted to meet him; to give him some advice about the business.

The two friends travelled down by train, and no sooner had they arrived than Phil, as Richard called him, took them off to the BBC in Cardiff, saying that he was going to give Tim an audition. He sat him down in front of a microphone in a small sound-proof room, gave Tim various scripts and asked him to read them. Hardy was under no illusions about himself, and his voice, he recalls, sounded 'like a desperately juvenile John Gielgud'.

'Right, thank you,' said Phil Burton's disembodied voice from the control room. Moments later he appeared. 'Well, it's no good,' he said. 'You've got a very, very, dull, dull English voice. There's no music in it – nothing to recommend it. I really can't recommend . . .'

Suddenly he was interrupted by a voice from a corner of the studio saying, 'Philip?'

'Yes, Aneurin', said Burton, and a man called Aneurin Abtalleron Davis came forward to meet them, a great doyen of the Welsh speaking genre.

'I heard what you just said, Philip, and I must beg leave to disagree. I was listening and I heard one of the subtlest voices I've heard in a long time.'

'Oh well, I suppose there may be some possibilities,' conceded Burton grudgingly. 'Anyway, your name: Tim. Tim Hardy. It's like calling a pussy cat under a table: Timothy, Tim, Tim, Tim, Tim. Have you got any other names?'

'Certainly,' said Tim.

'What?'

'Robert.'

'Yes,' said Burton, obviously mulling it over in his head. 'Robert Hardy; rather good.'

So Tim went away and changed his signature, changed his name at the bank and on his passport, and that very day became Robert Hardy. And he is convinced to this day that it was a set-up planned by Richard to put him off the idea of going into the theatre which, had it not been for Aneurin Abtalleron Davis, might well have worked.

When their six months at Oxford were over, the short-course recruits were sent off to RAF Babbacombe, a base on the south coast near Torquay, for a couple of months of further training. Filling in the student record cards, Nevill Coghill wrote of Burton, 'This boy is a genius and will be a great actor. He is outstandingly handsome and robust, very masculine and with deep inward fire, and extremely reserved.'

As at Oxford, a large proportion of the squadron were ex-public school who kept very much to themselves and excluded anyone they thought socially inferior. Burton presented them with a problem. He was clearly from a very different background, and made no pretence about it, and yet he was such good company and so self-possessed that they liked being with him. So they invented a background for him. They gave him a public school, Blundles, and they christened him Burton of Blundles, and as such he became one of them.

He had an aura of one in command. He had established a reputation for himself at Oxford as the personality to be reckoned with: the rugby-playing, Welsh-speaking lyricist, who could drink anyone under the table, woo any girl and flout any rule. And he quickly established himself as such in his new home too. While everyone else shared sleeping accommodation, he somehow managed to secure the only single room for himself, and he used it to entertain at night. One night he very nearly put paid to his airborne career. He came rushing up to Robert Hardy, ashen-faced and panic-stricken, and said he must talk, the most ghastly thing had happened. The following day Burton was taken out of line on parade and marched off by a very grave-looking Corporal Barker, normally a cheerful man and one of Richard's greatest fans. Everyone, including Richard, was convinced he was going to be court-martialled; but he talked his way out of it and the incident blew over. He never did admit precisely what he had been caught doing, but it was widely assumed that he had been entertaining the wife of one of the senior officers.

Richard directed his first play while he was at Babbacombe. He put on a production of *Youth at the Helm,* the play in which Philip Burton had directed him for the Air Training Corps the year before, and he cast his friend Robert in the leading role. He gave himself the small part of janitor, which he played with a blacked-out tooth. But everyone knew that he was a professional actor, and his reputation as a raconteur held good. He never failed to deliver. One day two hundred men or more were sitting in a hall waiting for a visiting lecturer to arrive. Time passed and there was no sign of him, and the men, growing tired of waiting, began to chant for Burton. Finally Richard rose to his feet and for the next fifteen minutes kept the room amused until the missing officer arrived and the lecture began.

It was at this camp that the recruits underwent exams and aptitude tests and the final decisions were taken as to whether they became pilots or navigators. These tests were clearly not foolproof. One of them involved fitting wooden shapes into the correct-shaped hole, rather like a child's toy posting box, which one boy on the course, who was hopeless in every other test, did in seconds. No one could understand this sudden flash of brilliance in someone who clearly had the wit to be neither a pilot nor navigator, until, much to the amusement of the entire camp, they discovered the boy had been a packer in a biscuit factory.

Few people could have had a poorer sense of direction, and yet after going through these tests himself, Richard was assigned the grade of trainee navigator, and as such set sail across the Atlantic to his posting in Canada early in 1945. Fortunately the war was very nearly over and his skills were never seriously put to the test, for the air-waves were alive with frantic air-traffic controllers trying to bring the errant navigator to order. Many were the times that he found himself over Winnipeg when he should have been in Toronto, or would tune into instructions to 'return at once to base, you are 206 nautical miles out'.

He kept in touch with Phil Burton by letter during the months he was away, but he would often forget to post a letter he had written, and friends were surprised by his lack of concern when he turned up something that was several weeks old. They thought he displayed a casualness about his relationship with Burton.

By the end of 1945 Richard and his fellow aircrew trainees were back in England. The atom bomb had fallen, the war was over, and the airforce was left with hundreds of highly trained young men who were posted to re-mustering stations around the countryside until their number came up for discharge. Richard was sent to an old bomber airfield in Norfolk called RAF Docking, where he languished for months with nothing to do but play rugby and challenge airforce rules. It was a frustrating time for everyone; they were in limbo, unable to use the skills they had spent the past two years learning, and unable to get on with the civilian careers that they had had to leave in order to come into the service. The airforce was sympathetic to the problem, and a directive had gone out from a senior level to leave these boys alone as much as possible, with the result that the authorities did turn a blind eye to the sort of behaviour that under normal circumstances would have warranted a court martial.

Richard established himself as lord of the manor, just as he had done at Babbacombe; he even became known as 'the Squire' and, instead of living in a cold damp Nissen hut like the rest of the unit, moved into one of the big houses in the centre of the village. If any visitors called on him he would immediately say, 'Right, let's go to the pub,' and they would set off for the local, which was invariably filled with RAF personnel in blue jackets with phoney ranks of air commodore, or air vice-marshal chalked or painted on them. They drank a lot, danced, bedded local girls if they were game, poached pheasants, and helped themselves to any produce in the fields they fancied to supplement scant canteen fare; and any non-commissioned officer who tried to discipline them was simply beaten up. One particularly unpopular sergeant was brought close to death in an incident.

There was no real work, so they spent their time doing menial ground tasks like cleaning lavatories and peeling potatoes. A few of the lucky ones, like Robert Hardy, with friends in high places who could pull strings, managed eventually to get themselves billeted in London, where they lived the high life, typing by day and enjoying the nightclubs by night. Robert asked Richard if he wanted to join him there, but the latter was happy to stay where he was for the time being, out in Norfolk where he could play in the RAF rugby team. Some of the country's best sportsmen perfected their games in these camps. Danny Blanchflower, who went on to captain the Northern Ireland football team, was at Docking with Burton.

This was also an opportunity for reading, one of Richard's greatest pleasures throughout his life, and for theorizing. He would often walk up and down the airfields with Robert Hardy, huddled up against the wind on freezing winter mornings, discussing Shakespeare. They continued to have a particular obsession with *Henry IV Parts 1 and 2*, making elaborate plans as to what they would do with the plays, largely based on Philip Burton's interpretation of them. Both agreed that Laurence Olivier, who had just produced both plays, had destroyed the balance of them by taking the part of Hotspur himself and getting a weak actor to play the part of Prince Hal. Robert did an impersonation of Olivier's performance which made Richard hoot with laughter. This was the traditional interpretation, that Hal, a bit of a prig, was a second-rate, boring part, and that the romantic figure and the more important part was Hotspur. Their theory was that this worked in *Part 1*, but what happens when you get to *Part 2* and you just have Hal – Hotspur having been killed off? Falstaff takes the centre of the stage, then Hal becomes King and rejects Falstaff; and you're on to *Henry V*. They felt that here were three marvellous plays about English life, apart from the wretched Prince. Their solution was to concentrate on Prince Hal, to turn the triptych into a detailed study of how someone trains himself for kingship, as Hal did, discarding friends on the way, and by the time you get to *Henry V*, whether you like the product or not, you've seen how a very young man learns to be a successful leader. In time, both men would put their theories into practice.

Richard's release from the RAF finally came through towards the end of 1947, but before that he had been given special permission to go to London for two weeks to appear in another Emlyn Williams play, *The Corn is Green*, being made for television by the BBC. This was Emlyn's autobiographical work about the way in which he was plucked from the valleys, groomed and educated by the Welsh schoolmistress who had taken him under her wing. His benefactor was Sarah Grace Cooke, and she was curious about this second 'Welsh peasant', as Emlyn described him, who had been seduced into the theatre. So he introduced Richard to her. Burton was on his best behaviour. When he left Miss Cooke, she turned to Emlyn and said, 'He's going to do well. What's more he's got the devil in him. You haven't.' He had remained friendly with Emlyn, his wife Molly, and their two sons, Alan and Brook, ever since *The Druid's Rest*, and went down to stay with them from time to time on weekend passes from the station. Their house was a home from home, and Richard later became Brook's godfather.

There were a couple of subsequent occasions, too, when he was given a day or two's release to record radio plays for the BBC in Cardiff. Philip Burton had become a full-time producer there by this time. The previous year he had given up teaching, left Port Talbot, and moved to a house in Cardiff, which was now Richard's real home – although after his twenty-first birthday on 10 November 1947, Burton was no longer officially his guardian.

When Richard's demobilization orders came through he swiftly found work in the theatre. Young male actors were thin on the ground in the immediate post-war period and, having already established some good contacts before going into the RAF, he was well positioned. He had fleetingly thought of going back to Oxford and taking a degree, as many of his contemporaries, including Robert Hardy, did. Indeed, he had told Donald Cullimore, another friend on the short course, that Emlyn Williams had vowed he would never speak to him again unless he did return to Oxford after the war; but by the time he was free to choose, he had been living on a pittance for longer than he had enjoyed, and he was eager to go out and earn some real money.

Thus his first port of call on reaching London was to his previous employers, H.M. Tennent Ltd, run by Hugh (Binkie) Beaumont, a legendary figure in the theatre world, and homosexual, as a great many of the most powerful men in the profession have traditionally been. His right-hand in the company was still Daphne Rye, who had spotted Richard for *The Druid's Rest*, and she played a central part in having him signed up now. He was given a year's contract at £10 a week, to be at Tennent's beck and call, like several other young actors at the time.

Now that he was back in London, Richard teamed up with Stanley Baker once again, and the two lived a wild existence. They found digs in Streatham, an unfashionable but cheap part of London south of the river, and drank, danced and dallied with Irish nurses on the common. Neither of them could dance to save their lives, but the local dance hall was the perfect place to pick up girls, and such was their record that they were known as the Palais de Danse Kings of Streatham.

Work brought their reign to an intermittent halt. Tennent's first claim on Richard was for a small part in a play called *Castle Anna*. It opened at the Lyric Theatre in Hammersmith in February 1948, directed by Daphne Rye, and Burton's performance went unnoticed. His second play, *Dark Summer*, toured the country, but again with very little success, either as a play or for Richard personally. Then, in the summer of 1948 Emlyn Williams came to his rescue with the offer of a reasonable-sized part in a film he had written, was going to direct, and would act in, called *The Last Days of Dolwyn*.

It was a light-hearted story about a Welsh businessman, played by Emlyn, who plans to flood a Welsh village to turn it into a reservoir for an English city. Burton played a part specially written for him. Dame Edith Evans was an old lady who stubbornly refuses to leave the village, and Richard was her foster son, Gareth, who hates cities. And although Emlyn had some problems in trying to get Richard to look innocent in one scene, he was generally delighted with his performance. When the film was released the following year, Burton was acknowledged by the critics for the first time, and hailed as an actor of promise.

Dolwyn was filmed initially at the London Film Studios in Isleworth, and then on location in North Wales, where they worked into the autumn. During the school summer holidays Emlyn's younger son, Brook, then aged nine, came to watch his first film being made, and spent a lot of time with Richard, whom he adored. It was also on the set of *Dolwyn* that Burton met Sybil Williams, a pretty young actress of eighteen.

Richard and Emlyn were sitting on the grass outside the studios one lunchtime. Emlyn asked what he had been doing the night before and, back came the inevitable reply, that he had been with some 'floosie'.

'Really, you know it's time you settled down,' said the older man, and suggested he take out 'one of the nice girls' who were in the picture. 'Now she's a real sweet girl,' he said pointing to Sybil, who was sitting on the grass nearby. Richard thereupon went over and introduced himself.

Like Richard, Sybil came from a small mining village in South Wales, coincidentally from the same village as Stanley. Sybil and Stanley had known each other all their lives – they were like brother and sister. Sybil's parents had both died when she was a child, and she was brought up by schoolteacher aunts in a strongly academic atmosphere. As a result she was unusually well educated and widely read. She was dark – with hair that was to be entirely silver by the age of twenty-five – almost Italianate in her looks, with a Roman nose, a long neck, and eyes and a mouth that always appeared to be on the brink of laughter, no matter what her mood. She charmed and infected everyone who knew her with her great love of life and bustling enthusiasm for everything that was going on around her. She had a style and an elegance of her own and, like Richard, she was someone everyone wanted to be with. They were a perfect match for one another; and made an enviable pair.

They were married within months of their first meeting, on 5 February 1949 at Kensington Register Office in London. Richard, typically, dismissed the event. He was marrying Sybil, he said, 'because it's what she expects me to do'. It was the day of the Scotland-Wales Rugby International at Murrayfield, something Richard would never miss for love or money – or marriage. Fortunately, it was also a working day for Sybil. She was an assistant stage manager in the comedy *Harvey* that was running in the West End, starring Sid Field. So, after a small reception given by Daphne Rye at her house in Pelham Crescent, where they were living, the new Mrs Burton went off to the theatre, while her husband settled down with the champagne and the radio to listen to the match. When it was over he went upstairs and drunkenly dallied with Daphne's maid, Sarah.

Burton was a great romantic; he revelled in poetry, wooing with all the extravagance of the English language but, recite as he might, love and sexual fidelity did not go hand in hand in his own life. As a fancy-free bachelor he went after girls with the dedication of many a red-blooded man on the make, with no discrimination, no emotion, no remorse, and scarcely time for an exchange of names. But while most men grow out of this single-minded desire for conquest, he never did. He retained an insatiable appetite for women: not to love them, not to be loved by them, but a need to possess them. He did not enjoy caressing them, he did not enjoy their company. He used women to boost his own confidence, to hide his insecurity, to feed his ego, and to make him feel wanted. He also used them to prove his heterosexuality which, like his intellect, he felt was threatened by his chosen profession.

Shortly before he and Sybil were married, Burton had his first chance to play the title role in *Henry V*. It was a Saturday Night Theatre radio production, directed by a young Oxford graduate, Frank Hauser, due to be broadcast on Shakespeare's birthday, 23 April. Instead of using one of the established 'heavies', Frank wanted a young Welsh actor for the part and his friend and contemporary from Oxford, Robert Hardy, suggested Richard. Frank had heard about Richard's performance as Angelo with OUDS but had never met him, so Robert arranged a meeting in London. They went out to dinner together, collecting Sybil en route from the Prince of Wales Theatre, where she was working on *Harvey*. They all got on very well together, quarrelling violently about Shakespeare, and Richard told Frank quite discreetly that his ambition was to have a thousand Everyman books and to have read them all. By the end of the evening Frank had decided he wanted Richard for the part, but he had first to convince his boss at the BBC, so they arranged a read-through.

Richard arrived for the reading slightly but noticeably drunk. He read the piece rather badly, but Marty Harding, Frank's boss, could see he was frightened and, backing his director's judgment, agreed to use him.

Richard was at a low ebb. He had just been fired from his first real West End production and was very depressed. This was a new Terence Rattigan play, *Adventure Story*, with Paul Scofield, a young actor just three years older than Burton, playing the lead. Frank asked why he had been replaced.

'Well, I was supposed to play Paul Scofield's older friend,' said Richard. 'And who on earth can play Paul's older friend? With a face like that, he looks 108 to start with.'

Eager to find him something else, Daphne Rye put him up for the next Tennent's production, a little verse comedy called *The Lady's Not For Burning* by an up-and-coming new playwright, Christopher Fry. No one thought it had much chance of running, but Daphne had faith in it and had cajoled 'Binkie' Beaumont into staging it at the Globe Theatre in the West End instead of out of town, and had managed to get John Gielgud to direct the play and to star in it.

The play was set in fifteenth-century England and concerned Thomas Mendip, a soldier of fortune who wants to die, and Jennet Jourdemayne, a beautiful witch who has been condemned to die but who wants to live. John Gielgud played Mendip, and Pamela Brown, Jennet, the witch. The part played by Burton was originally given to another actor, but after the first read-through Gielgud said he was unhappy with the boy, and also with the girl chosen to take the part of Alizon, and wanted to re-cast both. This was when Richard was asked to audition, along with a young actress called Claire Bloom who was up for the part of Alizon.

Richard arrived for the audition in a terrible state of nerves. He sat scowling with his legs wrapped round his chair like some contortionist, and gave a very indifferent reading of the part. Claire Bloom, just eighteen years old, by contrast, was the picture of composure; and Pamela Brown, sitting watching with Christopher Fry, said, 'Well, the girl's all right, but I don't think the boy's going to be any good.'

Fortunately Gielgud recognized how nervous Richard was and suggested, 'Have a chat with Christopher about the part, then come back tomorrow and read it again.' The following day he gave an excellent reading, and was awarded the part of Richard, a very likeable young clerk who falls in love with Alizon and runs off with her – two innocents in a sea of conniving, world-weary cynics. Burton played the boy with a perfect blend of simplicity, humour and truth; and with the stillness that was rapidly becoming his trademark.

The Lady's Not For Burning toured the provinces for two months before opening in London at the Globe on 11 May. It proved a huge success, running for the rest of the year, and only closed because Gielgud had commitments at Stratford the following season. Gielgud says he found Burton 'a born actor. A demon for hard work, and with limitless charm and promise. He was a joy to act with.' It was one of the best and most memorable performances he ever gave, but as Frank Hauser, who watched his career from start to finish, observed:

> Richard had the perfect part in *The Lady's Not For Burning*, and it's very rare for an actor to start off with the perfect role. The boy he played was modest, attractive and shy, with obviously a lot going on behind; and in his main scene he had to be very still while other people carried on around him. That is what Richard was best at, and later on productions were designed where he would stand centre of stage, and other people would work around him. Being still is one way of winning a reputation and getting a lot of parts, but it's not the way to be a great actor. Great actors have to stand and deliver.

Offstage, he did stand and deliver. Burton was never one to play the retiring new boy, even with such august company. As John Gielgud says, 'He was funny, gregarious and a bit of a show-off.' He got on especially well with Pamela Brown – they shared the same sort of humour – but it was a friendly company all round, and there would be parties and get-togethers, occasionally at Christopher Fry's house in Blomfield Road, when the conversation would invariably return to the subject of Richard's hard-drinking ancestors, or to the well-worn theme of his grandfather's demise, careering down the hill in his wheelchair. He never failed to raise a laugh, but as Gielgud observed, he could on the other hand be 'moody and unpredictable and had, I think, a dark Welsh streak of pessimism and carelessness'.

Richard left the play before the end of the run and his understudy took over so that he could begin rehearsals on another Fry play, again directed by John Gielgud, which opened at the Lyric Theatre, Hammersmith in January 1950. It was a one-act miracle play, *The Boy With A Cart*, based on the legend of Cuthman, a simple shepherd boy who wheels his elderly mother, played by Mary Jerrold, across the countryside in a cart to a site in Sussex where he has been instructed by God to build a church. It was a piece Fry had written for a village church jubilee twelve years earlier while he was still a schoolmaster, but this was the first time it had been staged. Richard played the part of Cuthman. John Gielgud had to do a lot of work on Richard's performance, particularly his first entrance where the character bounds in saying, 'This is the morning to take the air.' He tended to be rather muted, and took a lot of persuading to inject some spring and fire into the role. There were parts of the play where this understatement was perfect, and he did achieve extraordinary simplicity and freshness, but there were still places where Fry felt he should have taken off a little more.

While Richard was not singled out for lavish praise by the critics, he was noticed by Anthony Quayle, who was then casting an eye around for his forthcoming Shakespeare season at Stratford. Burton had also been noticed by one of the most prestigious theatrical agents in London, Major Vere Barker, head of Connies Agency, whose clients included luminaries like Ralph Richardson, Margaret Leighton, Eric Portman and Laurence Harvey. He invited both Richard and Stanley Baker to join him and although the eventual parting of the ways with Burton was unhappy, they remained together for many years. It was Vere Barker, who put up the money for Richard and Sybil to buy their first house, in Lyndhurst Road, Hampstead, where they moved early in 1950. To help pay for it, they rented out the top floor flat to a pair of lesbians. Richard would tell the story of how he had taken them breakfast in bed one morning and been absolutely entranced when they rolled over and began to make love to one another in front of him.

Early that year he had gone down to Brighton for a couple of weeks to perform in yet another Christopher Fry play, *A Phoenix Too Frequent* at the Dolphin Theatre, with Diana Graves and Jessie Evans. It was very informal, a spur-of-the-moment idea among friends, and they all spent a pleasant fortnight by the sea. Once again Richard's performance was muted, and his under-acting became a standing joke. As a first night present Christopher Fry, who was then living at Shipton-under-Wychwood, gave him a book with the following inscription: To Acting

Richard

from

Wychwood

Shipton

Sybil was in Brighton too. Work permitting, she went wherever Richard went. A little later in the year, however, *Harvey* went on tour and, as ASM, she went too. While she was away, Richard and Stanley were left living in the house in Hampstead. Although he was now married, Burton was still on the prowl, day and night, for new women to take home. Stanley meantime had met and fallen in love with a young actress called Ellen Martin, and she had come to live in the house to look after them both.

She was amazed by the way Richard behaved; by the way he blatantly slept around. He picked girls up all over the place, in cinemas, in pubs, in shops, in hairdressers. To this day Ellen drinks abnormal quantities of coffee because of the hours she had to spend sitting in cafés during that summer of 1950 when Richard turned her out while he entertained girls in the house. Yet he was always terrified that Sybil would find out, and Ellen, who had not yet met Sybil, was sworn to secrecy. One girl gave him a terrible fright: her hair colouring came off all over a very special pair of sheets that Sybil had bought, and Richard appealed to Ellen for help. The sheets had come from America and there was no way he could replace them, but try as they might the colour refused to budge. Ellen told Richard he had to go and find the girl and ask her what she had used on her hair. He couldn't bring himself to go, and pleaded with her to do it for him. So Ellen finally sought her out, in a café where she worked as a waitress, and, to their mutual embarrassment, quizzed her on the ingredients in the dye she used on her hair.

Ellen found him devastatingly attractive. Physically he was far from perfect: his face was pock-marked and pitted; his eyes, beautiful and staring though they were, were strangely cold; he was short and barrel-chested, with not much neck, and rather podgy paw-like hands. His posture was bad, and he walked with a sailor's roll. But for all his imperfections, he radiated pure charisma and sex appeal from every pore in his body.

It was Stanley that Ellen was interested in, captivated though she was, and she still maintains that she has Burton to thank for their marriage. She and Richard were travelling home together on a train from Ealing where they had both been working. Stanley was busy on a small film elsewhere. She had known him just two weeks.

'Do you want to marry Stanley?' Richard suddenly asked.

'Yes of course I do,' said Ellen, 'but he's not going to ask me is he?'

'Just leave it to me,' he said. 'I think he should be married. I'm married.'

That night he took Stanley aside and said, 'Are you going to marry Ellen?'

'I've only known her two weeks,' protested his friend, somewhat taken aback.

'Have you met her parents?'

'Yes,' said Stanley.

'Well you know what these English people are like.'

'What do you mean?' said Stanley.

'Where do they live?'

'Stoke Poges.'

'Well then,' said Richard, as if the mere mention of Stoke Poges had said it all. 'You know what they expect.'

That night Stanley asked Ellen if she would marry him.

'Tomorrow,' she said, 'provided you're not like him.'

'Darling,' he said confidently, 'nobody's like Richard.'

3

The Making of a Legend

The 1951 season at Stratford-on-Avon which opened on 24 March was a much-publicized affair. It was Burton's first opportunity to establish himself as a classical actor, and the culmination of two men's dreams. The Memorial Theatre was staging a cycle of Shakespeare's historical plays: *Richard II, Henry IV Parts 1 and 2, Henry V*, plus *The Tempest*, as its contribution to the Festival of Britain celebrations, designed to perk up the nation's morale and boost tourism. Stratford was expecting a record number of visitors, and large sums of money had already been spent on providing extra seats, building on additional dressing rooms for the actors, and in generally redecorating the theatre in preparation.

Richard, meanwhile, had been abroad for the first time, and had his first taste of America. He had crossed the Atlantic in some style aboard a Cunard liner to appear in *The Lady's Not For Burning* in New York, taking Sybil with him. It was with some regrets that he had to leave the company before the end of the run, in order to be in Stratford for the beginning of rehearsals.

Stratford was an exciting prospect however: his first real opportunity to play Shakespeare as a professional, and to play lead roles in the most prestigious theatre company in the world. Some would argue that the part he came home to play was the best performance of his entire career, the role which established him as the crown prince of the British stage. But by this time Richard had caught a glimpse of the good life. He had made four films in Britain, none of which was memorable, but which had earned him considerably more money on a daily rate than he had ever earned in the theatre. His appetite for big money had been whetted.

Richard was to play the part that he had talked so endlessly about while pacing the airfields of Norfolk with Robert Hardy – Prince Hal in *Henry IV*. The money was poor in comparison to his recent earnings, but it was a part he had been longing to play. He was much amused by the way in which Anthony Quayle had offered it. He had rung Sybil one day and asked her if she wanted to play the Welsh-speaking part of Lady Mortimer in *Henry IV Part 1*.

'Oh yes,' she had said enthusiastically.

'Well, you're very much on my list,' said Quayle. 'Now try and get your husband to play Prince Hal, and we'll see what we can do.'

Both husband and wife liked such a blatant ploy; and Quayle went up in Burton's estimation immeasurably.

'That's real common Welsh slyness,' he would say. 'If you want something go after it – none of this English fair play or decency.'

Richard was fiercely nationalistic. He loved anything Welsh. He wore red, the national colour, almost daily. He sang Welsh songs and, given a few drinks, he would recite in the language too; and the stories he told would invariably come back to the valleys. But of all things Welsh, the one he loved the most was the national sport. He would go for miles to watch the Welsh play rugby. He ranted and raved about the game, followed it assiduously throughout his life, listening to match commentaries on the BBC World Service when he was abroad, and anyone who shared his fanaticism was a friend for life.

Every free Saturday afternoon in the season a group would go off to a match, preferably an International; people like fellow Welsh actors Stanley Baker, Donald Houston and Meredith Edwards, and Euan Lloyd, the film producer, who was then publicity manager for a film distribution company which had handled Richard's films. They would try to find someone who didn't drink to drive them to the ground, and the afternoon would become one big party, starting in the car park before the match, and finishing long after everyone else had gone home.

High spot of the year were the Internationals at Twickenham and Cardiff Arms Park, with the stadium divided into English and Welsh supporters. The sound of myriad Welshmen in full voice, singing national songs, and drowning any song the English attempted, made Richard glow with pride. It was a sound he loved above all others, and he always sang heartily himself.

Most of his friends were Welsh at that time, and at Stratford there were a number of expatriates, generally referred to as 'the Welsh mafia'. One of these was the actor Hugh Griffith who with his wife had rented a big house, The Old House, some distance away – nearer Banbury than Stratford – in the village of Oxhill. Richard and Sybil lived there too along with Robert Hardy and a girlfriend. Robert was by now a fully fledged actor, embarking on his second season at Stratford.

It was a glorious summer: nightingales sang; friends dropped in; members of Richard's family came and went; Sybil's sister appeared from time to time; Philip Burton stayed on hand to give notes and coach his protégé; Charles Laughton paid a visit; Frank Hauser came up from London and spent the night on one of the Burtons' twin beds while they shared the other one between them; John Dexter bicycled over from Derby to see the plays and meet his friends; Stanley and Ellen Baker were around. Everyone sat around talking until the early hours of the morning, arguing about 'The Henrys'. There were parties, picnics on the banks of the River Avon, and daring midnight swims with no clothes on from the Duck Steps after the show.

Richard bought his first car during the season. It was an old and rather decrepit black Flying Standard, which he bought from another actor in the company, Ronald Marsh. He could not drive at the time, and lessons from Robert Hardy scarcely improved matters. They were driving into Stratford from Oxhill one day when Richard drove up a pile of chippings by the side of the road, and came to a grinding halt at an angle of 45 degrees.

The fact that he could not drive, and was never to be very safe behind a wheel, did not deter him, prompted by his friends, from wanting a better car in keeping with his status as a film star. So he approached Vere Barker, and he and 'Binkie' Beaumont between them lent Burton the money to buy a new car: secondhand and rather grandly black.

Having Sybil with him did nothing to stem Burton's desire for other women. If he couldn't take them home, as he had to their house in Hampstead while she was away on tour, he made do with a dressing room at the theatre, an empty room in the pub, a bedroom at a party, or the garden – anywhere that he could be sure of a few minutes to himself. He didn't need long, and had no inhibitions about calling on his friends to cover for him. He had no shame about the women he seduced either. The wives of friends fell as surely as his leading ladies.

Richard's performance as Hal received outstanding notices. Although he and his director, Anthony Quayle, came to blows on several occasions over his interpretation of the character, Richard played Hal as he had always said he would; as Phil Burton had taught him. His was not the traditional jolly, thigh-slapping Hal, but a powerful creature, with hidden strengths and moods. His great physical presence took the audiences by storm. Kenneth Tynan's review in the *Observer* was glowing:

> His playing of Prince Hal . . . turned interested speculation to awe almost as soon as he started to speak: in the first intermission the local critics stood agape in the lobbies. Burton is a still brimming pool, running disturbingly deep; at twenty-five he commands repose and can make silence garrulous. His Prince Hal is never a roaring boy; he sits hunched or sprawled, with dark unwinking eyes; he hopes to be amused by his bully companions, but the eyes constantly muse beyond them into the time when he must steady himself for the crown. 'He brings his cathedral on with him,' said one dazed member of the company. For all his bold chivalry this watchful Celt seems surely to have strayed from a wayside pulpit. Fluent and sparing of gesture, compact and spruce of build, Burton smiles where other Hals have guffawed; relaxes where they have strained; and Falstaff (played with affectionate obesity by Anthony Quayle) must work hard to divert him. In battle Burton's voice cuts urgent and keen – always likeable, always inaccessible.

Harold Hobson in the *Sunday Times* wrote, 'He had hardly got his performance started before I felt the Stratford audience that night was in the presence of no ordinary player. He had an interior force, so that he is doing everything when he appears to be doing nothing.'

The critics liked him, but he was not an easy actor to work with. He had a dismissive quality in his relationship with the other characters on stage. He appeared to be thinking of other things, uninterested in the play and the part.

He was not an easy actor to direct either, particularly when he had been drinking, which he thought nothing of doing while working.

Dress rehearsals in those days (before the actors' union put a stop to it) would go on until two, three or even four o'clock in the morning, by which time everyone would be tired, tense and longing to go to bed. During one such rehearsal, Burton drank eighteen half pint bottles of India Pale Ale, which had been brought in to him by his dresser. He was in full chain-mail armour, surcoat, belt, swords, helmet. They had just reached the Battle of Shrewsbury, an interminable scene, when Richard interrupted.

'Can we stop?' he asked, peering out front to the darkness of the stalls, where Anthony Quayle sat directing.

'No, no, no, Richard,' shouted Quayle with a certain desperation in his voice. 'It's very late; not now, Richard, please. We'll have a break in half an hour or so.'

'Right,' said Burton. 'Watch this.' And an incredulous company watched as he relieved himself, and eighteen bottles-worth of India Pale Ale seeped through his costume and collected in a large pool on the wooden floor of the stage.

His performance as Henry V, according to W.A. Darlington in the *Daily Telegraph*:

> Sets the seal on two years or so of promising work which began when he first caught the eye in *The Lady's Not For Burning*. His King Harry brings out a notable variety of talent and puts him in the front rank of the younger players.
>
> He has dignity and authority. He has a fine voice, rather like Laurence Olivier's, which is equally impressive both when he is quiet and when he is at full flood. He can give Henry brooding expression which brings out his sense of responsibility and makes it easy to believe in him as a leader of men.

Other critics, however, were less impressed. There was one in particular who commented that Richard Burton 'lacked inches' in his portrayal of the King, compared with the excellent performance Laurence Olivier had given in his most recent version at the Old Vic. Richard was mortified; but much cheered when a few days later he had a letter from Olivier enclosing the review that this very critic had written after the opening night of his own *Henry V* at the Vic. Laurence Olivier's Henry, he wrote, 'lacked inches'.

At much the same time Frank Hauser was being savaged for his first ever stage production of *Hamlet* with Alec Guinness. When he read the reviews for *Henry V* he wrote to Richard commiserating, and received this response:

> Dear Frank,
> The bastards didn't like me much. Thank you for your letter. I was delighted that you went to the trouble. I've discovered an extraordinary thing: I find difficulty in releasing the power which I know (I hope) I possess. I must work on it.
> Quayle has asked me to come back here next year and play *Hamlet*. I've declined. Instead I'm going to New York to play in *Point of Departure*. By the time I'm ready to have another crack at the Bard – I reckon about two years – you should be back in the picture again. Next summer I begin work for Korda as a film star. The first film is *The Last Enemy*. Richard Hilary.
> Like you, probably, I was shocked and infuriated by my first batch of bad notices. I'll teach the swine yet. I must work even harder to increase the range of my voice. It gets better all the time of course. The Korda business is not completed, by the way, so don't talk about it.
> I hope you are not too shattered by the failure of your first production. I meant to write to you before but I was afraid that my letter would appear condescending after the blue-eyed-boy notices I'd received. We'll be sorting 'em out together one of these days.

The reviews for his part as Ferdinand in *The Tempest*, however, were worse than those he had received for *Henry V*. It was the one play of the season he hated doing. He loathed being made up to be pretty, and refused to stick his wig on properly, with the result that it frequently slipped and looked decidedly amateurish. He disliked Shakespearean dress – short costume and tights – at the best of times, but to be dressed up in pink and blue with frills and ruffles was more than his masculine image could bear. And the critics noticed. But the performance which remained vividly in everyone's mind at the end of the summer was Prince Hal, and his reputation was in no way diminished by the subsequent notices. People came from far and wide to see Richard Burton's Hal.

When the Stratford season came to a close at the end of October, so, too, did Sybil's acting career. She had played a number of small parts during the summer, and had enjoyed them. She was a very talented young actress, but she realized that, with Burton's career taking him back and forth across the Atlantic, it would be impossible to work on a career herself if she ever wanted to see him. She had to choose whether to be a wife or an actress, and Richard held very orthodox views about wives. He had grown up in a society where the women kept house and devoted themselves to their men and, although he had joined the bohemian world of the theatre, at heart he was still a boy from the valleys. He wanted his woman to devote herself to him; and Sybil did, quite selflessly.

She was a very down-to-earth sort of woman, and she knew how to handle Richard. She would have just finished preparing the supper when he would put on his coat and announce he was going out.

'Oh no you're not,' she'd say. 'The food's on the table.'

'I won't be more than five minutes.'

'You'd better not be,' Sybil would say, 'or there'll be trouble.' And Richard knew better than to push his luck. He recognized that she was a match for him. She was also a great companion: quick, intelligent, witty. They were a delightful couple, speaking to one another in nursery talk, teasing one another, and playing the fool. They were always 'Rich and Syb' to their friends, always a pair. It seemed the perfect marriage. Everyone knew that Burton had other women, but they were brief affairs, one-night stands, and he kept them from Sybil. If she knew about them, she suffered in silence. She understood Richard: understood his inadequacies and his compulsions, and tolerated them. Friends admired her the more for it.

Their immediate future after Stratford was much as Richard had outlined in his letter to Frank Hauser. *Point of Departure* opened in New York after a brief tour in December 1951 under the title *Legend of Lovers*. It was a Jean Anouilh play (entitled *Eurydice* in France) in which Burton played the lead opposite Dorothy McGuire. His personal notices were excellent. He was hailed 'another Laurence Olivier', 'an actor of tremendous promise', and 'one of England's most gifted young actors', but the play itself was called 'cheerless, cynical and muddled' and closed within a matter of weeks. Thus by February Richard was back in London, filling in time with some radio work for the BBC, and appearing in Lillian Hellman's grim play, *Montserrat*, described as a 'study in torture', that came into the Lyric, Hammersmith, in April.

'This boy is a genius and will be a great actor. He is outstandingly handsome and robust, very masculine and with deep inward fire, and extremely reserved.'

Above: Youth at the Helm, RAF Babbacombe. Burton extreme left, Robert Hardy centre left next to Corporal Barker

Below: Richard aged seventeen in *The Druid's Rest*, his first professional part. Emlyn Williams, the advertisement said, was seeking Welsh actors and actresses for a new play

Opposite, above: On location filming *The Last Days of Dolwyn* with Emlyn Williams. 'As very special human beings tend to look at that age – he looked. . .imperishable.' *Below*: Emlyn's son Brook, with his father. The boy adored Richard and was a constant visitor to the set of *Dolwyn*

Richard with Sybil. They were a perfect match for one another, and he was a great romantic, but love and sexual fidelity did not go hand in hand in his own life

As Cuthman with Mary Jerrold in *The Boy with a Cart*, 1950. Burton achieved extraordinary simplicity and freshness in the role, attracting the notice of Anthony Quayle and one of the leading London theatrical agents

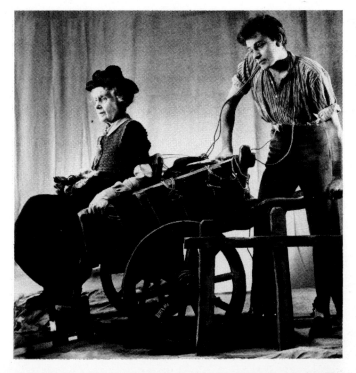

Burton in Christopher Fry's *A Phoenix Too Frequent* at the Dolphin Theatre in Brighton with Jessie Evans and Diana Graves. The performance was an informal, spur-of-the-moment idea among friends

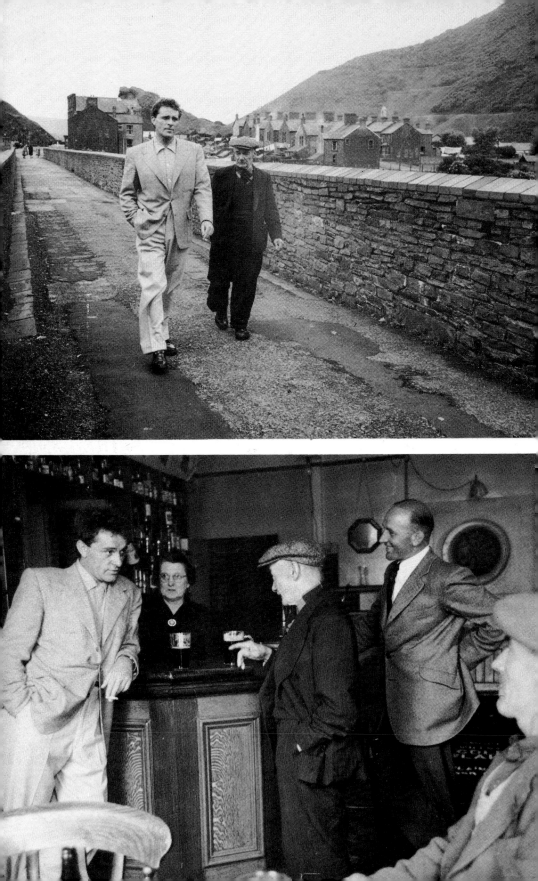

Richard returned home to Pontrhydyfen in 1953 a Hollywood star, happy to play the part of the boy-from-the-valleys-made-good. *Opposite above*: With his father, Dic Bach. The old miner lived in a small world of his own. They no longer even shared the same name. *Below*: Posing for a pint with the old man in the Miners Arms. *Above*: 'He had a dark Welsh streak of pessimism and carelessness.'

Richard's Hamlet, 'full of fire and passion and power', was the most popular production of the 1953 Old Vic season. Winston Churchill unnerved him one night by reciting the entire play from the stalls

With Claire Bloom, who played Ophelia. It was the beginning of an affair that lasted longer than any other

The Korda deal that he had spoken of to Hauser, however, did come to fruit that summer, although not the film, and not in quite the manner he had supposed. Nevertheless, he was turned into a film star. In a somewhat complex deal, Alexander Korda lent Richard to Darryl Zanuck of Twentieth Century Fox to make a number of films, the first of which was based on Daphne du Maurier's novel, *My Cousin Rachel*, starring Olivia de Havilland. The story was set in Cornwall, but the film was made in sound studios in Los Angeles. For the next year Richard and Sybil lived in Hollywood and rubbed shoulders with the stars.

The film was largely panned when it was released, but Burton's role attracted great excitement on both sides of the Atlantic, winning him three press and magazine awards and his first Oscar nomination. More significantly, it brought him the lead in *The Robe*, the film that assured his position as the beautiful and exciting new talent in Hollywood. In the meantime, he made *The Desert Rats*, a war film set in North Africa, but acted out near Palm Springs, with James Mason, but it was the third film he made in that year that was the most memorable: *The Robe* went into production in Los Angeles in the first part of 1953. It was a multi-million-dollar epic, based on the biblical novel by Lloyd C. Douglas about early Christians, and was the first film ever to use Cinemascope, a brand new photographic medium, which was shown on a slightly curved screen, two and a half times the normal size, and gave the impression of a three-dimensional picture.

A lot was riding on the film. It was a movie in the grand style of Hollywood spectaculars, like *Ben Hur* and *Quo Vadis?*. Darryl Zanuck was said to have staked the entire future of Twentieth Century Fox on it. It was the talk of Hollywood. The press, invited on to the set, kept interest percolating. And Burton had the lead. He played the part of Marcellus, the Roman officer who was in charge of the execution of Christ, and became so obsessed with guilt about what he had done that he became a convert to Christianity, and died a martyr's death.

Burton was the new star. He gave endless and romantic interviews about his Welsh background, his coal-mining ancestors, his rugby injuries, his passion for Shakespeare, his determination not to be seduced by films; and the press lapped it up. It was the same at the Hollywood parties. He was in demand, not just as a star, but as an entertaining star, who told shocking and amazing stories; and who was just a little out of his depth.

It was at one of these parties that Richard first met Elizabeth Taylor, then married to Michael Wilding. He set the scene in a book he wrote twelve years later, *Meeting Mrs Jenkins*. He had come a long way from Caradoc Street.

The house in California – it was in the Bel Air district of Los Angeles, I think – looked as if it had been flung by a giant hand against the side of a hill and had stuck.

From the main living room, master bedroom, guest bedrooms, dining room, kitchen level, the house jutted and dropped one floor to a 'playroom'.

The 'playroom' was not for children.

It was complete with bar and barman, hot-dog simmerer, king-sized double-doored two-toned refrigerator, drugstore hotplates, big-game trophies on the walls (the host was a big-game hunter who acted in his spare time), and huge, deep, low divans and easy chairs – villainously uncomfortable for men, but marvellously made for cute little women who could tuck their cute little legs away and blazingly efface their cute little pretty little pouting little personalities in niches of the vast furniture and make like cute little pussycats.

Below the 'playroom' the house again jutted and dropped to the swimming pool, the showers, and the changing rooms.

It was my first time in California and my first visit to a swank house. There were quite a lot of people in and around the pool, all suntanned and all drinking the Sunday morning liveners – Bloody Marys, boilermakers, highballs, iced beer. I knew some of the people and was introduced to the others. Wet brown arms reached out of the pool and shook my hand. The people were all friendly, and they called me Dick immediately. I asked if they would please call me Richard – Dick, I said, made me feel like a symbol of some kind. They laughed, some of them. It was, of course, Sunday morning and I was nervous.

I was enjoying this small social triumph, but then a girl sitting on the other side of the pool lowered her book, took off her sunglasses and looked at me. She was so extraordinarily beautiful that I nearly laughed out loud . . . .

She sipped some beer and went back to her book. I affected to become social with the others but out of the corner of my mind – while I played for the others the part of a poor miner's son who was puzzled, but delighted by the attention these lovely people paid to him – I had her under close observation . . . .

She was unquestionably gorgeous. I can think of no other word to describe a combination of plenitude, frugality, abundance, tightness. She was lavish. She was a dark unyielding largesse. She was, in short, too bloody much, and not only that, she was totally ignoring me. I became frustrated almost to screaming when I had finished a well-received and humorous story about the death of my grandfather and found that she was turned away in deep conversation with another woman. I think I tried to eavesdrop but was stayed by words like – Tony and Janet and Marlon and Sammy. She was not, obviously, talking about me.

Several other people were, however. Richard's appetite for women was well fed in Hollywood, and rumours of his sexual conquests became the talk of Beverly Hills. He worked his way through stars and starlets with indiscriminate abandon, as though desperate to prove something. Some were married, some were not, and sometimes he was found out. No married man felt totally secure when Richard Burton was around, not even his best friends.

One of the most brazen of his affairs was with his co-star in *The Robe*, Jean Simmons, then married to the actor Stewart Granger. Granger and his wife slept in separate suites and, after her husband had gone to bed at night, Richard would climb into their house through the wood shed, to make love to Jean on a big white rug in front of the fire.

'By God I wanted her,' Richard would say, recalling his escapades, 'but if you dismantle the entire contents of a wood shed, log by log, you've got to be pretty determined to do anything at the end of it.'

One day her husband discovered what had been going on, and confronted Burton. As Stewart Granger told the story some years later, he telephoned Richard at the commissary of Twentieth Century Fox and said, 'Get over here to my den tonight. I know all about you and Jean. You be here.'

Stewart Granger's den, as Richard well knew, was lined with hunting trophies and guns.

'I was going to kill the bastard,' Granger said, 'but I knew he was a tough guy, this Welshman, so I looked for something to protect

55

myself with, and opened the drawer of my desk and took out several rolls of dimes, and put them in my fist just in case he came at me so I'd be ready; and he came across to the house and he said, "Forgive me, forgive me," and he knelt down and dragged my knees and said, "Please, please, I promise, I promise I'll leave your wife alone. Don't hit me."

'And,' said Granger, 'I kicked him away and said get out of my house.'

'That's very interesting, Jimmy,' said his companion. 'It's not the way Richard tells the story.'

'What do you mean?' said Granger.

'It's one of Richard's dinner party pieces with Elizabeth,' he said. 'He says you phoned him in the commissary, and said, "Get over to my den tonight." And Richard said, "Of course I knew his den; there were guns and daggers and trophies, and I thought, 'Christ he's going to kill me. I don't possess a weapon.' Then I saw the cashier opening those nickle coins and I said, 'Here, I'll have two of those,' and I went to meet him with those in my pocket, and as I went into his den, Jimmy fell on his knees and came towards me, and said, 'Give her up, give her up. I'll give you anything.'"

'And Richard said, "You can have her you weak bastard. And I kicked him in the goolies and walked out."'

The one who actually put an end to the affair was Sybil. Sybil turned a blind eye to most of Richard's affairs, but this one proved too much. It was New Year's Eve, and everyone who was anyone was at a big Hollywood party. Richard was dancing with Jean Simmons, and as midnight struck everyone kissed their partners and toasted the New Year. In full view of all the guests, Richard kissed Jean slowly and passionately on the lips, while his hands slid across her breasts and buttocks and pressed her to him. Humiliated by so public and so flagrant a display, Sybil strode off the dance floor, left the party, packed her bags and took the next flight to New York. Four days later Burton came running after her and the affair was over.

There was one other liaison that Burton had to talk his way out of before leaving Hollywood. When the filming of *The Robe* was over, Twentieth Century Fox claimed that he was under an exclusive contract to them for seven years for a fixed sum of money. Richard denied it. They said they had a signed contract to prove it. He pointed out that his agent was the one who had signed the contract, and he had done so without Richard's permission.

The result of all this was that Twentieth Century Fox took their latest star to court for breach of contract.

Richard's described events later to a friend:

> On one side of the courtroom was Darryl Zanuck and half the corporation boys in America. On the other side was me, alone; I didn't have a lawyer. I played it very English, very Ronald Colman.
>
> At one point one of the lawyers jumped up and shook his fist at me and said, 'You shook hands with Mr Zanuck on this agreement. You shook hands with Mr Zanuck in his own office.'
>
> And I said, 'I don't believe Mr Zanuck said that because he's an honourable man. But if he did say it, then he's a fucking liar.'
>
> The place broke up in complete confusion. Strong men fainted and were carried off by weak men. And the next morning the phone rang, and there was a woman on the end of it. 'Did you call Darryl Zanuck a fucking liar?' she said.
>
> 'Yes, I think I did.'
>
> 'Then you need help. I'll be right round.'

The woman was a tough American lawyer who did help Burton out of the legal mess he had made for himself, and subsequently became his business manager.

Thus, in the summer of 1953, successfully disentangled from Twentieth Century Fox but with an agreement that he would return and make one film a year for the company for the next seven years, Richard returned to London with Sybil. The sunshine had been glorious, the sheer extravagance of their surroundings exciting, but they had missed their friends and family, and Richard was quite keen to get back to the stage and do some serious acting.

He had signed up for a season of Shakespeare at the Old Vic, beginning with *Hamlet*, in which he was to play the lead. But returning to London was a rude shock to his pocket. Burton had made three films while he had been away, and earned a total of £82,000. The Old Vic was paying him £45 per week, which was £95 less than he had been getting from the studio as a living allowance in the States. He was still acutely conscious of money, he often spoke about wanting his first million pounds – in those days a colossal sum of money, which friends thought simply laughable – and he was appalled when he worked out how much the British taxman was going to take from his year's earnings. Out of £82,000 he calculated he would be left with just £6,000. These were thoughts that prayed on his mind.

Rehearsals for *Hamlet* began in July, and in the preceding weeks Richard and Sybil went down to Wales to visit their respective families. *My Cousin Rachel* and *The Desert Rats* had both been released in Britain by this time, and Richard was already enjoying a certain degree of fame. He was happy to play the part of boy-from-the-valleys-made-good, and welcomed the attentions of the press. He went to stay with Cis and Elfed in Port Talbot, and visited the rest of the clan up in Pontrhydyfen. He willingly posed for photographers in any stance they chose: brooding wistfully against the backdrop of the Welsh hills; gazing into the middle distance with his brothers; and walking alongside his old father.

His brothers and sisters were all hugely proud. The whole village was proud. But his father's reaction somewhat saddened Richard. Dic Bach hadn't followed his son's progress with the same enthusiasm as the rest of the family; he didn't see films, didn't go to the theatre, wasn't interested in either, and the whole business was quite out of his ken. He lived in a small world of his own, and it was a world that Richie had left.

If Dic Bach felt he had lost a son, Richard had much the same sentiments about his father. He felt that he had no more had a father than he had had a mother. Dic Bach had sent him off as a small boy to be brought up by his sister; and had happily signed away his birthright at the age of seventeen when Philip Burton came into the picture. They no longer even shared the same name. There was a deep-seated feeling of rejection in Richard, which he could never quite shake off. Cissie had been everything he could have wished for in a mother; he loved her dearly and kept a photograph of her with him wherever he went, but it always troubled him that he couldn't remember anything about his real mother. But Richard found a father figure in his brother Ifor, who was nineteen years his senior.

Physically there were great similarities between the two brothers: Ifor frequently stood in for Richard at tailor's fitting sessions. Unlike Richard, he went bald early in life, and always spoke with a strong South Wales accent, but in build and looks there was little difference. In character, however, Ifor was a symbol of the qualities that Richard, in his darker moments, felt he lacked. He was kind, gentle, loyal, and a pillar of honesty and respectability. His wife, Gwen, was a gentle and intelligent woman. The great sadness in their lives was that they had no children.

It was Ifor that Richard began to turn to, to seek approval from, and to talk to. He respected his judgment; and in some ways, this elder brother became Richard's conscience. Philip Burton had never been a father figure in anything but name: a mentor, yes, a coach, a critic, a friend, and someone to whom Richard remained indebted, but never a man to whom he looked for pastoral guidance. In fact, now that he was established in the business, owned a house, was married, and no longer the new boy in London, he found Phil a bit of an old woman, and his pedantic ways a little irksome.

At the Old Vic Richard was back among friends. Many of the people who had been at Stratford were in the company, including Robert Hardy, who was to play Laertes. Claire Bloom, with whom he had last played in *The Lady's Not For Burning* four years earlier, was to be Ophelia.

Claire Bloom had not been greatly impressed initially by Burton. She was one woman on whom his charms had failed during their first association. She found Paul Scofield an infinitely more attractive proposition. When she heard that Richard was to play Hamlet to her Ophelia, she said, 'My God, that uncouth actor', a remark which someone in the company repeated to Richard.

He was furious. 'I'll make her pay,' he raged to a friend. 'I'll have her, I'll have her whichever way I like.'

And he did. They had an affair which lasted longer than any other, and which ended more acrimoniously than any other. He did, indeed, make her pay. But not during the summer of 1953.

After rehearsals at the Old Vic, the play opened at the Edinburgh Festival in August, to uncertain reviews. He had worked very hard at his part, not only with the director, Michael Benthall, but on his own with Phil Burton; but neither man had been able to control him. Richard's Hamlet was said to have been 'full of fire and passion and power', but because he took the great poetical passages at such a spanking pace, 'which prevented any emphasis from being laid on their musical quality', his performance fell flat, and was emotionally void. What did impress the critics, however, was the fight between Hamlet and Laertes. Robert Hardy was a fencer, which added a considerable amount of realism to their duelling, and although Richard had no natural poise or style, he was a born fighter, and looked so terrifying as Hamlet when he finally lost his temper in the scene that audiences used to gasp and wince, and start forward from their seats in horror. Once the blood they drew was real, when Richard's blade ran across Robert's brow; but it was a measure of their concentration that they had only one mishap in one hundred and one performances.

The most unnerving performance of all was the night that Winston Churchill came to see *Hamlet*. Much to Richard's amazement the Prime Minister appeared to be mumbling quite audibly from his seat whenever Richard spoke. Gradually he realized that the old man was mumbling Hamlet's lines – and much to Richard's terror, he was word perfect. In the interval Churchill came back stage. 'My Lord Hamlet,' he said, espying Burton in his dressing room. 'May I use your lavatory?'

Another visitor back stage was John Gielgud, master of the *faux pas*, who had not enjoyed his evening, but had arranged to eat with Richard after the performance. Worried about what he was going to say, he was much relieved to find a queue of people waiting to see the star at his dressing-room door, and determined to escape to the restaurant and delay the need to comment. 'Richard, dear boy,' he said, putting his head round the door, 'shall I go ahead, or wait until you're better – I mean, ready?'

Despite Fleet Street's misgivings, *Hamlet* was the most popular production of the season. But Richard's best reviews came for his performance in *Coriolanus*, which had him back once again as the bright young hope. The critics didn't like his Toby Belch in *Twelfth Night*, but the actor who really came in for some abusive reviews was Robert Hardy, playing Ariel in *The Tempest*. He played the part as near naked as anyone ever had to date, which drew howls of shocked outrage from the press. His performance was called 'obscene' and 'disgusting', and *The Times* refused to review the play unless it had the director's assurance that Ariel would be properly dressed for the next performance.

Robert Hardy was deeply upset, and took his crumpled ego to his friend for sympathy.

'Well there you are,' said Richard. 'Why read the bloody notices?'

'What's wrong? Am I really as awful as they say?'

'No!' he said angrily. 'You're too good. They don't understand what you're at. Stop worrying about it; don't panic.'

And Hardy went on that night and played as if the notices had never been; his confidence and his courage restored.

Burton was Caliban in *The Tempest*. The other role he played that season was the Bastard in *King John*. It is an odd part, a quasi chorus, and the director, George Devine, had him sitting still in a corner to one side of the stage between speeches, while the other actors got on with the play. It was a disaster. Richard sat in his corner doing nothing, and the audience sat watching him, rivetted. So he had to be kept off stage until his cue. It was a small part and he used to get very bored during the performance, and think of new ways to liven things up. At one point in the play, there is a series of long tiresome speeches by the barons, princes and counts at the siege of Moulins, during which the Bastard has to come on, and facing upstage go down the line of dignitaries addressing a word to each. Richard came on one night and, walking down the line of actors, said something outrageous to each, whereupon the entire cast turned its back on the audience as each member collapsed in uncontrollable giggles.

When the season came to a close at the end of May, the company went on a brief tour of England, and then over to Denmark for ten performances of *Hamlet* at Elsinore Castle. This entailed a glorious week of sleepless over-indulgence. Night after night the performers would go out to dine after the show, then go on to drink, and when dawn broke they laid down their glasses and leapt into yachts which they had begged and borrowed from the kindly but bemused Danes.

Richard had undertaken radio work during 1953, including the first recording on 25 January of Dylan Thomas's most famous work, his 'play for voices', *Under Milk Wood*. Thomas takes an affectionate look at a day in the life of a small fictitious Welsh seaside town, Llareggub, and its characters – people like Rosie Probert, the Reverend Eli Jenkins, Mrs Willy Nilly, Evans the Death, Gossamer Beynon and the retired sea-captain, blind Captain Cat – and all their thoughts, dreams and secrets are gently exposed by two anonymous narrators.

Thomas had worked on the play intermittently for nearly ten years, and died within a month of completing it, before he was able to revise the work, so that he never came to read the part he had written for himself. The part of First Voice, therefore, fell to Burton and was a gift. It represented everything he loved best: Wales, poetry, and a richness of language and music that were the very essence of the man. It was the perfect vehicle for his rich, brown, Welsh voice.

> *To begin at the beginning:*
> *It is spring, moonless night in the small town, starless*
> *and bible-black, the cobblestreets silent and the*
> *hunched, courters'-and-rabbits' wood limping*
> *invisible down to the sloeblack, slow, black,*
> *crowblack, fishingboat-bobbing sea . . .*
> *Listen. It is night in the chill squat chapel, hymning*
> *in bonnet and brooch and bombazine black, butterfly*
> *choker and bootlace bow, coughing like nannygoats,*
> *sucking mintoes, fortywinking hallelujah; night in the*
> *four-ale, quiet as a domino; in Ocky Milkman's loft*
> *like a mouse with gloves; in Dai Bread's bakery flying*
> *like black flour . . .*
> *Come closer now.*
> *Only you can hear the houses sleeping in the streets*
> *in the slow deep salt and silent black, bandaged night . . .*
> *Only you can hear and see, behind the eyes of the*
> *sleepers, the movement and countries and mazes and*
> *colours and dismays and rainbows and tunes and*
> *wishes and flight and fall and despairs and big seas of*
> *their dreams.*

Richard had loved Dylan Thomas and he loved the poetry. The poet's sudden death, just a few days after his thirty-ninth birthday, had come as a great shock, particularly in the light of their last conversation together. Burton had given and lent the poet money on innumerable occasions over the years, and Dylan invariably used it to buy drink. Shortly before his death, he was on the scrounge again, and had rung Richard from Phil Burton's flat in London wanting to borrow £200. He claimed it was for the education of his children. Richard knew better, and besides did not have the money readily to hand. Dylan offered him the rights to a play he had not yet written in return. Richard refused. It was the last time they spoke. Dylan left for America almost immediately, and the next month, on 9 November 1953, he was dead.

Soon after the final curtain had fallen on *Hamlet*, Richard and Sybil went off for another stint in Hollywood, which improved their bank balance if nothing else. Burton had begun to see films as a means of making 'money for jam'. He was being paid about £50,000 for each film lasting a maximum of three months. The effort required did not compare with that of a stage performance; there was no audience out there beyond the footlights who were going to judge each and every move. There was a director between him and the audience in the movies, and a film editor who would cut out the bad bits. There was no immediacy; by the time the film came out, Richard was long gone. If it vanished without trace, he was unconcerned. He was rich, and when the press wrote about him they called him a film star, which he loved.

Returning home to Wales for Christmas in 1954, however, he had an experience which shocked him to the core. *The Robe* had now been on general release for more than a year, and had reached the local cinemas, so that all Richard's friends and relations had seen it. It was the first film for which he had received good reviews for his part as Marcellus; it was also the first time for many years that the figure of Christ had been permitted by the British Board of Film Censors.

Richard did the usual rounds, visiting everyone who remembered him up and down Caradoc Street, including the Bagall family, who had a little boy called John. John was just five, and Richard had always had a soft spot for him. He loved children, and he and Sybil had been trying without success to have a baby for several years. So whenever he came home he would go and see little John Bagall and they would go and kick a football about in the street together. On this occasion the little boy hid behind his mother and refused to speak.

'Come on John,' said Richard, 'aren't you going to play football?'

'No,' said John. 'I'm not going to play with you any more. You crucified Christ.'

In January Burton was off to play *Alexander the Great*, a far more barbarous character, in another big Hollywood epic being made in Madrid, with Fredric March as Philip and Claire Bloom. She was playing the part of Barsine, one of Alexander's three wives, who, she explained to the press, was 'really his mistress'. Such, by then, was her position in real life too. Although Sybil was with him in Spain, he and Claire continued their affair. Claire was very much in love with Richard; she would do anything for him, yet he seemed bent on humiliating her.

One day on the set he announced that he was going to 'have her' in a stream that afternoon. 'Why don't you watch from over that hill?' he suggested. That afternoon he did indeed perform to an audience of film crew and stuntmen.

Alexander, written, produced and directed by Robert Rossen, was not as great as the publicists had promised.

> *Alexander the Great* is big, showy, overlong and unpleasant [wrote Campbell Dixon, reviewing it in the *Daily Telegraph*]. After sitting through 161 minutes I felt I, too, had marched to the Indus and returned saddle-galled.
>
> Alexander looks to me like Tamburlaine in a tunic. Mr Rossen seems to see him rather as romantics and power-worshippers have always seen him, almost, indeed, as he saw himself – the Greek god conceived to impose his will upon the world.
>
> Such a conception needs the poetry that Marlowe gave to Tamburlaine, superb direction, and an actor of genius; and these are not easy to come by.

Richard himself thought he had made a mistake. 'I know all "epics" are awful, but I thought *Alexander the Great* might be the first good one. I was wrong.'

Back in London, Robert Hardy, had had success at the Old Vic. He had stayed on for the new season when Richard had left for California, and had just opened as Prince Hal in *Henry IV* to rave reviews. They had now both played the part that they had talked about so earnestly at RAF Docking. They had both put into practice the premise they had plotted, and had both been vindicated.

As soon as he heard, Richard rang Robert from Madrid.

'I hear you've had a great success,' he said. 'Send me the notices – all of them, for *Part 1* and *Part 2*.'

Two weeks later he rang Robert at his home again.

'Fantastic notices,' he said. 'Congratulations. You know, next season, under Michael Benthall's system, I'm due to join the company and play *Henry V*? Well I'm not going to. I'm going to make Michael let you play it. I'll come and play Othello and Iago alternating with Johnny Neville.'

It was a generous gesture, but Burton did not yet have the power to dictate to his director who should play what. When he rejoined the Old Vic the following autumn, it was to play the part of Henry V himself.

In the meantime, after *Alexander*, Richard went back to Hollywood to make a film with Lana Turner called *The Rains of Ranchipur* in which he played an Indian doctor. It was a poor film, receiving poor reviews. When they appeared, a journalist, catching Burton for a word at the airport, asked what he thought of the dreadful reviews.

Richard paused for a moment, fixed the journalist with a wry smile, and said, 'Ah well, they do say it never rains but it Ranchipurs.'

He never saw his films, and he never read reviews. 'Forget critics,' he used to say. 'If they're good about you, they're not good enough. If they're bad about you they'll only upset you, so don't read them on either count.'

Along with earning his first million pounds, he had long dreamed of owning a Jaguar car. In 1955, shortly before making *Alexander the Great*, he bought his first Jag – a grey Mark 5. It was an exciting moment, the first time that Burton had bought a brand-new car – the others had been second hand – and quite undiminished by the fact that neither Richard nor Sybil could drive. But his brother Ifor could. He had recently moved up to London with Gwen to be Burton's personal manager, and they were living with Richard and Sybil in their house in Hampstead. They had joined them first in Hollywood during their last stay there.

It was an ideal arrangement. Sybil was enormously fond of her brother- and sister-in-law, and Richard knew that when he was out, there would always be someone to keep his wife company. It also made his sexual adventures easier. When he failed to come home until the early hours of the morning, he had Ifor for cover. He could tell Sybil that they met some of the boys and went for a drink, or dropped in to see friends and stayed up talking, secure in the knowledge that Sybil was not sitting by the telephone on her own. Ifor thoroughly disapproved of his brother's behaviour, but he was drawn into the conspiracy, as were all Richard's friends. They covered for him, and told lies for him, simply to stop Sybil being hurt.

Occasionally they made material sacrifices too. One of the Bakers' most prized possessions was the original sound recording of *Guys and Dolls*, which they had bought in America when Stanley was there in *A Sleep of Prisoners* by Christopher Fry in 1951. Since the musical had not yet hit Britain, the records were much in demand, and one night Stanley and Ellen had taken them to a friend's flat to provide music for a party. As Richard arrived, no fewer than three girls in the room burst into tears, and one of them seized the first thing to hand, which happened to be all eight records of the precious *Guys and Dolls*, she broke them systematically over his head.

There had been another embarrassing occasion the year before, when the Burtons were in America. English actress Dawn Addams was getting married in Rome to fabulously rich Prince Vittorio Massimo, head of one of the oldest noble families in Italy. It was the society wedding of the year, to which the Bakers had been invited. Ellen had written to Sybil and told her that she had had a new dress made specially for the wedding, and how fantastic it was going to be, and Sybil wrote back, telling Ellen to give Dawn their love. So when she and Stanley finally reached the top of the queue to congratulate the happy pair at their reception, Ellen immediately said, 'Oh and by the way, darling, Richard and Sybil send their love.'

Dawn, looking the dream bride beside her prince, replied, 'Well fuck him for a start.'

'Oh no,' said Ellen, in horror. 'Not you too?'

'Didn't you know?' said Stanley, steering her swiftly away. 'It was the talk of Hollywood.'

Despite the occasional shouting match, when Richard's behaviour became too much even for Stanley, the two men were still as close as ever; they were like brothers. Sybil and Ellen had become the greatest of friends too. They had a lot in common: both were married to wild Welshmen who were rugby fanatics; both were actresses who had forfeited their career for their husband; and, not least, both were extremely attractive women who nevertheless shared a thorough dislike of the shape of their legs – as their husbands, of course, knew only too well. Walking down the street,

Richard would make the women go ahead. ''Ere, Stan,' he would say, 'how can two sex symbols like us marry those two with ducks' disease: dropped bottoms, and a couple of legs like pianos?'

They would get their own back. The first time Ellen and Sybil had been in New York together, they went shopping in Woolworths and bought identical Maltese crosses made out of yellow glass for one dollar twenty. When Richard and Stanley came back to the hotel that night, they produced the crosses, stammered a little and said they didn't know quite how to break it to them, but they had been to Tiffanys. . . . Male wrath could be heard the length and breadth of Fifth Avenue.

The four continued to see a great deal of each other, and amongst them acquired a wide circle of friends, including most of the Welsh actors in London. They lived a very social existence. There would be parties, lunches, dinners, and a lot of time spent in pubs. Burton was also a cricket enthusiast, and when the rugby season came to an end, he would be off with friends to watch cricket instead. At home he would listen to the radio or music on the gramophone, and read books. If he had an audience, friends who had come to Sunday lunch for instance, he would sit them down after lunch and read poetry out loud. He loved conversation and debate, but he discussed acting less and less. Gone were the days of Stratford when he would argue about moves and motivation long into the night. If anyone began to talk about interpretation of a part these days, he would dismiss the subject. 'Yes, yes. Quite,' he would say, 'come along now, drink up, drink up.'

Shortly before the start of the season as the Old Vic in Waterloo Road, Richard made a flying visit to Port Talbot to show off the Jag. First stop was Cissie, then he collected Dillwyn and set off up the hill to see his father to take him out for a drink. The old man was eighty by this time, could scarcely see any more, and he had never been in a car in his life. They packed him into the back seat and set off down the Cwmavon road towards the pub.

'What do you think of the car then?' asked Richard, looking back over the seat at his father.

'Car?' said Dic Bach. 'It's not a car, it's a bloody boat.'

Shortly afterwards, the Burtons owned not one but two cars. Richard bought Sybil a bright red MG TF for her birthday, and parked it in the street outside their flat in Hampstead with a red ribbon tied round it. Sybil still could not drive, but quickly set about learning.

By December, *Henry V* had opened and Burton was back in harness at the Old Vic, drawing into the audience a whole generation of people who had never seen Shakespeare before, who came to see in the flesh their heart-throb from the movies. He was back in the tights that he hated so much, back with the grease paint and the make-up that he found impossible to do, and now at the age of thirty, he was beginning to question what he was doing with his life. Having struggled with such single-mindedness to leave the valleys, and having successfully freed himself from his working-class origins, he found they haunted him still. He could not shake off the knowledge in the back of his mind that the work real men did was difficult, dangerous, and dirty, taking them from their beds at dawn and bringing them home exhausted at the end of a day. Here he was dressing up, making up and parading on stage. Acting was not a job for a real man, no more than a draper's apprentice had been, and this feeling was to remain with him all his life.

Furthermore, he feared acting eroded his masculinity. The theatre world was, as it still is, liberally populated with homosexuals. It was commonplace for young actors, particularly good-looking ones, to be propositioned especially by men who were in a position to give them a job. Indeed, many of the men who had given Burton jobs were homosexual, as were a lot of his friends.

His *Henry V*, a stirring, romantic and majestic figure, proved another huge success. The reviews said that he had showed himself to be 'a leading actor to be reckoned with' when he played the part at Stratford. Since then, he had 'matured and developed'. His performance 'excitingly combined all the qualities of Shakespeare's ideal king'.

'What was gratingly metallic [at Stratford] has been transformed into a steely strength which becomes the martial ring and hard brilliance of the patriotic verse. There now appear a romantic sense of a high kingly mission and the clear consciousness of the capacity to fulfil it.'

These were his best notices yet and, to add official recognition, in January he won the *Evening Standard* Drama Award for the 'best performance by an actor'.

The following month he was rehearsing *Othello*, the second play in the repertory. Reviving a tradition which, with one exception in 1949, had not been followed in the London theatre for a century, the actors playing Othello and Iago, Richard and John Neville, alternated with one another. Once again, in the title role, Richard was accused of a flat delivery, of failing to make the poetry sing. It was a performance that one reviewer found 'was sometimes impressive and sometimes rather dull', while his Iago was 'unpretentious and therefore satisfying'. John Neville was the one who received the best notices for Othello.

Burton's third part of the season. Thersites in *Troilus and Cressida*, was never seen. Two weeks before the play was due to open, he was dropped from the production, ostensibly because he was suffering from exhaustion and doctors had advised him to slow down. This was not strictly accurate. The cause was a clash of personalities with director Tyrone Guthrie. 'Tony' Guthrie had never worked with Burton before and, because of his film-star image, he had started out with misgivings. Richard, who was never good at taking direction, balked at Guthrie's; the two came to blows, so Clifford Williams took over the part.

Richard carried on with the two plays he was already doing, which were more than enough. Both Henry V and Othello were demanding roles; and outside the theatre he was living life to the hilt, still seeing Claire Bloom, whom he had set up in a flat in Chelsea, still partying and drinking with friends who turned up to see the show, staying out half the night, and in addition, worrying about his financial position – toying with the idea of becoming a tax exile.

Frank Hauser was one friend who came to see him during this season at the Vic. He had left the BBC and was trying again to start up a playhouse in Oxford following the closure of an earlier attempt. He was trying to raise funds. The Arts Council had given him some money, the undergraduates had raised some, but he was still cripplingly short, and asked Richard whether he would come and act in a couple of plays to raise more.

Richard said he could not because he was contracted to the Old Vic, but would give the theatre some money instead.

'We'll make more if you come and act,' pressed Hauser. 'How much can you give?'

To his astonishment Richard said £2,000, which was then an

enormous sum of money, far more than Frank had ever imagined he would loan, and he returned to Oxford confident that he would have enough to start the company.

Several weeks went by and Frank heard no more, until one Saturday Burton's business manager rang and asked if he could come to the Old Vic to collect the money that night. Frank was going to a wedding in the afternoon, but said that, yes, he would come between the matinee and evening show. He found Richard in his dressing room; he was playing Othello that night. He handed Frank the cheque for £2,000.

'Have you seen it?' he asked, referring to the play.

'No,' said Frank, 'but I'll come one night next week, I'm supposed to be at a wedding right now.'

'You can't,' said Richard, 'it finishes tonight. You've got to stay and see it.'

And so he did. At the end of the performance he went back stage to congratulate Richard, imagining they would go and eat somewhere.

'Look I can't come out,' Burton said, 'but my business manager is going to take you out to dinner. Will you go with her?'

Puzzled, Frank set off with the business manager, the American lawyer who had come to Richard's rescue during the wrangle with Twentieth Century Fox.

'Look,' she said, unveiling the mystery. 'Richard wants you to forget about the cheque for the moment and come and make a film with him.' Burton needed the money himself but, rather than go back on his word and let his friend down, he had made the gesture of handing it over, and then hoped to persuade Frank to give it back. Unfortunately it was too late: the company was already formed, and the £2,000 allocated. Nevertheless he always thought Richard's behaviour the height of good manners.

In the end Burton found the finance from Twentieth Century Fox, but the film, *Sea Wife* from J.D. Scott's novel, *Sea-Wyf and Biscuit*, was another disaster. It was shot in Jamaica with Joan Collins, who played the part of a ship-wrecked nun marooned on an island with three men, one of whom was Richard. But, although the critics panned it, Richard made more money in a couple of months than he could have earned in a year at the Old Vic.

By now he had grown wise. His business manager saw to it that the taxman no longer took everything. He invested in projects, and formed a company in Bermuda where he could be paid money earned out of Britain. He did all that he could within the law, but the only way to get rich was to leave the country altogether. So he and Sybil went in search of a house in Switzerland.

4

Meeting Mrs Jenkins

They found a house in the small village of Celigny on the outskirts of Geneva. Out of sentiment they called it Le Pays de Galles, Wales in French, and although they could have afforded something bigger and better, the all-important factor governing tax assessment in Switzerland was the size of property, so the house was comparatively modest.

The savings were enormous. Richard reckoned that if he made £100,000 in a year in England, he would pay £93,000 in tax. Living in Switzerland, as a Geneva resident, his tax liability would be no more than £700 on the same amount. He could see no possible argument for staying in Britain. He realized they might miss a few things, but reasoned that nothing about the British way of life could be worth £93,000 a year: no rugby match, no Welsh hillside, no cricket season, no Hampstead pub, not even the pleasure of being with his friends and family.

Burton simply wanted to be rich, and he would never have made a million living in London. Besides, if he missed anything, he could be home within an hour and a half from Geneva, or in Paris within forty-five minutes, or Rome in two hours. If he could no longer pop down to Port Talbot to see his family, he could afford to fly them out to visit him in Celigny. The fact that neither Richard nor Sybil spoke French didn't matter either. Switzerland was attracting so many British tax exiles at that time that there was quite a sizeable English-speaking community in the area.

The other side of the coin, however, was that Richard was not entitled to own property in Britain, and could only spend ninety days a year in the country before he became liable to pay tax, so the work he did was strictly limited. Another season at the Old Vic, for example, was out of the question. Films shot on location in Britain were virtually out of the question too; and it was the strict limitation on the work they could take that decided other high-earning actors, like Stanley Baker, against tax exile.

For the time being, however, thoughts like that were pushed to the back of the Burtons' minds. Sybil was pregnant at long last. The baby was due in September 1957, and they were both thrilled. But shortly after the good news came the bad news in the spring that Richard's father had died in the local hospital in Neath. He was aged eighty-one, and had worked right up until the previous year. He had spent fifty years down the mines, and when he was retired from the pits, he took other jobs. His last job had been as night watchman for a company in Port Talbot, and until the very end he had walked the four miles back and forth from Pontrhydyfen.

Richard did not attend the funeral. 'My father was a very unsentimental person,' he said to those that asked. 'He would be shocked if he knew I had travelled more than seven hundred miles to go to his funeral.'

He was busy, there was film work to be done; yet another non-starter called *Bitter Victory*, filmed in Libya. There was talk of other films: George Bernard Shaw's *Saint Joan* with Jean Seberg in Otto Preminger's ill-fated production; an idea was mooted with Marilyn Monroe, and there were a number of other suggestions, but nothing came of them. The next venture that did materialize was another Anouilh play, *Time Remembered*, which took Burton back to the New York stage.

Richard left for New York a proud father. The previous day, 11 September, Sybil had given birth to a little girl that they named Kate, at a hospital in Geneva. Having seen his daughter safely into the world, he left mother and baby in Switzerland, with a nanny to look after them both, and flew to the United States. Sybil, Kate and nanny were to join him later.

A new production, predictably enough, meant a new love affair. The actress was Susan Strasberg, a junior member of the cast, who was just nineteen and quite taken in by the great Burton's charm. He rented an apartment where they could meet, he went home with her to meet her parents, and made no secret about their relationship. He introduced her to friends in New York, to Philip Burton, who had moved there on a permanent basis by this time, and even to visiting members of his family whom he brought out from Wales to see the show. He had taught her some Welsh, and when his relatives arrived, he made her recite what she had learned.

'Whom do you love?' he asked her.

'*Ti rwyn dy garu di* (I love you),' she replied, '*mwy na neb arall yn y byd* (more than anyone else in the world).'

She was madly in love with him, and shattered when he dropped her, but that was not for some time. The play ran for eight months and, although he was slightly more discreet about his movements when Sybil arrived, the affair continued. That Christmas he presented Susan with a white mink scarf and muff; he gave Sybil a full-length coat.

There was never any doubt with any of his conquests about whom Richard loved. He did not become involved with other women because he secretly wanted to replace Sybil or was in any way unhappy in his relationship with her. He didn't even pretend to other women that his wife didn't understand him; he didn't discuss her. His problem was that his wife did understand him; she understood him and she adored him, and he was entirely confident that no matter what he did, she would never leave him. And Sybil was confident that, provided she let him have his affairs, he would never leave her. She was aware, however, that he was easily led. Other people fed his ego, Sybil kept him in touch with normality.

His affair with Susan Strasberg came to an end when he went home in June, but she did not realize quite how dead it was until September when she paid him a surprise visit in London where he was making a film of John Osborne's play, *Look Back In Anger*. His co-star was Claire Bloom, and Richard found himself with an embarrassment of mistresses. He sent a studio car to collect Susan from the airport and bring her to his dressing room at Elstree where they were filming. No sooner was she through the door than he began a juggling act – bundling Susan into the loo when Claire came into the room – to keep each woman from seeing the other. By the end of the day, when he had driven her back to the Savoy Hotel and said he wouldn't come up to her room because someone might see them, Susan had well and truly got the message.

Burton had met John Osborne in New York a few months earlier, and the idea of doing the film had grown from there. They had bumped into one another, quite literally, as Richard was in the midst of a lively rendition of 'Knees Up Mother Brown' at a riotous party on the Hudson River. Their host was Laurence Olivier, who had been in the city playing in another Osborne play, *The Entertainer*, for much of the time Richard was there; and he had organized a midnight cruise up the river, serving two hundred-odd guests Cockney-style jellied eels and fish and chips in English newspaper.

Emlyn Williams, through whom had met a great many people in the profession, had first introduced Burton to Olivier. They had become quite friendly and Burton always claimed to have advised him, with reference to the bad films that they both made in their time, 'If you're going to make rubbish – be the best rubbish in it.' In turn Olivier had once said to Burton, 'Make your mind up. Do you want to be an actor or a household name?' And Richard had replied, 'Both.'

However *Look Back In Anger*, directed by Tony Richardson, provided a brief respite from the dross. The film was not everyone's idea of an entertaining night out: a stark picture of youth and disillusionment, pertinent to the late 1950s, with Burton playing the part of Jimmy Porter, the tormented angry young man, the intellectual barrow-boy who cannot cope with his wife's middle-class background. Richard was miscast. He looked too old and too obviously capable, but his voice and his remarkable presence earned him justifiable praise, and went a long way to restore his reputation as a serious actor.

Look Back In Anger had brought him to Britain for his first visit as a non-resident, and his new-found wealth was obvious. He drove down to Wales in a Rolls Royce, and spoke about his life in Switzerland: his Cadillac convertible, his house, his Swiss bank account, and the thousands of dollars nestling inside it. He was like Father Christmas come to the valleys; drinks all round.

In the long term he provided more than drinks. For Cissie and Elfed Richard bought a detached house overlooking the sea out on the Baglan Road, and a life pension for Elfed. He bought a house for Ifor and Gwen at Squires Mount in Hampstead; a bungalow for his eldest brother Tom; and a terraced house in Pontryhdyfen for Hilda, the sister who had taken care of their father before he died. He gave substantial presents to the rest of the family, – a car each for Will, Verdun, David and Graham – and cheques, which eventually began to arrive regularly. In addition, there was the promise of £25 to any of his nieces or nephews if they passed their 11-plus exam, which would see them into grammar school.

The generosity did not stop at the family. Richard organized and paid for a coach trip to take the old people in Caradoc Street to the seaside at Porthcawl for the day. This became an annual summer outing that he continued to sponsor for most of his life.

1959 brought another stint in America and two more poor films: *Bramble Bush*, which had nothing to commend it from the start; and *Ice Palace*, based on the novel by Edna Ferber about feuding families in Alaska, which over-ran its schedule and at least made Richard a lot of money, but plunged his sagging reputation deeper still.

Then towards the end of the year, he had a call from Moss Hart, who had written the screenplay for *Prince of Players*. Moss was now working on a project with lyricist Alan Jay Lerner and composer Fritz Loewe – creators of classics like *My Fair Lady* and *Gigi* – and they wanted to come to talk to him about it. The project was *Camelot*, based on T.H. White's book *The Once And Future King* about the legend of King Arthur. Although they had not yet started writing, Julie Andrews had already agreed to play the part of Guinevere, and they wanted Burton to play King Arthur.

Richard had never done a musical before, but Alan Jay Lerner had once heard him sing. It was at a Hollywood party given by George and Ira Gershwin, where Richard and Sybil had sung a collection of Welsh folk songs which he had found enchanting. So, when Moss Hart, who was to direct the production, suggested Burton for the part, Alan readily agreed. Richard was enthusiastic about the idea, and signed to play the part for a year. In the meantime he did some television work on both sides of the Atlantic, including another John Osborne play for the BBC, *A Subject for Scandal and Concern*, an hour's drama for which he was paid £1,000 – peanuts, as he was quick to point out, compared with what the American TV companies had paid him, but the highest fee to date that the BBC had ever paid for two weeks' work.

By the end of the year Richard was a father for the second time. It had seemed at one point as though he and Sybil would never have children, and now within two and a half years they had two little girls. Richard had been hoping it would be a boy this time – he always longed for a son – but was nevertheless delighted with his baby daughter, whom they called Jessica.

Before *Camelot*, Burton made a twenty-six-part series about Sir Winston Churchill for BBC Television and ABC in America, *The Valiant Years*, in which he spoke the voice of the Churchill reading from his war-time memoirs. There are some who believe it was the best work he ever did. He did not try to impersonate Churchill: 'I based my voice,' he told Roderick Mann in the *Sunday Express*, 'slightly on a Peter Sellers imitation I once heard of an upper-class Englishman, dropping aitches and changing "R"s into "W"s.' The effect was extraordinary, and earned him high praise.

Rehearsals for *Camelot* started in September 1960. They were originally due to begin in the spring, but if ever a production was dogged by bad luck it was *Camelot*. Alan and Fritz were rewriting throughout the try-out in Toronto, in Boston, and right up until four days before they opened on Broadway two months later. On the first night at the new O'Keefe Centre in Toronto the show ran for four and a half hours. The curtain did not come down until twenty minutes to one in the morning. *Camelot* was officially designated 'a disaster area' by the Broadway jackals who can make or break a show over a drink in Sardi's Bar, the famous show business restaurant.

It needed radical surgery, at least one and a half hours' worth. Two days later Alan, principal surgeon, was in hospital himself, having collapsed over dinner, and was out of action for two weeks. He had only just got over a nervous breakdown, so his health was frail in any event. The day he came out of hospital, Moss Hart was wheeled into the room he had just vacated with a heart attack, which put him out of the show for the rest of the run. And Fritz, the remaining member of the trio, had only recently recovered from a heart attack, too, so was not yet running on full steam. With no director, an audience to play to nightly, a cast of sixty-one people, and an entire musical to rework, the strain took its toll. Alan and Fritz, who had been together through thick and thin for eighteen years, began to fall out.

It was a miracle that the show ever reached Broadway. When it finally did, the notices were indifferent, audiences began walking out of the threatre not just by the dozen but some nights by as many as two or three hundred, and *Camelot* seemed doomed to die.

Noel Coward was in the audience that first night on 44th Street, packed in among the other stars and celebrities, and he was the first person Alan saw after the final curtain fell. One of Richard's party pieces had been impersonating what various theatre people said when they met one after a first night, and he had mimicked Noel Coward repeatedly. He came up to one, according to Richard, patted one on the shoulder, and said, veddy, veddy softly, 'Mahvellous, darling, mahvellous.' Alan met Coward in the alley just outside the stage door. 'He came up to me,' said Lerner, 'patted me on the shoulder, and said, veddy, veddy softly, "Mahvellous, darling, mahvellous."'

A few weeks later, Moss Hart reappeared on the scene, fully recovered and able to cast a fresh eye on the show. He suggested some changes and encouraged Alan and Fritz to rewrite some more, which they did.

The final saviour was 'The Ed Sullivan Show', the most popular television variety programme in the States at that time. To mark the fifth anniversary of *My Fair Lady*, Ed Sullivan had decided to devote a whole hour to Lerner and Loewe, and allowed them *carte blanche*. So they brought on half the cast of *Camelot* and devoted the bulk of the show to its best songs, including the title number sung by Burton, and 'What Do The Simple Folk Do?' by Julie Andrews. The following morning there was a queue for the theatre box office that ran halfway down the block, and *Camelot* was a smash hit. Burton gave 'a majestic performance' as King Arthur, one critic said it was among the best in his career, and although his singing had never been as good as his younger brother, Graham, he had a fine voice.

Richard had behaved impeccably throughout the ordeal, and Alan Jay Lerner says to this day that the show would never have made it even as far as New York without him. Far from playing the temperamental star, he would go to Alan, who, as well as rewriting the show, took over as director when Moss disappeared, and say, 'Listen, love, you won't have time to do the understudy rehearsals. I'll do them for you.' He was endlessly patient and tolerant about being messed around, having lines and songs changed night after night and, by keeping his own spirits high, did a great deal to prevent company morale from plummeting.

He also kept himself high on spirits of the liquid variety. 'When any normal man would have been placed on the critical list,' says Alan, recalling the amount of alcohol he put away during *Camelot*, 'Richard could stand firmly in the centre of the room, recite Dylan Thomas from "hello" to "goodbye" and rattle off any Shakespearean part he had ever performed.'

As a doctor friend in Boston, who had once come across someone else with Burton's extraordinary capacity, later explained to Lerner, 'Welsh livers and kidneys seem to be made of some metallic alloy, quite unlike the rest of the human race. One day,' he added, 'like aeroplanes, they eventually show metal fatigue.'

Yet, although he frequently arrived at the theatre several drinks into the wind, Richard never missed a single performance. The only way in which the alcohol manifested itself was that his voice would go croaky. There were occasions when he turned up with no voice at all, and Alan would tell him to go home. But he would insist he could do the show, and the moment he walked on to the stage, sure enough, his voice returned and sounded as strong and as fresh as if he had just come back from a month's holiday.

There was one occasion, however, when he lost his voice because of a cold which turned into laryngitis. It was during a matinee in Toronto and, to give his throat a rest, he did the final scene of the first act in a whisper. It was the moment in the story when Arthur reveals that he knows that his wife, Guinevere, and Lancelot are passionately in love with each other, but decides that because he loves them both, he will do nothing about it, and with God's help they will live through it. Spoken in a whisper it proved exceptionally moving, so much so that an elderly lady sitting in the front row felt an uncontrollable desire to comfort poor Arthur. She stretched out arms to him and began to climb over the orchestra rail. Fortunately the conductor saw her coming and managed to restrain her before she plunged headlong into the first violins. Richard also saw her coming and somehow managed to control his mirth just long enough for the curtain to fall. Thereafter the first few rows of the stalls were stunned by the sound of poor, sad King Arthur roaring with laughter from behind the curtain.

As usual, once out of costume poor, sad King Arthur had the rest of the company entranced. Like the Pied Piper, they would gather round him at the bar or in his well-stocked dressing room at the Majestic Theater, and out came the stories of his grandfather, of anyone else's grandfather, of Oxford, of Hollywood, of the plays and the films and the actors he had acted with. And, as usual, there were chorus girls who succumbed to his advances. So well known was his philandering that when the chorus sang of King Arthur, 'I wonder what the King is doing tonight?' they frequently sang, 'I wonder who the King is screwing tonight?' Burton enjoyed the refrain, and boasted of it later.

Such was his prowess that when Robert Goulet, playing the part of Sir Lancelot, the knight who falls in love with Guinevere, developed a passion for the Queen in real life, and was given the brush-off, he went to seek a few hints from Richard. Richard sent him packing. 'Why did he come to me?' he asked. 'I couldn't get anywhere either.'

Richard was under contract to *Camelot* for a year, but in July 1961, a month before it was completed, he went to Alan and told him he wanted to leave early. He had been approached by Walter Wanger, a senior producer from Twentieth Century Fox, and offered a quarter of a million dollars for three months' work in Rome, playing the part of Mark Antony in the much-publicized film of *Cleopatra*. In addition, he would be given one thousand dollars a week living expenses, and a villa and staff for Sybil and the children.

Cleopatra was another production that had been plagued by misadventure, and it had been hitting the headlines. Shooting, which should have begun the previous autumn at Pinewood Studios, was delayed because Elizabeth Taylor, playing the title role, had been repeatedly ill. They began filming bits without her, but bad weather and other problems thwarted these, and, after spending over two million dollars thus far, it was decided to call a halt. In the new year the director resigned and Joseph Mankiewicz was brought in at great expense to rewrite and direct. Peter Finch and Stephen Boyd, the actors playing the parts of Caesar and Mark Antony, were no longer available by this time, so he had to re-cast, and wanted Richard for the part of Antony. But before Mankiewicz had time to approach him, Elizabeth Taylor, had collapsed with pneumonia in her suite at the Dorchester Hotel and for a week it was touch and go over whether she would survive.

Elizabeth Taylor was a star who had captured the public imagination since childhood, in films like *Lassie Come Home* and *National*

Velvet. English by birth, she was the daughter of a prosperous London art dealer who had moved to the United States at the outbreak of war. Now twenty-nine, she was at the height of her beauty and one of the most famous, most publicized women in the film world. Her marriages – and the public declaration each time that this one was for life – were not the least cause of her fame.

At the age of eighteen she had married her first husband, Nicky Hilton, heir to the famous hotel chain. 'Your heart knows when you meet the right man,' she had said. 'There is no doubt Nicky is the one I want to spend my life with.' Nicky lasted eight months, and Elizabeth moved on to husband number two: English actor Michael Wilding, twice her age and married to Kay Young at the time. 'I just want to be with Michael, to be his wife,' she said. 'He is so mature and that is what I need.' Elizabeth had two sons by Michael Wilding, Michael and Christopher, before moving on to a new love, film producer Michael Todd, whom she married in 1957. He was another man more than twice her age, divorced from Joan Blondel at the time when they met, and engaged to Evelyn Keyes. One baby, a little girl called Liza, and fourteen months later, he was killed in a plane crash, and she turned to his best friend, singer Eddie Fisher, then married to Debbie Reynolds, for comfort.

Debbie Reynolds was everyone's darling, and Elizabeth's public was outraged. Vitriol was poured upon her, she was branded a 'scarlet woman', a wicked widow, a marriage-breaker – despite the fact that this particular marriage had been empty for years – and the pressure was so intense that she had no alternative but to marry Eddie. They married on the same day as Debbie Reynolds divorced him, 13 May 1959, with Elizabeth declaring, 'We will be on our honeymoon for thirty or forty years.'

She had made romantic vows like this before, and public wrath was not much appeased. The climate was so hostile that the Theater Owners of America, who had named her 'Star of the Year' for her performance in *Cat On A Hot Tin Roof*, thought better of it and withdrew the award.

Then came her brush with death and all was forgiven. Influenza turned into *staphylococcus* pneumonia and it was only the action of a quick-witted young doctor attending a party at the Dorchester that saved her. He rushed to her suite and fed a thin plastic tube down her throat so she could breathe before she was whisked to hospital for an emergency tracheotomy. On four occasions in the course of the operation she stopped breathing, and bulletins about her condition were issued every fifteen minutes to the scores of reporters waiting round the clock outside the London Clinic. Her parents flew in from America to be by her bedside, the Queen's physician, Lord Evans, and ten other doctors were on hand; and when the drama was over, less than a week after it had begun, Dr Carl Goldman explained to the press that, 'Out of every one hundred who have Miss Taylor's type of pneumonia, rarely do two survive.'

Her public had forgiven her everything; letters, telegrams and flowers arrived by the gross. She was even bigger news than she had been before. As if to put the official seal of approval on her return to favour, she was scarcely out of hospital when she was awarded an Oscar for her role in *Butterfield 8*.

Twentieth Century Fox, who had been considering replacing Elizabeth, suddenly realized they had a considerable asset on their hands, even if it did mean delaying production yet again. They were paying Elizabeth more than any actress had ever been paid in the history of the film industry: a million dollars for sixty-four days' work, plus three thousand dollars living expenses per week, and a dozen other fringe benefits, like penthouse suites, villas in Rome and Rolls Royces to take her to and from the studios.

It was turning into an infinitely more expensive production than the company ever envisaged at the outset. Extricating Mankiewicz from his commitments had cost three million dollars, and Twentieth Century Fox had had to pay fifty thousand dollars to buy Burton out of his contract for *Camelot*. But by September the show was finally on the road, and Richard was told to stand by in Rome at the end of the month.

So he and Sybil and the children, plus Ifor and Gwen, sped to Rome, installed themselves in a villa on the Appian Way, and for the rest of the year Richard was standing by with nothing to do. The director was busy shooting the early part of the film with Elizabeth and Rex Harrison, playing Julius Caesar, and the most Burton had to do was make the occasional appearance from behind a pillar. In nineteen weeks he spent five days on the set, and by the time he was needed for any real work, it was January, and under the terms of his contract, Richard was into very lucrative overtime.

He was thoroughly bored and frustrated during the weeks of inactivity. But he and Sybil had friends in the city, and he was never short of drinking chums: Roddy McDowell, playing Octavius, with whom he had been in *Camelot* for the last year; Rachel Roberts, a friend from Stratford days, who fell in love with Rex Harrison during *Cleopatra* and subsequently married him; Katlin, Dylan Thomas's widow; and Stanley Baker, who was in Rome making *Eve*, with the French actress Jeanne Moreau.

Producer Joseph Losey had been terrified that Richard would make a bee-line for Jeanne Moreau and wreck his film, and had pleaded with Stanley to keep his friend away from her. But Losey had picked the wrong leading lady. A group of friends were having tea across the road from the studios one afternoon when Richard left the party and went off to watch Elizabeth Taylor doing her nude scene. He came back like a man possessed, raving about her beauty, and everyone knew that in no time at all he would get her into bed.

It was not long before the whole world knew that he done so. Richard made a fundamental mistake. This was the first time he had ever been to Rome, and he had never encountered the 'paparazzi' before – the freelance Italian press photographers, who specialize in digging dirt in the stars' private lives, and materialize with a magnifying lens to record and relate their every gesture. He had never been excessively discreet about his other affairs, and he made no secret of this one.

He made one other mistake. Elizabeth Taylor, for all her marriages, had a strict code of personal morality. She had always made much of her lack of promiscuity in a notoriously promiscuous profession. This simply meant that she married the men she slept with, whatever their marital status at the time; and Richard Burton was no exception.

Richard thought he could handle it. Friends told him he was out of his league, that this one was different, but he ignored them. He insisted that he had had affairs before and never come unstuck. Sybil would not leave him. What was so different about Elizabeth Taylor?

But she was different. There is scarcely a person who has met Elizabeth Taylor who has not been spell-bound by her. Whether the spell is cast by the woman herself, or the magnetism of what she represents – such glamour and such fame, or a mixture of both – she has admirers of every age and sex, who may condemn the way she behaves, but profess great love for her nevertheless.

Richard was attracted by the mixture too. All his adult life he had been proving his masculine prowess, proving that he could take any woman he wanted, irrespective of the cost or the risks, as though driven by some fury. Elizabeth was the ultimate prize: the most beautiful woman in the world, the most famous, the most desired. And he, Richard Burton, son of a Welsh miner from Pontrhydyfen, could have her.

He had been sold to her as the Shakespearean actor, the new Olivier, the wild Welshman with the poetry and the voice, and the reputation of a great lover. The man everyone wanted to be with. Her marriage to Eddie Fisher had been a mistake. She had bowed to public opinion, and was looking for a way out, for some romance in her life. And it was perfectly apparent that Richard was available; Richard was always available. Elizabeth decided that she wanted him – the first time the boot had been on the other foot – and Elizabeth had seldom been denied anything in life.

Sybil knew what was going on long before it became public knowledge, but tolerated it in silence, as she had all his affairs, and kept her unhappiness to herself. He would climb into bed beside her in the early hours of the morning, sometimes too drunk to take his clothes off. One night he got into bed with a lighted cigarette and fell asleep with it still in his hand. Sybil woke up some time later to find the room full of smoke from the smouldering bedclothes. She tried to wake Richard, but he was so deeply asleep that she couldn't move him. So she ran through the villa to find Ifor and alert the rest of the household, and she and Ifor between them carried Richard to the safety of the garden. In all the drama they suddenly realized that no one had brought out Jessica, who was asleep on the top floor. Sybil dashed back into the smoke-filled house and rescued the little girl in the nick of time.

Jessica was two. She was a beautiful child, but she was not yet talking, and Sybil had been growing increasingly worried about her. Initially she had been telling everyone that it was quite normal, that a lot of children didn't talk until late. Then she had kept her friends away from the child; Jessica was just never around when they went to visit. But she had now reached the stage where she had

As Sir Toby Belch in *Twelfth Night*. He was hopeless at applying wigs and make-up, so Robert Hardy did it for him

As the Bastard in *King John*. His remarks on stage were so outrageous that the entire cast had to turn its back on the audience as each member collapsed in uncontrollable giggles

Burton was back at the Old Vic in 1955, drawing into the audience a whole generation of people who had never before seen Shakespeare

His Henry V won Burton lavish praise and the coveted *Evening Standard* award for Best Actor. 'He combined all the qualities of Shakespeare's ideal King.' He is seen here with Zena Walker playing the Princess of France

In *Othello* Richard and John Neville revived a tradition by alternating in the part of Othello, as he is here with Rosemary Harris

Known by their friends as Rich and Syb, they seemed ideally suited. Other people fed his ego; Sybil kept him in touch with normality

Reading was Richard's greatest pleasure. His ambition was to have a thousand volumes of the Everyman library

In 1957 Richard and Sybil bought a house at Celigny in Switzerland, and Burton became a tax exile

Opposite, above: Playing Jimmy Porter in *Look Back in Anger*. But Burton was miscast; he looked too old and too obviously capable

Below: 'I am, after all, the authentic dark voice of my tortured part of the world, Wales.'

Above: As Mark Antony in *Cleopatra*: 'all sound and fury, and what he signifies is the sad waste of a major talent'

Richard and Sybil with their elder daughter Kate in 1962: a happy family on the verge of break-up. For months he was torn between his duty to Sybil and his infatuation with Elizabeth Taylor, and for months he havered

Burton and Taylor in the early days of their relationship. Richard is wearing the suit that he went out and bought specially to meet Elizabeth's posh friend, Sheran Cazalet

Burton in John Gielgud's production of *Hamlet*. The opportunity to perform Shakespeare with no wig and no tights was enormously appealing

Elizabeth with Richard and his adoptive father, Philip Burton in 1964. She had effected a reconciliation between the two men, and won the older man's lasting affection

to face up to the fact that something was wrong with her younger daughter.

Early in February Richard and Elizabeth dined quite openly together at a restaurant called Alfredo's. The rumours that had been circulating the city now appeared in black and white on the pages of the morning papers all over the world. Two days later Sybil packed her suitcase and left for New York to try to rally some support from Philip Burton. Richard was due in Paris to finish filming *The Longest Day*, and before he left he told Elizabeth that their affair was over; Sybil came first.

Elizabeth took the news badly, and that night she was rushed to hospital having taken an overdose of sleeping pills. Richard realized for the first time that he was out of his depth; and when Philip Burton sent his former ward a cable from New York, expressing his strong disapproval, Richard picked up the telephone and told the older man, in no uncertain terms, to mind his own business. It was the beginning of a rift which lasted more than two years.

It was not the only relationship strained past its limit. In the following weeks there was much coming and going. Sybil returned briefly. Eddie Fisher left, then reappeared to throw a big thirtieth birthday party for Elizabeth at the Hostaria del'Orso, then left again, and was taken into hospital to rest. Emlyn Williams flew to Rome to try to reason with Richard. But, driving from the airport in the car, Richard turned to him and said very calmly, '*Dwi am briodi'r eneth 'ma* (I am going to marry this girl)'. Stanley Baker tried to make him see sense. And Ifor begged him to stop before it was too late. There were innumerable denials and counter-denials in the press. Eddie Fisher told reporters there was no substance to the rumour that his marriage was breaking up, and telephoned Elizabeth from New York while the press were with him so they could hear her deny it first hand. She refused.

Sybil could take no more. She packed up her belongings, and cleared out of the villa and out of Rome, taking the children with her and Liliana, the Italian nanny who had been looking after them. Ifor and Gwen flew out on the same flight, and they all returned to Squires Mount together.

Ifor left no room for doubt about whose side he was taking. The brothers had a monumental row over Richard's behaviour, so impassioned that they came to blows. This gentle, tolerant man whom Richard so adored was appalled, and said so. Of all the criticism, all the anger, all the advice that came from friends, relatives and colleagues, Ifor's was the censure that hurt the most. Ifor refused to see or speak to Richard and it was more than two years before the rent in their relationship was healed.

Burton was left on his own in Rome. He had no alternative, whether he would have chosen to follow Sybil and make it all up or not. He was still needed on the set every day, as was Elizabeth, and the affair continued under the full glare of the press. They lunched, they dined, they went to the beach and to nightclubs, they drank champagne, they kissed, they quarrelled – every detail was faithfully recorded.

Back in London, Sybil was learning the truth about Jessica. After a series of consultations and tests, the specialists had diagnosed autism. Autism is a complaint that is still little understood. Children who suffer from it are perfectly normal physically and intellectually, but because of some kind of inner trauma, they shut themselves off from the world, and their only form of expression is anger. It varies in intensity, but Jessica, they said, was one hundred per cent autistic; she would in all probability never talk, and never grow out of it. She would remain cut off from the world; she would always be very difficult to handle.

Richard went to pieces when he heard the news, and took refuge, as usual, in the bottle. He could not cope. He felt guilty, responsible in some way for what had happened. It was the bad blood he had always feared, and his instinct was to turn and flee. For months he was torn between his duty to Sybil and his infatuation with Elizabeth, and for months he havered.

When the filming of *Cleopatra* came to an end in July, he and Elizabeth went off to spend a few weeks with Rex Harrison and Rachel Roberts in Portofino. Then they went their separate ways: Richard back to Sybil and the children, who came out to join him in Celigny; and Elizabeth to her house in Gstaad, just an hour's drive away. In no time at all, they were meeting again, and Sybil decided to leave him to it, and return to London. She still loved him and had been prepared to forgive him for all the hurt, all the indignity and humiliation, but now he was asking too much of her. The press, watching every move, were driving her out of her mind. If Richard wanted her he knew where to find her, and she would wait for him to make up his mind.

Meanwhile she endeavoured to forget. She moved out of the home she had shared with Burton in Squires Mount, leaving the children with Liliana and Ifor and Gwen, and went to stay with friends. She had dozens of friends, and was never short of an invitation. Everyone adored Sybil and was eager to do whatever possible to cheer her up. She based herself in a rented flat in Brompton Square. She embarked on a hectic social life, dancing by night and sleeping by day. She went to every first night in London, she went to restaurants and to parties, and when all of that was over, she would go on to the Ad Lib, the most fashionable nightclub in town, and dance until dawn. For a time she stayed with writer Bert Shevalove in Pelham Square while *A Funny Thing Happened On The Way To The Forum*, which he wrote, was being staged, and the house was never empty. Visitors came, like Princess Margaret and Tony Snowdon and Dirk Bogarde, who fell madly in love with her. Older friends rallied around, too: Emlyn and Molly Williams, Robert Hardy and his wife Sally, Frank Hauser, Stanley and Ellen Baker, the singer Alma Cogan – all friends who had known her as part of a permanent partnership, as 'Rich and Syb', and were stunned by what had happened

Zenith of Sybil's time in London was her thirty-third birthday. Dirk Bogarde and Alma Cogan organized a surprise birthday party for her at the Ad Lib. It was the first time the club had ever been given over to a private party, and it was to be the party of all time, with nearly sixty of the most famous and glamorous people in London. One person who was not at the party was Ellen Baker. Her birthday present to her friend was to take Kate off her hands for a week, so she could forget about loose buttons and school runs and what to cook for supper. She took Kate with her own children, Adam, Martin, and Sally, who was Richard's goddaughter, to stay in their house in the South of France – and every day Sybil rang to see how Kate was.

Richard and Elizabeth, in the meantime, had incurred the disgust of the American public. Elizabeth was right back to square one, as unpopular as she had been for coming between Eddie Fisher and Debbie Reynolds; and Richard was not far behind. A female member of the House of Representatives suggested they should both be barred from entering the country. She said the American people had the right to 'ostracize those who show no concern for either flag or people, particularly innocent children, or show no respect for either cherished institutions or God'.

Whether it is good or bad, publicity is the stuff of which fame is built, and Richard discovered he enjoyed the attention that he and Elizabeth attracted. Producers were not slow to see the advantage of the situation – there were people who had thought that their romance was nothing more than a publicity stunt dreamt up by Twentieth Century Fox to try to boost *Cleopatra* – and by October other producers were trying to use them both again. The first was a film of Evelyn Waugh's novel, *The Loved One*. Elizabeth wanted her usual fee of £357,000 plus ten per cent of the profits; and Burton held out for half that sum with ten per cent of the profits. He had put himself into a new league, and one which that particular producer was not prepared to pay. MGM, however, were prepared to pay the price, and in December Richard and Elizabeth were both signed up to co-star in *The VIPs*, a film to be made at Elstree Studios. It was yet another rather indifferent film about a band of celebrities stranded at Heathrow Airport by fog.

Richard and Elizabeth arrived in London by train. Elizabeth never travelled light. She had three children with her, two secretaries, and enough baggage to clothe a small army. The press were waiting for them at Victoria Station and, after an ugly altercation in which cameras and photographers were knocked to the ground, they drove to the Dorchester. Elizabeth was also a Swiss tax exile and, like Richard, barred from owning property in London, so that the Dorchester had been her base on every visit to London since the age of nineteen. For the sake of appearances, they stayed in separate suites overlooking Hyde Park, the Terrace and the Harlequin Suites. This ploy did not fool anyone, but unmarried couples being seen to sleep in the same bed, particularly when they were married to other people, was not as acceptable in 1962 as it is today.

Elizabeth had to work hard to be accepted, not just by the public, but by Richard's friends. No one blamed her for what had happened; they all knew him too well. They were simply sad because of what they had both done to Sybil, and they found their allegiance split down the middle. She tried hard not only to be accepted by friends, but also to be what Richard wanted her to be. She wanted him, and was well aware that he had not yet cut the ties with Sybil. She went to rugby matches with him, two during their first week in London, and drank pints of beer with the lads. And, as so many of his other women had done, she tried to learn a bit of Welsh.

One of the first people Richard rang was Robert Hardy, who had seen a lot of Sybil.

'I've got a young woman here,' said Richard, 'who's determined to meet you.'

'Oh who?' said Robert. 'Elizabeth who?' And with some trepidation he invited them over for sausages and mash at his home in Chelsea. As they were leaving, Elizabeth turned to Robert, who was showing her into the car, and said, 'Tim, please don't hate me.' It was, he said, impossible not to like her.

Yet on another occasion it would be Sybil sharing the Hardys' evening meal. She was drinking more than she normally did during this time, and there was one night when they had all had rather too much. They suggested she stay the night, but she insisted upon going home. Robert offered to drive her back to Hampstead, so they all piled into his car, Sybil, Sally and their enormous Dalmatian dog, and set off for North London. Their route took them up Park Lane, and as they drew abreast of the Dorchester, Sybil burst into tears and said, 'Look, there they are, they're in there, they're up there in that suite. Oh get him out,' she sobbed. 'Get him out.'

'You want him out?' asked Hardy imperiously, sounding not unlike Burton. 'Then I'll get him out.' And with that he swung the car across the southbound carriageway, screeched to a halt outside the Dorchester, snapped his dog to his heels, and pushed in through the doors. It was nearly a quarter to four in the morning, the vacuum cleaners were whirring and the rug from the centre of the foyer was in a giant roll by the desk. Robert strode up to the night porter standing behind it, who asked if he could help.

'Yes,' said Robert. 'I want to speak to Richard Burton who is upstairs in his suite. I've just arrived from America.'

'We're putting no calls through,' said the man.

'Tell him who it is,' said Robert, 'and he will speak to me.'

The man remained unmoved, and Robert began to get impatient. He was determined at all costs to get Richard out, although he hadn't quite worked out what would happen next. The problem was solved, however, by the appearance of an under-manager, bearing down on him in full morning dress, to find out the cause of the commotion. Robert was prepared for combat, when he looked down and noticed that his dog was calmly cocking his leg on the roll of carpet at his feet. So, without another word he stepped nimbly over the puddle, and continued on his way to Hampstead.

Robert Hardy was not the only one with crazed schemes to mend the marriage. Stanley and Ellen were sure that if only they could get Richard and Sybil together again, Richard would come to his senses. So they persuaded them both to come to Stanley's birthday party. Richard sent a car to collect Sybil from Squires Mount, which went on to pick him up at the Dorchester, where he was waiting in the foyer. Elizabeth was upstairs, and she telephoned him three or four times during the course of the evening. Richard was very funny as usual, and charming to Sybil. She looked beautiful but strained. On the way home the car dropped Richard back at the Dorchester once more, and took Sybil on to the house in Hampstead.

Yet for all her unhappiness, Sybil was determined that she was not going to let Richard off the hook by asking for a divorce. If the marriage was going to die, he must be the one to kill it. He continued to haver. Then, finally, at the end of March they arranged to meet on neutral ground, in the foyer of the Savoy Hotel in the Strand, and Richard told her that he had made up his mind. He had chosen Elizabeth.

Sybil went straight home, telephoned her best friends, and said, 'I'm going to New York tomorrow. Come and help me pack.'

The next day she was gone. She took Ifor and Gwen with her, plus Liliana and the two girls, and made a clean break. She cut herself off from the past completely: from her home, her memories, and, with a few exceptions, from her friends, and made a new start in America. The financial settlement was more complicated, but the deal she made with Richard was that she should have the run of New York. He could have the rest of the world, but New York was hers, and if he ever planned to go there, he was to give her prior warning so that she could leave before he arrived.

Sybil found herself the toast of New York. She was recognized and congratulated everywhere she went. Shoppers would stand on chairs to get a good look at her; people would come up to her in the street and say, 'You're marvellous. I so admire you.' Actress Joan Crawford stopped her in Saks, the exclusive Fifth Avenue department store, one day, and said, 'You have integrity. You know what integrity means, Sybil?'

'Yes, Miss Crawford.'

She bought an apartment at the Eldorado Towers overlooking Central Park, and her lawyer, Aaron Frosh, who also represented Richard and Elizabeth, moved into the floor above, while her great friend Roddy McDowell bought the one below, so she was protected on all sides, and had friends around while she found her feet.

English actor Edward Woodward, in New York with a play, met Sybil at a first-night party after the show. He was so terrified of putting his foot in it, he scarcely knew what to say to her. He began on safe ground discussing the play, in which he wore a very distinctive suit, which he explained he had had great trouble finding. 'Where did you get it in the end?' asked Sybil.

'Burton,' said Woodward, then suddenly realized that he had mentioned the very word he had been at such pains to avoid, and blushed to the roots.

'It's all right,' she said. 'It could have been worse. You could have said "Burton the Tailor".'

Back in London, soon after work on *The VIPs* came to an end, Richard went on to film *Becket* with Peter O'Toole as Henry II of England and John Gielgud as Louis VII of France. The film was based on another Jean Anouilh play, set in twelfth-century England and focussed upon the battle between Church and State as represented by the personal quarrel between Henry and the Archbishop of Canterbury, Thomas à Becket. When the film was first mooted, Laurence Olivier's name was suggested for Becket, but in the end it was Burton who played the part. It was ironic that the choice should have been between the two for, although Olivier was nearly twenty years his senior and, to most actors of Richard's generation, a figure to emulate rather than to compete with, Burton always saw himself as an equal.

Most of *Becket* was filmed at Pinewood. It was the first time Burton and Peter O'Toole had worked together, and they became firm friends. O'Toole was the son of an Irish bootmaker, eight years younger than Burton, and had just hit the heights in the title role in

Lawrence of Arabia. They had a lot in common, not least of all their considerable appetite for alcohol. Elizabeth was also a seasoned drinker. Richard boasted that he could drink any man under the table, and so he could, but not every woman. Elizabeth's tolerance was remarkable, learnt through years of practice, but Richard never gave up trying to better it.

Every day that he was needed on the set, Elizabeth would go down to the studios too, usually later in the day. Early mornings were not her strong point, so she would join Richard for lunch in the pub or a restaurant in the village of Iver, frequently with her children, and then stay and watch the shooting in the afternoon. They behaved like young lovers, purring about one another's assets, teasing each other, then suddenly turning on each other. If Elizabeth's drinking capacity was a match for Richard's, so too was her vocabulary. She used language that made strong men blush. She was certainly a match for Richard. He had always been volatile, and when he lashed out, she could more than stand up for herself.

One of her biggest hurdles was meeting Richard's family down in Wales. Ifor had refused to meet her. Richard had been to Squires Mount to try to talk to his brother, but Ifor would not even open the door, and Richard was left shouting through the letter box. The rest of the family were disappointed by what had happened, and hurt because they were all so fond of Sybil, but Richie could scarcely do wrong in their eyes. Besides, here he was bringing someone even more famous than he was to the valleys. Elizabeth handled them well, and made noises about how nice it would be to have a house nearby. They were warm, kindly people, but the family en masse, with husbands and wives and assorted children, could be very over-powering. The one thing that brought a smile to Sybil's face about the entire fiasco was the fact that Elizabeth would get the family: there was some justice in the world after all.

The closest to family Elizabeth had in England were the Cazalets. The Taylors had known them for years, from the time when they lived in England, and Sheran Cazalet and Elizabeth had virtually grown up together. Sheran's father was Peter Cazalet, the Queen Mother's race-horse trainer, and her step-grandfather the novelist P.G. Wodehouse.

Elizabeth took Richard down to Kent to meet her friend over lunch one Sunday. He was on his best behaviour. He was wearing a suit, he explained, that he had bought specially for the occasion because Elizabeth had told him that the Cazalets were the sort of people who wore suits, and he didn't have one. His best behaviour lasted for about ten minutes. In no time at all he had the assembled company in fits of laughter. He was telling stories, taking off Sheran's upper-class accent, telling jokes about Welsh miners, relating the sorry tale of his grandfather's last ride, and hardly drew breath the entire afternoon. By the end of the day he had made a firm friend.

Another old friend Elizabeth went to visit with Richard was Professor Nevill Coghill. Richard had corresponded with his former tutor over the years, and he was keen to show Elizabeth Oxford, so they went and lunched together, and discussed working together again. The Oxford Playhouse was trying to raise money again and, with his customary bravado, Richard conjured up a scheme: he would act there in Marlowe's *Dr Faustus* if Coghill would direct. But it was a scheme that had to stay on the shelf for a while. Richard's time in Britain was up for the year, and he was off to make another film for MGM in Mexico, and after that he was booked to play *Hamlet* in New York.

Other friends found it less easy to accept Elizabeth. Ellen Baker was one. Whenever they met she would accidentally find herself calling Elizabeth 'Sybil', and want to die with embarrassment. But Elizabeth was understanding. 'Look, Ellen,' she would say, 'don't worry. Everyone does it.' And when Ellen finally decided that it was better if they didn't meet, and left Stanley to pursue the relationship on his own, Elizabeth was sympathetic.

The man handling Burton's commitments now was an English agent, John Heyman, whom he had met through Elizabeth. Heyman was the man who negotiated Elizabeth's first fee of a million dollars. He had left Vere Barker nearly five years earlier, and shortly afterwards, to his great shock, Vere inexplicably committed suicide. They had been together a long time, and Vere had done a great deal for Richard in the early days, but it was he who had ensnared Richard in the seven-year contract with Darryl Zanuck, although at the time he had been delighted by the deal.

When *Cleopatra* was released at the Rivoli Theater in New York in June 1963, the biggest and most publicized film premiere Broadway had ever seen, the critics condemned it. By the time the film was complete, it had cost fourteen million pounds – the most expensive film ever made. The European premiere followed a month later, and the critics were just as unkind. 'Seeing *Cleopatra* at long last,' wrote Philip Oakes in the *Sunday Telegraph*, 'is rather like watching the birth of an elephant. In each case the interest is clinical rather than aesthetic. In each case the gestation period runs into years. And in each case the end product is big, costly, and clumsy. All things considered, I prefer the elephant.'

The only actor to come out of it comparatively unscathed was Rex Harrison. Richard Burton, said Oakes, 'rages like a bull in a Roman china shop. Despite a dozen or so films, he remains a stage actor (and a very good one). Here he treats the camera as an enemy; as a Peeping Tom, to be harangued, to be bawled out of existence. He is all sound and fury, and what he signifies is the sad waste of a major talent.'

The most savage remarks were saved, however, for Elizabeth. One critic encapsulated what a dozen other hinted at, 'Overweight, overbosomed, overpaid and undertalented,' he wrote, 'she set the acting profession back a decade.'

Sheila Graham, the influential Hollywood columnist, said, 'After seeing her Cleopatra, I'm wondering how many producers are still willing to pay her a million dollars a picture.'

Richard paid no attention. He was sorry for Elizabeth, who was so upset by the reviews that she refused to go to the first night in London, so they both stayed away. He was unshaken in his belief, however, that critics were not worth bothering about. On this occasion, because of all the time and money that had been spent on the film, he felt they were going to pull it to pieces no matter what they found, and he could not care less.

The reviews for *The VIPs* were no better when the film was released in September, but by then Richard was on his way to Mexico and another half million dollars for twelve weeks' work. That was the only part of film-making that he paid attention to; the money.

The film was based on Tennessee Williams's play *Night of the Iguana*. Burton played a priest who has been defrocked for committing adultery, and is now in charge of a busload of women tourists, one of whom tries to seduce him. His seductress was seventeen-year-old Sue Lyon, who had last played *Lolita*, and his co-star was

Ava Gardner. Not surprisingly, Elizabeth made certain that he was not alone for long with either of them. She settled into the pretty little village of Puerto Vallarta, with two secretaries, a cook, a chauffeur, a nanny, and her children.

Elizabeth now had four children. The first three had been delivered by Caesarian section, and she had been told that she could have no more. So, during her marriage to Eddie Fisher, they had looked for a child to adopt. The actress Maria Schell eventually found one for them, a little German girl who had been discovered abandoned in a laundry basket, suffering from malnutrition and a crippled hip. Eddie and Elizabeth named her after Maria Schell. She was nine months old when she was found, and her official adoption was completed three months later, in January, just as the *Cleopatra* scandal was about to begin, and Elizabeth's marriage to dissolve. Maria had then gone into hospital in Munich for the first of a series of operations to correct the hip; but she was now living with Elizabeth and was a much cherished part of the family.

Before director John Huston chose this particular area of jungle on the mountainous Pacific coast for *Night of the Iguana*, Puerto Vallarta was a quiet fishing port with no telephone, and its only contact with the outside world was a daily aeroplane that flew in from Mexico City, three hundred miles away. The location for most of the filming was eight miles deeper into the jungle, on a wild peninsula called Mismaloya reached only by boat. The cast and crew worked in intense heat, fighting off fierce biting insects, and playing their scenes with parrots screeching overhead. Off-duty, they swam in the sea, which was like a warm bath, albeit filled with barracuda, and lazed on the soft, sandy beaches. Richard and Elizabeth fell in love with the place, and bought themselves a house there.

In the meantime, lawyers were working out the details of their separate divorce settlements. Elizabeth's was held up because of a disagreement about money with Eddie Fisher, which turned into an ugly slanging match played out on the front pages of the daily press. Richard's, on the other hand, was straightforward. In her absence, Sybil was granted a Mexican divorce by a judge in Puerto Vallarta, on the grounds of her husband's 'abandonment of the home, and cruel and inhumane treatment'. She claimed that he had frequently been seen 'in the company of other women'. There was no mention of Elizabeth. The divorce was granted, and in settlement, Richard gave his wife everything he had, with the exception of the house in Celigny, plus £50,000 a year in alimony. It was blood money; he was buying his way out. He knew he had treated Sybil shamefully, and he knew he was running out on his responsibilities towards Jessica, of whom Sybil retained custody, along with Kate.

But Richard paid dearly for his folly. His wife accepted a settlement; it was not so easy to pay off his conscience.

5

Selling a Soul

Richard and Elizabeth spent Christmas 1963 in their new home in Puerto Vallarta. *Night of the Iguana* was finished, the film contingent had left, and the pretty and once-peaceful little village had returned to as close as normal as it could ever be with two superstars encamped.

They were surrounded by children. Elizabeth's brother, Howard, and his wife had joined them with their family of five, which brought the children count to nine, and they spent their days lying in the sun, swimming, reading, eating well, and drinking. Richard was beginning to drink heavily, beginning each day with a Bloody Mary at 10.30 a.m. The last year had been a nightmare, and he knew this was the lull before the storm. Tucked away in Mexico they were spared the full force of the press, and the criticism of the public; and Richard was somewhat apprehensive about returning to the lion's den.

He had agreed to perform in *Hamlet* with John Gielgud in the summer while they were working on *Becket*. Indeed, it had been his idea. The first Hamlet he had ever seen was Gielgud's, back in 1943 while he was at Oxford, and he had been mightily impressed. He told John when they were rehearsing later that in the 'To be or not to be' speech, when he came to 'When we have shuffled off this mortal coil', Gielgud made such a magnificent gesture that the friend he was with gave up drinking on the spot.

Gielgud had long nurtured a plan to produce *Hamlet* not just in modern dress, but as if the whole play were a rehearsal run-through, with no costume, and no scenery. Richard liked the idea. The opportunity to do Shakespeare with no wigs and no tights was enormously appealing. The scheme was duly sold to one of Broadway's most successful producers, Alexander Cohen. The production was destined for New York, but rather than rehearse there, which was certain to excite publicity, they decided to rehearse in Toronto, where they would then open, followed by a short run in Boston, and on to Broadway.

So in January, Richard, Elizabeth, secretaries and bodyguards, moved camp to the King Edward-Sheraton Hotel in Toronto, two days ahead of the rest of the company. They had stopped over in Los Angeles en route, and been mobbed at the airport. There were about two hundred photographers on the tarmac, and another two hundred or so frenzied teenagers outside waiting for them to get into their car: screaming girls pushing and shoving past one another in an effort to touch Elizabeth's coat. One was knocked to the ground in the crush.

Richard had a tendency to lose his temper under these conditions. He would shout at the crowds and lash out at reporters and photographers with his fists. His evenings with the shared pair of boxing gloves at the old Taibach Youth Club had stood him in good stead, although his aim was a little rusty. His first punch that day at the airport missed the man thrusting a microphone in his face, and landed on a very surprised policeman.

Fearing the same reception in Toronto, they decided to arrive early. This proved an excellent idea, for once again, on the day it had been announced that everyone was arriving, the foyer of the hotel was packed with photographers and hysterical teenagers all desperate to get a glimpse of them. They were still rating front-page news with the slanging match over Elizabeth's divorce dragging on. There were stories that Eddie Fisher was demanding a million dollars; that Eddie Fisher denied demanding a million dollars; that Eddie Fisher said Elizabeth was a liar; that Richard Burton said that Elizabeth was not a liar; that Eddie Fisher said that Richard Burton deserved an Oscar for sheer gall.

It was March before the settlement was finally worked out and the divorce granted, like Sybil's, at Puerto Vallarta on the grounds of 'abandonment'. By then it seemed that Richard was in danger of losing his right to work in the United States, which would have scuppered the production of *Hamlet* and seriously endangered his earning capacity. Having given away most of his money he was dependent upon what he made from the production.

Burton had started afresh. He later said that he had given away £500,000 when his divorce came through; and what he hadn't given to Sybil, he had donated to charity.

'I didn't really know why I did it then,' he told Barry Norman, 'and I still don't know today. I simply felt the need to do something purgative.'

'I wasn't very popular at the time, I can tell you. After all, there were Elizabeth and the children, the nannies, the secretaries . . . they all had to be supported. Obviously Elizabeth wasn't hard up but I felt it was my job to support them, even though I had nothing. Moneywise I was just hoping.'

For a while the fate of the entire company hung in the balance, and they were all just hoping. A congressman called Michael Feighan was insisting that the State Department should revoke Richard's non-immigrant visa because of his scandalous association with Elizabeth.

One morning Burton came into rehearsals to find some member of the cast had anonymously pinned an editorial from *The Washington Post* on to the call board. It said it all:

SLINGS AND ARROWS

Congressman Michael A. Feighan of Ohio strongly feels that the State Department ought to show its regard for propriety by revoking the visa issued to Mr Richard Burton, the British actor. Mr Feighan points out, correctly, that publicity has attended Mr Burton's friendship with Miss Elizabeth Taylor. The American people's deep moral repugnance toward this entire episode may be measured by the minute and voluminous detail in which the American press has described every aspect of it. The Department announces that it will 'reexamine the case'.

Both Mr Feighan and the Department have missed the more substantial threat to our national morals. If Mr Feighan thinks that the past publicity is deleterious, what will he think of the perfectly shocking play that Mr Burton proposes to bring to New York in April? Reeking with scandal and passion, it revolves around an eccentric young man whose mother is guilty of incest and whose uncle, a politician, won power by poisoning his rival. His fiancée commits suicide. The script is sown with off-color jokes. In the last act there is a duel; the vicious custom of dueling is fortunately illegal here, whatever may be the law in the notoriously wild and bloody Kingdom of Denmark. The play ends with four more murders. The tone throughout is one of unbridled violence and pessimism.

Worse still, this play reflects political ideas wholly foreign to our American democracy. No doubt Mr Feighan and the State Department will, upon reflection, find it more profitable to leave the actor to his own devices, and instead investigate the playwright.

A week later it was announced that Richard's visa would not be revoked after all. The Department had found no grounds which would make him ineligible; and the play went on.

The closer they came to opening, the more nervous Richard grew. He had not played Shakespeare for ten years, and had not stood in front of a live audience for eight. He had difficulty remembering the lines and, despite his bravado about critics, he was worried lest he repeat the faults they had found in his previous production of *Hamlet* at the Old Vic. He was anxious about his voice, his tendency to speak the lines flatly and to kill the music in the poetry. There was no learned technique for voice control, any more than for movement. The effect that Burton achieved on stage was largely the result of instinct, and the more people expected from him, the more nervous he became of his talent.

He found himself identifying with the tortured Prince of Denmark. 'I know myself,' he told Gielgud, 'that one day I'm absolutely bubbling over and making jokes and being rather coarse and jumping about, and the next day I'm very down. And I think that's Hamlet's problem too.'

'Yes,' said Sir John. 'First, he lashes himself for his own stupidity and then he becomes despondent and feels that he doesn't care one way or another and tries to determine if everything is worth it. "Shall I kill myself and get rid of the problem?" And then he decides at the end of the speech that he will go on living in spite of all the drawbacks of life – the fears, the doubts, and the sufferings.'

Elizabeth was a great support to Richard about his fears and doubts. She only sat in on a couple of rehearsals because it was impossible to leave the hotel without having to fight her way through crowds of people, but he talked it through with her endlessly and rehearsed half the night in their suite. But what he really needed was Philip. This was the first time he had set foot on stage without the pedantic schoolmaster guiding him from somewhere in the wings. But he and Philip had not spoken since Rome and the beginning of *la scandale*, as Richard called it, and he was far too proud to ring and ask for help now.

Elizabeth, however, was not so proud. She took her courage in both hands and rang Philip Burton at his home in New York. She explained that Richard needed him desperately. Could he come?

Philip behaved with impeccable manners. He was only too eager to get on the first plane to Toronto to help Richard, to mend the gulf in their relationship, but he had seen a lot of Sybil since she arrived in New York, and did not want to do anything that might upset her. Sybil, however, was equally magnanimous. In all the years she was with Richard and throughout all the years she was divorced from him, she never said anything unkind about him, not even to close friends. She never blamed him and, what is more, she never allowed her children to believe he was anything but the best.

And so Philip flew to Toronto, arriving there on a Saturday, three days after the opening night. It was an easy reunion, no great speeches or excuses or soul searching, and they quickly got down to work. Richard had received a mixture of reviews, but on the whole the production was panned. Philip saw the matinee that afternoon, and then went back to the hotel with Richard to meet Elizabeth for the first time. He gave his former pupil some notes about his performance, which he thought as magical as ever, although he did not care for the production very much; but then he was a purist, and to see Hamlet dressed in black trousers and a sweater, wearing a wristwatch, was not his idea of Shakespeare.

Philip did not stay long. He had decided to take out American citizenship, having just started up an acting school in New York, the American Musical and Dramatic Academy, and was due back in the city to swear an oath of allegiance. But he left Toronto a happier man, and relieved, as Richard was, that their friendship had been restored.

Although Elizabeth had not seen more than a couple of rehearsals, once the play was running she hardly missed a performance. Night after night she went to the theatre with Richard – the O'Keefe Centre, where he had appeared in *Camelot* four years earlier – and helped him and some of the other actors with their make-up, and then watched from the wings. She almost became one of the company, friends with actors and stagehands alike. So much so, that on the night of her birthday, 27 February, they presented her with an enormous cake, decorated with flowers and the inscription, 'To our Mascot and Den Mother – Love and Happy Birthday – The Company'. Elizabeth, dressed in a black V-neck sweater and trousers, ran to the prop table and returned with Hamlet's sword. 'Now might I do it pat,' she said, delivering a perfect impersonation of Burton's Hamlet, 'now he is a-praying – and now I'll do't.' And with that she swung the sword in an arc above her head and brought it down on the cake, cutting it clean in half.

Two and a half weeks later, on Sunday, 15 March, Elizabeth and Richard chartered a plane and flew to Montreal to get married. At first they had planned to wed in New York, but there was some doubt about the validity of their Mexican divorces in the United States. Toronto was also difficult. They would have had to obtain permission from the Provincial Secretary for Ontario, who would have had to ascertain first that their divorces were valid in their normal places of residence; and Mexican divorces were certainly not recognized in Switzerland. Montreal, however, being in the province of Quebec, had different rules and they were able to marry there with no licence.

It was a quiet ceremony, performed in their suite at the Ritz-Carlton Hotel by a Unitarian minister, with just ten other people present, including the best man, Bob Wilson. Bob Wilson was a black American whom Elizabeth had known for years. His wife had been her dresser and, when she died suddenly, Elizabeth found a job for Bob. He became Richard's dresser and general right-hand man, staying with Richard, on and off, for the rest of his life.

They spent that night in Montreal and flew back to Toronto for the performance the following day, to find Burton's dressing room filled with presents from the company: an array of kitchen equipment – pots, pans, an onion chopper and two rolling pins. That night after the curtain call, Richard beckoned Elizabeth on to the stage, and presented his wife to the audience, 'for the first time on any stage'. Then quoting Hamlet's line to Ophelia in the nunnery scene, he said, 'I say we will have no more marriages.'

When the play had first opened in Toronto, Elizabeth had sat in the auditorium and caused a sensation. Richard reckoned her presence there had added eighteen minutes to the running time of the play because the audience was shouting and screaming and watching her rather than what was happening on stage. Hamlet was playing second fiddle.

Throughout their partnership, Richard always found himself playing second fiddle to Elizabeth; and although he lived with it for years, this was not the role that his childhood in the valleys had prepared him for, and it grated. Try as she might to be the 'little woman', which for a while she did, in private at least, it was not a role she was cut out for; and it was certainly not a role that the public were prepared to allow her.

Their arrival for the opening in Boston was even more traumatic than before. The company flew together, and three thousand people were waiting at Logan Airport to greet them. The crowd broke through the terminal gates on to the runway, and it was an hour before they were sufficiently under control for the plane to be taxied into a hangar and everyone off-loaded into limousines. A police escort took them to the hotel, but there were more than a thousand people waiting there too, and as Richard and Elizabeth came into the lobby, the crowd surged towards them. Richard's hair was pulled and his shirt torn, but Elizabeth took the full force of the crowd. She was swept across the lobby and pushed and shoved and pulled at, until her face was jammed against a wall. It took Richard, eyes blazing with rage, nearly five minutes to manage to rescue her.

Expecting more trouble at the opening night, police moved in to keep the crowds back outside the theatre. So vigilant were they that when John Gielgud tried to go back stage to talk to the company, he was stopped and told to move along. 'But I'm the director,' protested Gielgud. 'Sorry, buddy,' said the policeman, 'no one gets in that door.' In desperation, Sir John went back to his hotel and wrote a note to the stage manager calling a rehearsal. It seemed the only way he was going to be able to speak to the cast.

The night the play opened in New York, no one was even allowed to get close without a ticket. A hundred policemen kept control outside the front of the Lunt-Fontanne Theater, with an additional ten on horseback. The crowds were unprecedented; they entirely filled 48th Street, spilling into Broadway at one end and Eighth Avenue at the other. Inside, the theatre was filled with glittering and glamorous celebrities. Burton was more nervous than he had ever been on stage before. The lavish party laid on afterwards by Alex Cohen on the sixty-sixth floor of the Rockefeller Center proved equally nerve-racking. Richard and Elizabeth had to run the gauntlet of New York society for the first time since the rumpus of their affair.

As he reached the entrance of the Rainbow Room, where over six hundred of the most illustrious names in the theatrical, financial and social worlds were waiting to meet them, Richard turned to Elizabeth and said, 'Let's get away from this rubbish.' He played the cheeky Welsh boy, the role that he always slipped into when there was a tricky situation to negotiate, and the ice was broken.

On the whole, his Hamlet was also well received. That night the audience gave him six curtain calls, and most of the papers carried glowing reviews, although there was considerable criticism of the production. Most rapturous of all was *Newsweek*, which said of Burton:

> His timing is flawless, his range immense; he is fully up to great diapasons of passion and despair. But what lifts his performance above that of any Hamlet in memory is his reinterpretation of the familiar. Time and again he takes a speech or an action we had thought fixed forever in an unshakable conception, and daringly hurls it into new life.
>
> He is humorous when we expect solemnity and withdrawn when we anticipate aggression. . . . The entire performance is overwhelming, a revelation of what Shakespeare can be like, a monument to the actor's art, and a new base from which our imaginations can recover from their sleep.

Walter Kerr in the *New York Herald Tribune*, however, was disappointed:

> Richard Burton is one of the most magnificently equipped actors living. . . . He places on open display not only all of his own reverberating resources . . . but also all of the myriad qualities which the man Hamlet requires. All except one. Mr Burton is without feeling. . . . The absence of genuinely felt heat – the kind of heat that will actually inform a raging soliloquy instead of reporting it at an adopted pitch – splits the performance, and perhaps even the produc-

tion, in two. The wit is there, the intelligence stands clear. . . . But when mind is not enough, when passion must clamor up through mind and burst it asunder, Mr Burton does no more than open another organ-stop and shift speeds: faster, faster. . . .

Mr Kerr had come close, not just to Burton as Hamlet, but to the very essence of Burton himself. Richard did lack feeling. He had an abundance of Celtic emotion and sentimentality, which he could pour out at the drop of a hat, but he allowed himself very little real depth of feeling.

John Gielgud privately thought it was a pity that Richard had chosen *Hamlet* as the vehicle for his return to the theatre. He felt he would have been better suited to *Macbeth* or *Coriolanus*. Nevertheless, the play was a sell-out and the run extended until August, which made it eighteen weeks in all – the longest-running *Hamlet* ever to play in New York, and the most profitable in stage history.

Throughout the run police had to hold back hordes of fans that congregated outside the Lunt-Fontanne Theater every night, waiting for the Burtons to come and go. Richard stopped Elizabeth coming to the theatre to try to make them go away, but still they came, in their thousands. Alan Jay Lerner came to see the show one night and was stopped for his autograph as he went back stage. 'You are a friend of Richard Burton?' asked the frenzied girl, suddenly uncertain. 'Yes,' said Lerner, highly amused, as he signed her book, 'A friend of Richard Burton.'

Richard hated it: hated his freedom being cramped, hated being unable to walk across the street to a bar after the show. Elizabeth, on the other hand, seemed to get a positive thrill out of fighting a path through fans.

One fan who appeared after the show one night was Spyros Skouras, chairman of the board of Twentieth Century Fox. 'My dear Richard,' he said, flinging his arms out in greeting. 'You were always my favourite actor.'

'In that case,' said Richard, 'why are you suing me so much?'

He and Elizabeth were thick with lawsuits over *Cleopatra*. Twentieth Century Fox was claiming a total of fifty million dollars in damages because their conduct had depreciated the value of the film. But in another lawsuit, four large film exhibitors had cited Twentieth Century Fox, with Richard and Elizabeth, in their claim for six million dollars. Their conduct, they alleged, constituted an affront to good taste and morals and made the film an inferior product. Richard found the whole business rather comical, pointing out that if Fox won its claim against him, they must lose against the cinema owners; and since the film had already taken forty million dollars, he failed to see how they could have depreciated the value very much.

Elizabeth was content for the time being to do nothing but be Mrs Burton. Despite her high public profile, in private she was quite introverted and shy, and Richard boosted her confidence, brought her out of herself. She idolized him. She would sit at his feet and listen to him talk, never tiring of the same stories, always laughing on cue. But, apart from poetry, which she also enjoyed, sex, and a rather coarse sense of humour, they had very little in common. Their backgrounds were different, their experiences, their friends, their tastes, even their careers were at variance. Indeed, Elizabeth lived her life on a different plane from the rest of the world. She had been a star for almost as long as she could remember. She was used to getting her own way, and knowing that if she was late for a lunch or a film or a plane, which she always was – sometimes as much as two or three hours late – both in her private and professional life, everything would be all right, and they would still love her.

The first Mrs Burton, meanwhile, having given up her career for Richard and been content to play the supportive, stay-at-home wife for thirteen years, was discovering a talent and a life of her own. She had developed a taste for clubs during her last few months in London, and one of her regular New York haunts was The Strollers Club, where a satirical group called The Establishment played. Sybil became friendly with one of them, Jeremy Geidt, and together they turned the upper floors of the club into a theatre, formed The Establishment Theater Company and, as co-directors, produced successes like *The Knack* and *The Ginger Man*.

Sybil went from strength to strength. When, some months later, The Establishment moved out of town, Sybil took over the lease on The Strollers Club, invited some of her wealthy showbusiness friends to invest, and turned it into a discotheque, which she named 'Arthur's'. It very quickly became the most fashionable and the most talked-about nightclub in New York. Richard and Elizabeth longed to go, but it was the one place in the city they would never visit.

They desperately wanted to be friends with Sybil, but she wouldn't speak to them. They communicated through Aaron Frosh and, on the occasions when Richard wanted to see Kate or Jessica, Sybil took them to Aaron, and Richard collected them from him. Kate was a delight, but he found any encounter with his younger daughter deeply upsetting. The older she grew the more devastating it was to see no inkling of recognition in her pretty little face, no response to anything, no trace of affection.

Sybil found it even more upsetting to be with her child day and night, and never see so much as a smile, or an indication that they were related. She also found her increasingly difficult to control. She tried to take her out to see friends and mix with other children, to go to restaurants and cinemas and lead as much of a normal life as possible, but Jessica was quite likely to create havoc, to stand on a chair and scream or to lash out and smash everything within reach. As she became bigger and stronger, she became harder to restrain. Sybil coped with her bravely, and Kate was very adult about her little sister, but it was emotionally destroying. Sybil was advised that everyone would be better off, Jessica included, if she were to live in a home for autistic children on Long Island, where she would be cared for by people who had special training, and who had the facilities to cope. And she could, of course, visit her as often as she liked.

During his four months in New York, Richard patched up two more of the relationships severed when he had left Sybil. Emlyn Williams, playing in New York in *The Deputy*, received a telephone call one night from Elizabeth, who had once again boldly taken the initiative, inviting him to join them for a drink. Emlyn, like Philip Burton, was only too pleased by the approach. Taking Molly with him, they walked in through the door to the closely guarded Burton suite at the Regency Hotel on Park Avenue, Richard kissed them both and the rift was healed. Now that Richard and Elizabeth were married and there was some permanence to their affair, Emlyn thought it only sensible to accept the situation.

It was Richard's marriage to Elizabeth which also led Ifor to accept the situation and make it up with his brother. Once Sybil had settled down in New York, he and Gwen had returned to London,

107

although they remained in constant touch with her. But her marriage to Richard was clearly over and dead, and remaining at crossed swords with him would not do anyone any good. So, when Richard made a tentative approach, Ifor responded, and to Richard's immense relief, they soon reverted to their former closeness.

His relationship with Philip Burton was completely repaired too. They saw quite a bit of him while they were in New York. He had now got his citizenship, and the drama school was going well, but it was short of funds. Elizabeth thought of a scheme to help him; she and Richard would give a poetry recital at the Lunt-Fontanne Theater one Sunday night, when there was not a performance, and invite celebrities to pay one hundred dollars per ticket to hear them.

It was to be the first time they had ever worked together in front of a live audience, and Elizabeth, who had never performed on stage before, was extremely nervous and very keen to do well. Philip coached them both, and found Elizabeth hugely receptive. She was being paid nothing for the piece, yet she worked day and night for several weeks to perfect it. Richard did no work. He thought, as he often did, that with his voice, all he had to do was stand up and say the words. Philip Burton readily admits that Elizabeth did the better reading. Even Richard was surprised. 'I didn't know she was going to be this good,' he said at the end of the evening. 'I've never had an ovation like that before.'

Richard constantly needed someone to goad him. Sybil had recognized that from his early days at the Old Vic, but the more famous he became, and the more money he earned for a job, the less the directors he worked for appeared to push him, particularly in films. In *Hamlet* he had been disciplined by Gielgud, but when the final curtain came down on the play after 136 performances, Richard headed straight for Hollywood, intent on remaking his fortune the easy way.

At the end of the summer he went straight into a film with Elizabeth, *The Sandpiper*. Her days as a full-time wife were over. They had had several offers, but chosen this project because, although the script made them cringe with embarrassment, MGM was prepared to film outside the United States to accommodate their tax problems. Richard could not earn any more in America during the current financial year without becoming taxable. So the entire unit moved to Paris and most of the film, set on a beach in California, was shot in a French studio.

It was another second-rate film, but because the Burtons were still such a box office sensation, *The Sandpiper* made money. It did nothing for Richard's newly restored reputation as an actor, however. Margaret Hinxman in the *Sunday Telegraph* praised Elizabeth for taking a dud script and working hard to make the best of it:

> In the commercial cinema, it's what you can make of the dim stuff, not how you shine in the good roles, that separates the useful pros from the unpredictable dilettantes.
>
> By contrast, Richard Burton acts as if it's codswallop: a naughty old habit of his, dating back to the days when he passed off *The Rains of Ranchipur* as 'It never rains but it Ranchipurs' and played his part in it in like style.

He didn't care. Elizabeth's fee was a million dollars, Richard's was half a million, plus several thousand dollars for living expenses.

Their living expenses required several thousands. Elizabeth had always lived extravagantly. She was no businesswoman; she earned higher salaries than any other actress in the world at that time, yet she never had any money. It came as quite a shock to Richard to discover that economy was not a word she knew. She spent lavishly on clothes and creature comforts, but the bulk of her fortune went on wages. She employed two secretaries, a photographer, a hairdresser, a valet, a make-up artist, a chauffeur, a tutor for the older children, a governess and a nanny. In addition, there was a bodyguard. Quite apart from her own safety, Elizabeth was always terrified that one of the children would be kidnapped. Then, of course, there were hotel and living expenses for this entourage, and she always stayed in the best hotels.

Richard adopted the same style. They shared some of the staff but, as well as Bob Wilson, he now had two secretaries of his own. When they moved to Dublin early the following year for Richard to begin work on his next film, they needed four suites at the Gresham Hotel, three single rooms and one double, to accommodate them all.

'You must have someone to answer the phone and read the mail,' Richard told Barry Norman in justification, 'or your life's not worth living.' It was certainly true that they were both bombarded with mail wherever they were, and the phone seldom stopped ringing. If he was ever to do anything else with his day, such as writing, he did need someone to filter the letters and the calls. But by living in this style, Richard slowly became inaccessible to his friends, isolated from everyday life, and out of touch with the real world.

Richard enjoyed writing, and in his frequent denunciations of acting had often said he would rather have written for a living. A small portable typewriter travelled everywhere with him, and sat prominently on a table in his suite, as often as not with a clean sheet of paper in it, awaiting inspiration. He had kept a diary on and off since the age of fourteen, sometimes wrote poetry, and would read both out loud to friends. He wrote occasional articles which were commissioned by magazines, including *A Christmas Story*, about his memories of Christmas in Wales as a child, and *Meeting Mrs Jenkins*, which were both subsequently published as small books. But most of the writing he did was letters. He never much liked using the telephone, and would always write in preference. He loved words and the sound of language, so his writing tended to be florid, and sometimes pretentious, filled with superlatives and protestations of affection; and often unchecked, so the grammar and spelling were sometimes unorthodox.

But Burton used the telephone when there was some urgency. In June of that year, 1965, the Bakers were in the midst of a party at their home in London, when Richard telephoned. He had heard that Sybil, now thirty-six, was planning to marry again, and was outraged.

Sybil had hired a sensational group to play at 'Arthur's' called The Wild Ones, and had fallen in love with its leader, Jordan Christopher. Jordan was a Macedonian from Ohio, twelve years younger than Sybil, who had made her happier than she had been for years. Their marriage would mean Richard would no longer have to pay alimony. He would be richer by fifty thousand dollars a year. Yet, he was nearly hysterical on the phone.

'You've got to stop it,' he thundered. 'Go out there, Stan, and stop her marrying that boy. Please don't let her get married.' It was some time before either Stanley or Ellen could calm him down enough to point out that it was really none of his business any more what Sybil did with her life.

The film that took the Burtons to Dublin, then London and Bavaria, was *The Spy Who Came In From The Cold*, a John Le Carré thriller; a counter-balance to the first of the glamorous James Bond films that had just been made. Burton played the part of a shabby, disillusioned spy by the name of Alec Leamas; a character with the face of a man whose body is still alive but whose spirit is dying of sickness and self-disgust. Richard said he found the part very liveable. One day on the set he broke what he called all his own admirable records. 'I had to knock back a large whisky,' he said, describing the scene to journalist Peter Evans. 'It was the last shot of the day, and I decided to use the real hard stuff. We did 47 takes. Imagine it, luv, 47 whiskies.'

Drunk or not, this was the first film performance that the critics were unanimous about. Leonard Mosley, writing in the *Daily Express*, said, 'His performance makes you forgive him for every bad part he has ever played, every good part he has ever messed up, and every indiscretion he has ever committed off the screen or on.

'If he doesn't win an Oscar for it this year there is not only no justice left in Hollywood, but no judgment either.' Alas, there was no judgment in Hollywood.

Burton's co-star in *The Spy* was Claire Bloom, whom he had not seen since his involvement with Elizabeth, and who was now, as she quickly discovered, a thing of the past. At their first meeting off the set, Richard snubbed her with such callousness that she never forgave him. He was capable of great unkindness at times, particularly when he had been drinking. He was also capable of physical violence; several of his women suffered blows from a drunken quarrel.

Richard was so intoxicated after dinner in a restaurant one night that he fell down the steps on his way out. Elizabeth and Stanley Baker were with him, and having had every bit as much to drink herself, Elizabeth fell about laughing. Richard was furious, and brutally snatched off her wig. (She wore a wig frequently.) Back at the house, Richard told her to come to bed. She refused, saying that she wanted to sit and have a drink with Stanley, and he stormed off in a rage. Close to tears, she sat and poured out her heart to Baker, about how much she loved Richard, and how hard she had tried to overcome everyone's resistance to her, because they were angry at what she had done to Sybil. She realized the hurt it had caused, but she loved him.

Sober, Richard was a different man: gentle, kind and infinitely generous.

That April Richard and Elizabeth formed a production company together. Throughout filming of *The Spy*, he was planning their first film, which was to be called *The Greatest Train Robbery in the World*, based on the real Great Train Robbery in Buckinghamshire two years earlier. He was very excited about it, particularly the prospect of being both sides of the camera. Sam Wanamaker was to direct and Burton would play the ringleader; the first time he had ever played a criminal.

'It's a funny thing,' he told journalist Duff Hart-Davis, 'I come from the humblest of Welsh families. My father was a miner, and I was the twelfth of thirteen children. I'm shortish, thick-set and bow-legged: I couldn't be more Welsh. Yet I've almost always played princes and kings, like Hamlet and Alexander the Great. I'm looking forward to getting back to a working-class part.'

He was also hugely impressed by the subject. 'I remember at the time of the robbery feeling rather good that we – the British – had brought off the biggest raid ever made, and I've never met anybody who wasn't delighted that the robbers managed it.'

The project was scheduled for November, but first he and Elizabeth were contracted to make a picture in Hollywood. He was still drinking heavily. Playing the part of yet another man who drank did not help. From Alec Leamas in *The Spy*, he had gone on to play the part of George in a film of Edward Albee's disturbing play, *Who's Afraid of Virginia Woolf?* It is a study of a marriage, of two human beings destroying one another, in a dialogue of pure invective. Their conflict is played out for the most part as a game, in which they take turns to expose the tender spots in their partner's defences, then kick hard. George is a down-trodden, middle-aged, mediocre professor of history. Martha, his fat, vicious, domineering wife, is the daughter of the college's president, yet despite her influence he has still failed to become head of the department. She has failed to have children. There is plenty of scope for destruction; and in the course of destroying each other, they also cruelly savage an innocent young couple whom they have invited home for a drink.

Elizabeth was cast as Martha. She was offered the part before the producer Ernest Lehman ever considered using Burton. In fact, it was she who first suggested Richard for the part, and persuaded him to take it. It did not take much persuasion. His fee for a film had now gone up to three-quarters of a million dollars, plus all the usual living expenses and the trappings that he had learned from Elizabeth to insist upon.

They lived in a very grand Hollywood villa at the rear of the Beverly Hills Hotel, lavishly furnished and staffed, with a great, sweeping staircase, and fabulous views.

Robert Hardy was in London and had plans to adapt a book, *The Golden Warrior*, about William the Conqueror into a film. It was the first time he had ever done anything of the sort, but he had the author's permission and felt Burton was a perfect William. He rang him from London and said he wanted to show him the treatment he had written. Richard immediately invited him to bring it out to Hollywood and stay with them for a few days. He was constantly inviting friends and family to visit, wherever he might be in the world. He loved being surrounded by people.

'I can't,' said Robert, who didn't have that sort of money in those days.

'Don't worry about the expense,' said Richard. 'Tell me what day you want to come and a ticket will be at the desk at Heathrow.' Sure enough it was.

Richard and Elizabeth were both working very hard at that time, learning lines, going to bed early, albeit full of vodka.

Before he met Elizabeth, Richard's drink had always been beer. Elizabeth, on the other hand, had always drunk spirits and it was not long before she had given up her token appetite for beer, and reverted to the drink she really enjoyed, vodka, and also wine. Richard joined her.

But filming ran long over schedule and, although it meant running into 'golden time' financially, it also meant that they were unable to make *The Greatest Train Robbery in the World*, which was a great disappointment. Besides, after five months, Albee's play was beginning to spill over into their lives. Friends had warned that it would be a mistake to do the film together. No marriage, however good, they had said, could withstand the hatred of Albee's lines. And, having spent the day fighting viciously with one another on the set, it was hard to come home, share a bottle of vodka, and play happy families.

There were compensations. *Virginia Woolf* not only earned them vast sums of money after it was released with their cut of the takings, it also earned Elizabeth a Hollywood Oscar. Burton won an award from the British Film Academy for his performances in both *Virginia Woolf* and *The Spy Who Came In From The Cold*.

Amongst his oft-told repertoire, one of Richard's most constant themes was Oxford. He told stories of his time there, he talked about how one day he would give up acting, go and be an academic, and live in Oxford for the rest of his life. It was a constant fantasy: like the fantasy that he would give it all up to become a writer; or that he was only making bad films so he could earn enough money to produce good films like *Macbeth* and *Coriolanus*; or that he would one day play *King Lear*.

'I have to play Lear as a kind of obligation,' he once said. 'I am, after all, the kind of authentic dark voice of my tortured part of the world, Wales, and I have to play Lear because Lear is the only Welshman of any interest that Shakespeare wrote about. Lear, when he lets off steam, when he really lets go, is utterly Welsh. Hamlet is not. Hamlet is English, but Lear is a Welshman.'

In February 1966, Richard did go back to Oxford, however, to take part in the long-awaited production of *Dr Faustus* promised to Nevill Coghill more than two years previously. It was an OUDS production, and he and Elizabeth, who was to play the non-speaking part of Helen of Troy, had agreed to give their services free in order to raise money for the University Theatre Appeal Fund.

Over the years, Richard had been approached for money to support various aspects of the university. Like every big star, a good proportion of his daily mail was from or for some good cause or another, begging for support, but Richard was especially keen to do something special for Oxford. He felt he had some debt to repay for his time there which, as the years passed, he looked back on with increasing nostalgia. He had a romantic vision of the place: Oxford was his real home, his intellectual and spiritual home, and he had been away a long time.

By the time the Burtons arrived in Oxford and installed themselves in the Randolph Hotel, the rest of the cast had been rehearsing for weeks. The project had been much talked about both on television and in the press, and even the most blasé of the students were in a state of some excitement at the prospect of meeting the famous pair. To have gone from instant coffee out of chipped mugs by a single-bar electric fire in their college rooms to a suite at the best hotel in town, with Elizabeth Taylor saying, 'How would you like your drink fixed?' and then watching while she fixed it herself, was an experience few of them would forget.

They were both excessively friendly to the students, giving parties for them, and taking them on outings. Elizabeth seemed somewhat over-awed by the place, and being surrounded by so many people 'with brains'. Richard simply had a new audience for his stories; he was sharp and witty and kept everyone entertained.

Superficially he was the life and soul of the party, but some of the students sensed a dangerous quality about the man, that he was not a person to cross. They found him distracted, as though he were constantly waiting for something, bored, but not just with what was going on around him in the present; it was as if he had an inner boredom, a cosmic desperation.

Yet he appeared to enjoy his weeks in Oxford. He took Elizabeth drinking in all the local pubs, driving through the countryside in their Rolls Royce. He joined in any activity offered. He didn't play the big star, he was happy to chat to the undergraduates, and there was talk of him becoming an honorary fellow of one of the colleges.

Professionally he was a disappointment. He had talked a lot about *Faustus*, about how he loved the play, how he knew it so well, and how he had been wanting to play the Doctor for more than twenty years. Yet when he stepped on stage for his first rehearsal, it was apparent that he had made no preparation, and had taken no trouble to learn the lines. Furthermore, he rehearsed with no emphasis or projection in his voice at all, which made it very difficult, as well as unnerving, for the rest of the cast to play against. It was not until the first night that he gave any sort of performance, although he still did not know the lines. Every night it was a different play: he would transpose lines, leave out chunks, ad lib a few, and on one night left out a speech in the first act which cut someone else's entrance out completely; a character Marlowe had invented never got on stage at all.

Elizabeth had two entrances, and while she was on stage her dresser stood in the wings with a vodka and tonic balanced on a cushion at the ready.

The production was damned by eight out of ten national newspapers. Alan Brien, concluding his piece in the *Sunday Telegraph*, wrote, 'Even the pleasure of hearing the famous anthology passages spoken with classic eloquence was finally denied us. Long ago I compared Mr Burton's Old Vic delivery to that of the man in the I-Speak-Your-Weight machine, too perfectly modulated to be real. Now that effortless flow has been interrupted by his new habit of pausing in the middle of almost every phrase as though dictating to a secretary whose shorthand was rusty.'

Undeterred, Richard and Elizabeth left for Rome with plans to put their own money into making a film of *Dr Faustus*, the profits of which would also go to the workshop project. Their week at the Playhouse had already given the fund £3,000; but they had given a lot more than that in terms of lost earnings. By being out of gainful employment for three weeks (two to rehearse, one to play), it was estimated that they had lost something in the region of £700,000.

The management of the Randolph were a little shattered by the experience of having two volatile superstars under their roof, but all in all they had gone down well with the city, and Nevill Coghill was delighted with the outcome, 'Now with this money . . . I can realize a drama for a cultural laboratory for Oxford. A special building, for exhibitions, performances, string quartets. With a library and a restaurant.' As for the critics, he said, 'What do you expect from a pig but a grunt?'

Burton felt he had a special relationship with Faustus. He had found the last two film characters he had played, Alec Leamas and George, a little too like him for comfort, but this was more fundamental. '*Faustus* is the one play I don't have to do any work on,' he told friends. 'I am Faustus.'

Doctor Faustus is man who sells his soul to the Devil in exchange for knowledge and power, but who forgets his worthy aspirations, is taken in by toys and has a childish delight in showing off. Mephis-

tophiles takes advantage of his weaknesses; he blinds him with illusions, distracts him with spectacular visitations and gaudy gifts, and
frightens him with sudden terrors to stop him thinking of God and
repenting, and so finding a way out of his pact. Faustus is overcome
by his own vanity and wastes the riches that he has traded his soul
for. His final folly is to summon the figure of Helen of Troy, the
most beautiful woman in history, to be his paramour. After that he
esteems himself lost, for though he feels remorse, he has lost the
faculty for repentance. Despair has mastered him. The hour strikes
and he is damned.

Having met his own Helen of Troy in Rome, and sworn he
would never go back to the city, Richard was soon installed with
Elizabeth in a luxurious villa on the Appian Way, guarded as closely
as Fort Knox. When asked what had happened to his resolve, he
said, 'We got plastered and middle-aged, I suppose, and forgot.'
More important, he was finally going to produce his first film. It
was Shakespeare's *Taming of the Shrew*, in which he would star,
with Franco Zeffirelli directing. Yet another story, albeit a more
vintage version, of marital strife and the sex war, with Elizabeth
playing the part of Katharina, the shrew, with 'a child's ungovern-
able temper in a woman's body. . .', Richard playing Petruchio,
who tamed his shrew, 'For I am he am born to tame you, Kate, and
bring you from a wild cat to a Kate conformable as other household
Kates.'

From *The Taming of the Shrew*, which was the first film for which
Richard had put up any of his own money – though Columbia also
put up a sizeable chunk – he and Elizabeth stayed on in Rome to
make *Dr Faustus*, which they entirely financed themselves. *Faustus*
was also the first film that Richard directed; indeed, it was the first
time he had directed anything since RAF Babbacombe and his
Youth at the Helm production back in 1944. It was also the last; he
found the experience exhausting. His co-director was Nevill
Coghill. They used the same student cast and the premiere was
held, suitably enough, in Oxford the following autumn. The critics
were no kinder than they had been to the stage production, and the
film was never much of a commercial success.

The Taming of the Shrew did prove a success, although on the
night of its first showing in London, Richard paid for a hundred and
fifty of the cinema seats himself. It was a Royal Film Performance at

the Odeon in Leicester Square, which raised £36,000 for the Cinema and Television Benevolent Fund, and Richard invited all his relations up to London for the weekend to see it. He took over fourteen double rooms at the Dorchester and held a party for them the night before the premiere which went on until dawn, with a second party the following night. Their suite was overflowing with merry singing Welshmen, who by morning had drained every bottle in sight.

Princess Margaret attended the showing, and Richard, his head still swimming with the excesses of the night, took to the stage. 'My real name, of course,' he said, 'is Jenkins and my wife is known as Lizzie Jenkins. Sitting up there in the circle is Maggie Jones. When we took over the Dorchester it was only a desperate attempt to try to keep up with the Joneses.'

It was a joke, of course, but the Burtons had moved into a league of their own; they had become the royal family of the cinema. They held out for vast fees on each film, for a percentage of the gross, for a myriad of extra perks, they had director approval, and their contracts were a jungle of exceptions and sub-clauses. Once they were on the set and working they were both extremely professional – sub-clauses permitting – but off the set, they lived the legend.

It was Elizabeth's legend, Elizabeth's world of tinsel and temperament, and Richard, the most leadable of men, as Sybil had once remarked, was fast joining it. He had always been ambitious for money, but Elizabeth made him ambitious for stardom, made him want to be given the best suite in the top hotels and the best table in the most expensive restaurants. Surrounded by a circus of aides and secretaries whose sole purpose was to keep the world at bay, Richard was gradually being stifled.

6

One Ego too Many

By the end of 1967 Burton had added two more unmemorable films to his name, despite good authors: *The Comedians*, from Graham Greene's controversial novel about political dictatorship in Haiti; and *Boom*, adapted by Tennessee Williams from his play, *The Milk Train Doesn't Stop Here Anymore*. Richard and Elizabeth worked together in both. They had begun coercing producers and directors who approached one of them for a film into casting the other as well, with the result, particularly noticeable in *Boom*, that he was badly miscast.

The first location for *The Comedians* was Dahomey, in West Africa, a small state which the Burton fame had hitherto eluded. One of Richard's favourite stories was the night he 'went out on the booze with some of the lads. When it got late, Elizabeth got our chauffeur Gaston to ring various places to find out where I was. He called one hotel and asked for me.'

'Who?' they demanded.

'Burton,' he said. 'Richard Burton.'

'Is he black or white?'

Richard frequently went out on the booze as he put it, and had to be retrieved from some bar or another. There was one occasion in Sardinia, where they were filming *Boom*, when he disappeared for the entire evening. Elizabeth had arranged to meet him at the hotel when he came off the set in the afternoon, and by 8.30 there was still no sign of him. Kidnapping was rife in Sardinia at that time, and Elizabeth was frantic with worry; she didn't know where to turn next. The police were alerted, all the hospitals rung, but there was no sign of him. He was finally found by the police at ten o'clock at night outside a bar in the centre of Alghero, standing on a table reciting Shakespeare to an audience of bemused Italians, and promising a drink to anyone who could tell him which play the speeches came from. Bob Wilson was standing on the ground beside him, desperately trying to get him down.

It was Burton who was first approached for the *The Comedians*, and suggested they use Elizabeth too. With *Boom* it was the other way round. Elizabeth was the first to be offered the film. Joseph Losey, who was directing, producer Norman 'Spike' Priggen, and Tennessee Williams all flew down to Portofino to discuss the script with her. She and Richard had hired a yacht for a week's holiday, and they were all due to meet up at Santa Marguarita on the day that they returned. But the Burtons did not return. An entire week went by; the trio waited, the man who had chartered them the boat waited, and the people who had booked her that week waited. Finally they appeared. Elizabeth had fallen in love with the *Odysseia*, and Richard was going to buy it for her. They were sorry if they had inconvenienced anyone, 'But you know how it is when Elizabeth wants something,' he explained.

The 279-ton yacht had an interesting history. She was sixty-one years old and had been built for an eccentric Englishman to house his organ, so he could take her to sea in stormy weather and get the right atmosphere for Bach. She had also been used as a Mediterranean patrol boat in both World Wars. In recent years, the six-suite floating pleasure palace had been used for charter. Richard paid £75,000 for her, took on a crew of nine, and almost immediately put her into Genoa to be cleaned up, re-painted and given her new name: *Kalizma* after three of their daughters: Kate, Liza, and Maria.

Joseph Losey and 'Spike' Priggen were shown aboard and found Richard on the after-deck, where a bar formed part of the bulkhead. 'You've got a good girl there,' said Richard, referring to Elizabeth, 'You couldn't do better.' Then sorting through a mound of scripts and books that were piled on top of the bar, he found what he was looking for, and held up a cheque which he thrust at Spike. 'This'll give you an idea. This is one of her profit participation cheques for *Virginia Woolf.*' The cheque was for a little over two million dollars.

Elizabeth was to play the part of a fabulously rich, much married, ageing, dying widow who lives in isolation on an island. Her solitude is disturbed by the arrival of a young, handsome stranger, who has a knack of turning up just before rich widows meet their maker. The actor they had in mind for the handsome young stranger was James Fox. Elizabeth said she wanted Richard to play the part. At forty-two Burton was considerably older than the character should have been, but Elizabeth was adamant and Losey, the producers and distributors all agreed.

Thus the Burton/Taylor circus, including the new yacht, moved down to Sardinia for the summer. The older children were now at boarding school in England, but they flew out for the summer holidays, and added to the fear of kidnapping. Having Richard and Elizabeth together on the film already meant exorbitant insurance premiums, and if any of the children were kidnapped, the parents would obviously stop working and the whole picture would be in jeopardy. So the children had armed guards looking after them, and threw everyone into panic if they wandered off by themselves, as the boys frequently did.

The production had other insurance problems too. Elizabeth refused to wear fake jewellery. So John Heyman and Spike, who were co-producers on the film through Heyman's company, World Film Services, had no alternative but to try to find the genuine article. They managed to persuade Bulgari, the famous Roman jeweller, to lend them two million dollars' worth of jewellery, which went into a special safe sent down from Rome, with an armed guard standing over it twenty-four hours a day.

What Elizabeth wanted, Elizabeth tended to get, no matter what the cost or the inconvenience. There was a journalist in one of Burton's scenes in the film, who interviews him on board the boat that first brings him to the island. Elizabeth persuaded them to use her brother, Howard, whom she had invited out for a holiday with his family. Spike pointed out that he was not an actor; he was actually a marine biologist. 'No, but he's a Taylor and he's got beautiful eyes,' she said. The alternative would have been to bring an actor down from Rome. That settled, they got down to his fee for the job. Elizabeth calculated what an actor would have cost, including the airfare, and mentioned a figure. Spike agreed. Then she said, 'Ah, but he's a Taylor, and you'll get a lot of publicity out of it. You'll have to double that.' Then she went off for lunch. 'Spike,' she said when she came back. 'I've been thinking. It's got to be a thousand dollars.' They had started at 150 dollars.

There was no question about who wore the pants. Spike went to Burton and asked if he would be prepared to do a shot at 5.30 in the morning one day, because they needed the dawn light. Burton, who was always amenable over a couple of drinks, agreed. A little later Elizabeth appeared. 'I hear you're trying to call Richard at 5.30. I don't think so, darling,' she said; and that was the end of the matter.

They were both drinking heavily, and frequently rowing in public. One night Elizabeth told Richard to come to bed because he was drunk. They started to quarrel about it. They often fought about who could drink more. Finally Elizabeth went off to bed and left him on the terrace with the rest of the party. Their room was two floors above and, some time later, Elizabeth appeared on the balcony, dressed in a filmy negligee, and called him to bed once more. Thereupon they repeated the row they had had on the terrace, within earshot of everyone in the bay.

Elizabeth never showed any ill-effects from her drinking. She began with Bloody Marys almost as soon as she was up in the mornings which, if she was about to begin filming, could be as early as 8.30. They were made for her by her make-up artist, Frank Larne, with special salt and pepper flown in from America to whichever country she was in. 'He makes the best Bloody Marys in the world,' she used to say. At noon she moved on to Jack Daniels whisky.

The first day of filming in Sardinia she was extremely nervous, and had three outsize Bloody Marys before arriving on the set. In the first scene she had to be lounging about with a drink while dictating to her secretary. Joe Losey asked her what she would like, and suggested ginger ale, which would look like whisky.

'No darling, it's noon,' she said, looking at her watch. 'Jack Daniels.' So she was brought a whisky. It took seven takes to get the scene right, and each time Elizabeth knocked back a large Jack Daniels.

At the end of the morning, she enquired what time she would be needed on set the following day.

'Don't worry about that now,' said Spike, 'there'll be plenty of time to discuss that when we finish this afternoon.'

'But I've just had a word with the continuity girl,' said Elizabeth, 'and she tells me that we've already shot three minutes of film today, and I never shoot more than two and a half minutes in a day. It may even be in my contract.'

This was one detail not in her contract, and one battle she lost.

Burton simply missed his first day of filming. They were scheduled to go to a little harbour on the far side of the island, to film the boat shot with the journalist. The unit was set up, everyone was ready to go, but there was no Richard. He was at the hotel and in no condition to do any work. Finally Elizabeth sent a message apologizing, but they would have to count him out for the day. He would be there tomorrow.

After *Boom*, Burton played a small part in *Candy*, a film with Marlon Brando made in Rome. Then he and Elizabeth moved the ménage to London. He was to star in *Where Eagles Dare*, an Alistair Maclean film with Clint Eastwood that guaranteed him a million dollars, plus a percentage of the gross, with the usual living expenses and perks. Elizabeth was to star in *Secret Ceremony*, for the usual fee. Living, however, was to cost rather more than usual on this visit. Elizabeth had wanted to bring their dogs with them – two Pekingese – but because of British quarantine regulations, they were unable to land on British soil. *Kalizma* was in dry dock being refitted, so the Burtons hired a yacht, the 191-ton *Beatrice and Bolivia*, costing £1,000 per week, and kept the dogs on board, moored at Tower Pier on the River Thames.

They were both filming at Elstree: Richard at the MGM studios, Elizabeth at the ABC studios (now EMI) half a mile away. But this was no coincidence. If they made separate films, they insisted upon making them in the same place so they could meet for lunch. It was in the contract.

Secret Ceremony did not begin, in fact, until a few weeks after Burton started work on *Where Eagles Dare*, so initially Elizabeth was driving down from London for lunch. Someone else who joined them for lunch two or three times a week was Robert Hardy, who also happened to be working in the ABC studios round the corner at the time.

'Do you want a part in my film?' asked Richard one day, knowing that Robert's film was almost finished. 'Pat Wymark's ill. You can have his part. Do you want it?'

'No, I can't,' said Robert. 'I'm going on holiday – five weeks in Greece – I've promised Sally; we haven't been away for ages.'

Richard changed tack. 'Take the plane,' he said.

'Yes, we're going to fly,' said Robert. 'We'll fly to Athens, then hire a car.'

'Don't be fucking silly,' said Richard, 'I mean, take my plane. I've got a jet. I've got six jets.' He explained that he had part share in a company that operated out of Switzerland. Robert havered.

'Go on, do what he says,' said Elizabeth. 'Now Rich, pick up the phone; you'll only forget if you don't do it now.'

A telephone was brought to the table where they sat, and three days later Robert and Sally were sitting in the VIP lounge at Heathrow, awaiting their private jet to Athens.

This air charter firm in Switzerland was just one of the many business ventures that Richard and Elizabeth had gone into together. They had also set up a variety of trusts and funds, and given away a great deal of money to individuals they felt deserved help in some project or other, like American fashion designer Vicky Teil (who married Richard's make-up artist, Ron Berkley), whom they helped to establish in a boutique in Paris. One of their ventures was in Harlech Television, a consortium of businessmen and actors, including Lord Harlech and Stanley Baker, which took over the franchise for Wales and the West of England from the existing holder, TWW. The Burtons guaranteed £25,000 for five years, and Richard became a non-executive director. He was not the most dedicated businessman, and although his association with the venture started happily enough in May, with an opening made even more sensational by Elizabeth's latest acquisition, the Krupp diamond, glistening under the flash bulbs, it came to a premature end.

His investment sense was not foolproof either. When he met Frank Hauser ten years after putting money into the Oxford Playhouse, he said, 'You know when I gave you that money I was very flush and had very, very good expert business advisers, and I invested in a lot of things. They've all gone bust. The Playhouse is the only thing that's still extant.' Every year the £2,000 loan from Richard Burton came up at the Playhouse annual general meeting, and although Richard went on to give many thousands of pounds to Oxford in one way and another, he never wrote off the debt.

The diamonds and other jewellery Richard bought for his wife were partly acquired as an investment, as were the works of art and the books, which formed his vast library in Switzerland. Books were the only one of these from which Richard derived any pleasure. Elizabeth had always bought paintings when she had any money. Her father having been an art dealer he advised her on what to buy. Amongst her enviable collection, she had a Monet, a Degas, and a Modigliani. A lot of the paintings were on loan to a gallery in Geneva because of the cost of insuring them anywhere else; but even they were a bone of contention between them. As Richard told Duff Hart-Davis, 'My trouble is I can't understand art. I've tried and tried, but I still can't tell the difference between a Rembrandt and a Picasso. Some time back Elizabeth bought a Van Gogh for around £100,000. I said to her: "A hundred thousand pounds? Twenty-six inches by twelve? Good God."'

Yet he was quite happy to spend as much on diamonds. The 33-carat Krupp diamond cost £125,000. For Elizabeth's thirty-seventh birthday, he spent £15,000 purchasing the famous La Peregrina pearl, which had been given to Mary Tudor by King Philip II of Spain. He also acquired for a million dollars the fabulous inch-long, inch-thick, 69.42-carat Cartier diamond.

Elizabeth was wearing the Krupp diamond, which Richard called 'the ice rink', on the day of Sheran Cazalet's wedding. Princess Margaret was also a guest, and told Elizabeth she thought it was the most vulgar thing she had ever seen.

'Want to try it on?' offered Elizabeth.

'Yes, please,' said the Princess.

Elizabeth's passion for jewels amused Richard. He would often tell the story of waking up at 6.30 one morning, mystified to find Elizabeth out of bed, sitting up at the window. 'I'm playing with my diamonds,' she explained.

Occasionally he would see the immorality of it all. It was not just jewellery: Elizabeth was a compulsive buyer, and he would sometimes look at her latest purchase, yet another shirt or another pair of shoes, and say, '120 dollars. That was fourteen weeks' wages for my father in the thirties.'

Sheran married Simon Hornby, a member of the giant chain of booksellers, W.H. Smith, whose father and grandfather had been instrumental in building up the firm. It was a society wedding, held at Fairlawne, the Cazalets' lovely house near Tonbridge in Kent. The Rolls Royces sat two abreast in the drive and the guest list read like a page from Debrett's Peerage, starting with Her Majesty Queen Elizabeth The Queen Mother, and working down. Richard never wore suits, and had no morning dress for the occasion. He tried to hire one, but failed, and so for the second time bought a suit specially to visit Elizabeth's posh friend.

The two couples got on extremely well. Richard loved having someone to talk to about books, and Sheran was always an enthusiastic audience for his stories, with the result that Richard and Elizabeth would never come to London without dining or spending a weekend with the Hornbys. They returned hospitality in Rome, in the South of France, or wherever they had taken a villa, and shortly before they were married, Sheran and Simon spent a holiday in the house in Puerto Vallarta. They spent their honeymoon in Portugal and Venice, and were due to fly back to Heathrow between countries, because there was no commercial flight that flew direct. The day before the changeover, they had a surprise telephone call in their Portuguese hotel room. It was Richard's secretary, Jim Benton.

'I'm told you're not to be trusted on public transport,' he said. 'We're sending the jet to collect you.'

They not only sent the jet; there was a Rolls Royce waiting for them at Heathrow to take them to the *Kalizma* at its mooring on the Thames, and the following day they were taken back to the airport and flown out to take up their reservation in Venice.

Only two people had known their travelling arrangements. Richard had happened to meet one of them, and immediately thought of sending the jet.

The Burtons now had two houses in Puerto Vallarta. This first house, Casa Kimberley, had proved too small to house everyone, so they had built a second on the other side of the road, 'The New House'. Both had breathtaking views across the Bay of Vallarta; and both were colourfully and luxuriously furnished by Jill Melford, the London-based interior designer who decorated all their houses.

One house was Elizabeth's, the other Richard's, and they built a bridge which connected the two, running from Elizabeth's swimming pool area to Richard's first floor, where he went with his typewriter to work in the mornings. It was an exact replica of the Bridge of Sighs in Venice. The road that ran under the bridge was very minor, and scarcely saw any traffic from one week's end to the next, but if ever a lorry came down it, the structure was so low that the lorry would have to unload in order to pass underneath.

Puerto Vallarta had changed dramatically since the Burtons had made a home there. From a dusty Mexican fishing village, it had grown into a thriving tourist town, of which Richard had become a major figure. He was treated like a mayor – echoes of his days in the RAF as the 'Squire' of Docking – and his drunken antics were well known to the locals, who were frequent dinner guests. He loved going there, and quite frequently suggested it as the location for films he was working on.

Where Eagles Dare was largely panned by the critics for its excessive and mindless brutality. 'The only response,' wrote Eric Shorter in the *Daily Telegraph*, 'is laughter; and depression that so much action in the simple physical sense can be so devoid of drama, wit or tension.' Several projects were discussed after *Where Eagles Dare*, and one for which he suggested Puerto Vallarta was *The Man from Nowhere*. It came to nothing in the end. After a lot of expensive ground work, which included Richard choosing as director Sam Osteen, the film editor he had worked with on *Virginia Woolf*, he decided he was unhappy with the script. The producer was having difficulty finding the money anyway, so they dropped it.

Staircase was the next project that did come to something. It was a film of the play by Charles Dyer about two sad, ageing, homosexuals who live together as man and wife – basically yet another examination of a patchy marriage, in which the dialogue is all. Burton played Harry, a hairdresser and the 'wife' of the team, and Rex Harrison was Charlie, who is summoned by the police during the course of the play for some sort of indecent behaviour.

It was a curious choice of film. Burton was aggressively anti-homosexual. He would refer to people as 'My homosexual friend' – and a large proportion of his friends were gay. 'This happened,' he would say, 'before he decided he would become abnormal' or, 'Of course, that was in his homosexual days before he decided to reform and get married.' Friends found his constant reference to the subject unnecessary and intrusive, as though he were trying to eradicate some incident from his past, or the germ of homosexuality in himself. He did once say he thought perhaps most actors were latent homosexuals, 'and we cover it with drink'.

Set in a barber's shop in London, *Staircase* was actually shot in Paris because of Richard's tax problems. His time in Britain for that financial year was up. In keeping with their terms of employment, Elizabeth's next film, *The Only Game in Town*, had to be shot in Paris too, although it was about Las Vegas.

Richard went to New York to sign the contract for *Staircase*. Because Kate was staying with him and would be returning to her mother in New York, Richard suggested taking with him Sally Baker, Stanley's daughter and his goddaughter, so she too could go and see Sybil.

Sally was physically handicapped. It was not a secret, and not something that the Bakers were in any way trying to hide. Sally coped with her disability very well. She was pretty and extremely bright, and Stanley and Ellen were fiercely proud of their daughter. They simply wanted her to have every chance to lead a normal life, and not be exposed to unwanted publicity. For fifteen years they had succeeded, so that when Richard suggested taking her with him, Ellen and Stanley were nervous. Elizabeth, however, was in hospital and would not be going, so there was unlikely to be the usual blaze of publicity, and Richard would hand the girls over to Aaron to give to Sybil as soon as he arrived.

At the last minute Elizabeth decided she wanted to go too, which meant taking a nurse, so their plans to fly were dropped. Instead, they booked suites on the *Queen Elizabeth*. Stanley knew his friend only too well, and sat him down at their house in Epsom and made him promise to keep Sally in the background. 'Look Richard,' he said, 'your taking Kate and Sally to New York by plane and handing them over is one thing, but going on a boat with Elizabeth in a wheelchair and a nurse is another. Promise me – Sally's not used to this at all – promise me, no nonsense, no interviews.'

'I promise, I promise,' said Richard. 'Would I do that to you?' And so with some misgivings, they let her go.

The Bakers then went off on holiday themselves to their flat in Cannes. The arrangement was that Richard would bring Sally over to Paris when he had finished his business in New York, and Stanley would collect her there and drive her down to join the rest of the family.

One morning Ellen went downstairs to buy some milk and a paper. To her horror she noticed a pile of French newspapers with a picture of Richard, Elizabeth and Sally walking down the Champs Elysées spread across the front page, and the headline, 'The mysterious girl with one arm and one leg.' She read on.

'This is my goddaughter,' explained Richard Burton. 'I'm taking her to Russia. She is the nearest thing to my heart after Elizabeth. She is the granddaughter of a one-legged coalminer. Her name is Sally. The finest professor in the world is in Russia, and if it's the last thing I do in my life, I'm going to take her to see him.

Shocked beyond belief, Ellen got into the car and drove around the newsagents of Cannes buying up the town's entire stock of newspapers, and took them upstairs to Stanley. He was appalled. He immediately picked up the phone and rang Richard in Paris, and they had the most searing row in over twenty years of friendship. In the end Ellen said it was their own fault, they knew Richard, what did they expect? But Stanley couldn't forgive him: Richard had promised, he had specifically given his word that there would be no interviews. Their friendship was never the same again.

Sally had not spent her holiday with Sybil at all; in a whole month, she had been with her for a total of four days. The rest of the time she was with Richard and Elizabeth in their suite at the Regency Hotel, or in nightclubs. She didn't go to Central Park, or the Zoo, or the Metropolitan Museum of Art. Her only outings were to see *Gone with the Wind*, with a maid, and to Saks to buy 144 pairs of tights with Elizabeth's charge card, when she was almost arrested because they thought she had stolen it.

Elizabeth had behaved like a fairy godmother to Sally, and, although it had not been the holiday her parents might have wished for their fifteen-year-old daughter, Sally had had a wonderful and unforgettable four weeks and had fallen soundly in love with Elizabeth.

This was one of a number of heavy blows that knocked Burton at the end of the 1960s. Stanley had been a brother to him throughout the ups and downs of his career, of his marriages, of his affairs. They had been drunk together, irreverent together, and Richard was shattered and slightly bemused to have lost his approval.

Towards the end of 1968, another incident shook him. Since his marriage to Elizabeth, Richard had scarcely been to the house at Celigny, because, whenever they were in Switzerland, they would stay in Elizabeth's house in Gstaad. One day he decided on the spur of the moment to take Kate to see Le Pays de Galles, and pack up Sybil's books, which he had never given back to her after their divorce. Elizabeth was busy, so he, Kate and Ifor took the jet to Geneva, and a couple of hours later they were in Celigny. It was lunchtime and Ifor suggested that Richard and Kate start ordering some lunch at the station buffet while he went ahead to open the house up and switch on the heating. He would be back to join them.

Richard and Kate waited for him to come back, but he was taking longer than expected so they began their meal, then they had coffee. Still there was no sign of Ifor. Eventually they went up to the house to look for him. They found Ifor lying with a broken neck in the snow where he had fallen nearly two hours earlier. Richard had asked for a snow grill to be put on the front door, which was hidden by the heavy snow. In reaching up to get the front-door key from its hiding place on the lintel, Ifor had caught his toe in the grating and fallen.

He was in a poor condition but still alive, and was quickly whisked to an intensive care unit in a hospital in Geneva. Gwen and Elizabeth flew out immediately. As soon as his condition was stable enough to risk moving him, they flew him home to Stoke Mandeville, the spinal injury hospital in Buckinghamshire. Ifor was paralysed from the neck down and was unable to move for the rest of his life. He was only sixty-one, and at times became so depressed that he begged to be allowed to die.

Burton went to pieces. He began drinking more and more heavily, unable to face up to the enormity of what had happened. His life seemed to be falling in ruins around him. This was now the second of his relatives in an institution, and he found them both equally upsetting to visit. Ifor he could at least talk to. Jessica, on the other hand, still showed not the faintest glimmer of interest or recognition, and in the end he gave up going to see her.

With Ifor out of action, a new figure joined the entourage to take his place. He was Emlyn's son, Brook Williams, who had hero-worshipped Richard, his godfather, ever since he was a boy. He was an actor, but also a heavy drinker, and he had been having a difficult time getting work. So Richard took him under his wing. He was a good conversationalist and Richard enjoyed his company. Brook therefore joined the great Burton/Taylor payroll, and became Richard's minder, drinking companion and general lackey. In almost every film Richard made thereafter, a part would be found for Brook.

Burton made one film throughout the whole of 1969, Maxwell Anderson's *Anne of the Thousand Days*, which he and Hal Wallis, who produced *Becket*, had discussed five years previously. They filmed at Shepperton, and Richard, Elizabeth, Brook and the rest of the retinue stayed at the Dorchester, driving down each day in the Rolls Royce that was specified in the contract.

It was a film he enjoyed making. He was fond of history: apart from poetry and Shakespeare, most of his reading was historical – and very thorough, he would read books several times over. He had a particular fondness for Churchill and he knew his writings intimately. Novels he seldom read, and newspapers did not influence him much apart from the sports news. Most of the daily news he heard on the radio, a constant companion. Whatever part of the world he was in, he would tune into the BBC World Service.

In *Anne of the Thousand Days*, Burton played the part of Henry VIII, the much-married Tudor monarch, obsessed with his wives' failure to produce a son for him. He was a figure Richard had considerable admiration for. 'For all his sins, I find him very attractive,' he told journalist Margaret Hinxman. 'Such courage. It's difficult now to appreciate the enormity of what he did, cutting not only himself but his country off from the Church at a time when men really believed in hell and damnation.'

His screen wife, Anne Boleyn, who lost her head after a thousand days, was played by a beautiful French-Canadian actress of twenty-six, Genevieve Bujold. Burton took more than a passing fancy to his young co-star, which did not improve relations with his off-screen wife. Elizabeth did not share Sybil's attitude to infidelity – physical or mental. She was not prepared to turn a blind eye to anything, becoming insanely jealous if she so much as caught him looking at another woman. Ironically, he was even more possessive about her. He flew into a rage out of all proportion to the offence, whether real or imagined. The fabric of their marriage was beginning to wear thin.

Burton talked about retiring in a couple of years. Elizabeth said he was taking a year off. He said he was fed up with acting. Talking to Barry Norman, he pointed to his contemporaries, Olivier, Gielgud, Richardson, Scofield.

They love acting. Me, I'm different. Much of the time it's just tedium for me.

Last year I had a few months off in Mexico, the first holiday I'd had in fifteen years, and I suddenly realized that doing nothing was marvellous.

What I'd like to do now is appear in two plays – Jean-Paul Sartre's *The Devil and the Good Lord*, and *King Lear* – and then just disappear from view.

It was not just acting. Life too was growing tedious. He wanted to be surrounded by vibrant intellectuals, who could share his enthusiasm for literature and feed him new ideas. As it was, he was being stifled by an entourage of sycophants, starved of intellectual stimulation, and plagued by his fundamental suspicion that dressing up and saying other men's lines was no job for a man. Yet he knew that he did not have the moral fibre to do anything about it.

He was constantly offered work in the National Theatre, then under the directorship of Sir Laurence Olivier, where he could have performed *Macbeth* or *Lear* or Sartre's play. Many were the times that he would spend weekends with the Oliviers at their home in Brighton and, over a bottle of whisky or two (which Olivier could hold better than Burton), map out his future in the theatre. Olivier's wife, Joan Plowright, was frequently heard to remark before his arrival, 'Now Larry, you are not to offer Richard the directorship of the National Theatre again this time.' They devised exciting schemes, major productions, but Richard was never seriously tempted. Though he talked grandly he was only too aware of what he would have to pay in back tax. And money was only a part of the problem.

He was nearly forty-five. For the last quarter of a century people had been forecasting that he would be the next Olivier, the greatest actor in living memory, and the fear of not living up to that forecast was colossal. Hidden behind bad scripts and the big screen, he could put off the chance to prove himself. He could take the money and run, and any criticism could always be diluted by being spread over the plot, the director, the editing, the co-stars. Out on an open stage, with Shakespeare's script, he was alone, and, like many an actor with far less depending on his performance than Burton, he was frightened. The longer he stayed away, the longer he hid behind the celluloid, the more difficult it became to go back.

Nervousness of the stage was not the whole answer, either. Richard's Welsh cheek, his wild exhibitionism, his devil-may-care bravado, all masked a basic and deep-rooted insecurity. His ego needed constant attention, and Elizabeth was not the woman to provide it. She had an ego of her own that needed care. She enjoyed the idea of nesting with Richard and tending his needs, and did genuinely love him very dearly. She tried hard, but Richard was not an easy man to live with, nor an easy character to understand, and she found the going too tough.

There was one further problem that was insoluble. Elizabeth was the bigger star: she earned more money, she drew bigger audiences, and was far, far more famous. No matter how much either of them might have wished it differently, Richard could never compete. She was the princess, he was nothing more than consort; and this gnawed at his fragile equilibrium.

He temporized by spending money on her, buying famous and fabulous jewels which brought a fame of their own. The world knew that he had given them to her, the world even knew what they had cost, and when she wore them in public, they shone like a brand-mark, as if to say that Elizabeth Taylor belonged to Richard Burton. By the time he had added a vast pear-shaped diamond to her collection, which cost £437,500 and went on public display in Cartier's, and £125,000 worth of smaller pieces as a peace-offering following a quarrel, Elizabeth's haul after six years of marriage came to about £4,500,000. But Richard's insecurity ran too deep to be patched up by millions of pounds, and his ultimate solution to any problem in his life was to escape from it. He escaped in the only way he knew how, with drink.

When *Anne of the Thousand Days* was over, the Burtons retreated to Puerto Vallarta, where they spend a good part of 1970, keeping a comparatively low profile, not even appearing for the premiere in February. Twelve-year-old Liza went in their place, and took her headmistress from Heathfield, a boarding school at Ascot in Berkshire. Michael Wilding, Elizabeth's elder son, now seventeen, had attended Millfield, the progressive co-educational school in Somerset. His brother Christopher, two years his junior, had started at

Millfield too, but was now at school in Hawaii, where Elizabeth's brother Howard and his family lived. But even there he was not doing well.

One factor that bound Richard and Elizabeth together was the children. He was enormously fond of them, although he was never a very tactile person and when he did hug them he did not do so with any real warmth. His role was that of paterfamilias: he was concerned about their education, their behaviour, and their overall welfare. Elizabeth was the one who romped with them, gave them treats, spoilt them, and derived most fun from them.

Richard gave Christopher an ultimatum. It was time he did some work: he either went to a serious boarding school in England, or he would have a private tutor and work at home. Christopher opted for the latter, and so Richard wrote to Nevill Coghill for help in finding a tutor. Coghill recommended a young man called John David Morley, who went out to Casa Kimberley in February, and taught both Christopher and his cousin, Christopher Taylor.

Shortly before the Oscar presentations the following month, Richard stopped drinking. It was the first time since he embarked on beer at the Jug and Bottle in Taibach in his early teens that he had spent a full day without a drink. Without alcohol he was a different man. He looked better, he thought more clearly, he took an interest in what was going on around him, and his stories were less repetitive. He was also considerably less menacing. His violent temper and sudden outbursts, which could be ignited at any moment, were temporarily defused. It was a great relief to the entire household, not least to the children, who hated being around when he was drunk.

The Oscar ceremony was in Los Angeles, and Burton had been nominated for his part in *Anne of the Thousand Days*. This was the sixth time he had been nominated, and for the sixth time he missed it. The award went instead to John Wayne. Richard was disappointed, but did not begrudge the legendary star of Hollywood his prize. He mimicked other actors, he sent them up, he told anecdotes about them, but Richard had a generosity of spirit which was rare in such a competitive industry.

By the summer he was still 'dry' and making a film in the Mexican desert, *Raid on Rommel*, which took just twenty days to shoot, as it was an amalgamation of new material with previous footage from another war film. Burton's fee was not as large as usual, but he was moving towards a new system of payment. By the next film, he was on a deal whereby he took nothing for the film, except living expenses, but enjoyed a large percentage of the profits when the film came out.

The film was *Villain*, a British gangster movie made for Anglo-EMI, which conveniently took Burton to London in time to collect a Commander of the British Empire decoration from the Queen on his forty-fifth birthday in November. The award was for services to the theatre and, dressed up in a morning suit and top hat, Richard took Elizabeth and his very proud sister Cecilia with him to Buckingham Palace.

Elizabeth and Richard were back at their base at the Dorchester for the autumn. He was drinking again, for he had only intended to give up for three months, and he was rapidly making up for lost time. He also caught up with a lot of friends they had not seen for some time. Robert Hardy was one whom he rang to invite to a party at the hotel. Robert had been to his parties at the Dorchester before and declined. 'I'd love to come and see you,' he said, 'if ever there's a time when there will just be a few of us. I'm afraid your giant organization defeats me.'

'Sure, wait a minute,' said Richard. 'Come for lunch on Friday when there'll just be us and the children.'

It was agreed, and Robert arrived at the Dorchester to find about a hundred and fifty people in the Burtons' suite, and the biggest mound of caviar he had ever seen in his life: it stood about five feet high. Gradually, as the mound was whittled down, so too were the guests, until no more than six were left, sitting and chatting.

'Right, that's it,' said Richard jumping to his feet at about four o'clock. 'The rest of you can go now, I'm going to fuck my wife.' His slightly startled friends beat a hasty retreat.

The next day Robert wrote his friend a note, saying how lovely it had been to see him, and to thank him for the opportunity of staying on for a chat. 'But getting to see you nowadays,' he wrote, 'is rather like getting through the protocol of a mid-eighteenth-century minor German court.'

The following morning a telegram arrived from Richard, 'Bugger "minor". Rich.'

Richard could never given it all up to go back to the Old Vic, or be a don, or a writer, or to fulfil any of his other fantasies. Intellectually he wept for his lost soul, but physically he enjoyed every minute of being Richard Burton the film star. He loved the wealth, the attention, and proximity to royalty.

Through Sheran and various of her friends, Richard and Elizabeth met Princess Margaret repeatedly. Richard revelled in the friendship, and she enjoyed him. On one occasion she overheard him refer to her as Princess Elizabeth by mistake.

'Now let's get this right,' she said. 'My sister, who was Princess Elizabeth, is now the Queen. My mother is Queen Elizabeth The Queen Mother. And I am Princess Margaret. Got it?'

On another occasion he was rather drunk in her company. He suggested she should tell Robert Hardy a story she had once told him. 'Have you ever heard Princess Margaret's Welsh accent?' he asked. Robert said he hadn't. 'Tell Tim your story,' he urged. 'Go on.'

Princess Margaret demurred.

'Tell Tim your story,' roared Richard, pounding the table with his fists. Equerries appeared from nowhere and swiftly invited the Princess to dance, but she held her ground and eventually, in a very soft voice, she told her story.

After two relatively inactive years, 1971 was busy. First, a film version of *Under Milk Wood* was made in Wales. Burton just had time to appear in it before his limited time in Britain was up. He was back in his element again, playing the First Voice, and working with his old drinking pal, Peter O'Toole, who played the part of Captain Cat.

> *Captain Cat, the retired blind sea-captain, asleep in*
> *his bunk in the seashelled, ship-in-bottled, shipshape*
> *best cabin of Schooner House dreams. . .*
> *Captain Cat, at his window thrown wide to the sun*
> *and the clippered seas he sailed long ago when his*
> *eyes were blue and bright, slumbers and voyages;*
> *ear-ringed and rolling, I Love You Rosie Probert*
> *tattoed on his belly, he brawls with broken bottles*
> *in the fug and babel of the dark dock bars, roves with*
> *a herd of short and good time cows in every naughty*
> *port and twines and souses with the drowned and*
> *blowzy-breasted dead. He weeps as he sleeps and sails.*

By May, he and Elizabeth were back in Mexico to make *Hammersmith Is Out*, arguably his worst film. It was a black comedy about a madman called Hammersmith, who escapes from an asylum for the criminally insane, and goes off on a trail of havoc across America, making him ever more rich and powerful. Burton was Hammersmith, and Elizabeth played the part of a blonde waitress who takes off with her lover in pursuit of him. It was directed by Peter Ustinov. Before they began shooting both Elizabeth and Richard, unbeknownst to the other, had taken Ustinov aside and warned him about the problems he could expect from their partner. Despite the inauspicious start, they got on well together, as they did with most directors, and when filming came to an end there was an exchange of gifts. Ustinov gave Elizabeth a modest ring, and Richard a pair of cuff-links. In return they gave him a painting by the Mexican artist Rufino Tamayo, which Richard passed off as nothing too special. Several weeks later, Ustinov discovered from the shipping manifest that the painting was actually worth ten times what Richard had led him to believe.

From a bad film in Mexico, Burton went straight on to another disaster in Yugoslavia playing President Tito as a wartime guerrilla. The film was called *The Battle of Sutjeska*, and was sponsored by the Yugoslavian government. Burton was approached independently, and rang John Heyman to ask him to negotiate a contract. It transpired that he had not even bothered to read the script. He thought Tito was a great man, so he would do the film, and Richard and Elizabeth subsequently went to stay with Tito. Fortunately for his swiftly sinking reputation, however, the Yugoslavs ran short of money and the film was put on the shelf for a few years.

His next subject was the Russian leader Leon Trotsky. The film depicted his assassination in 1940 at the hands of a Stalinist who found a way into his hideaway in Mexico, and murdered him with an ice pick. Once again Burton accepted the part without reading the script. But this time he was working with friends, Joe Losey and Spike Priggen; his co-stars were Alain Delon and Romy Schneider.

The production walked a political tight-rope in Mexico. They had to get permission from the President, and his censor was on the set daily to approve every scene, so only those shots that could not be reproduced anywhere else were filmed in Mexico. The rest was shot in Rome, where a complete house was built in stone, a faithful reproduction of Trotsky's villa in Mexico.

When Burton joined the unit in Rome he was on the wagon. Spike had been forewarned by Gaston, his chauffeur, who had been in Sardinia and was a permanent member of the retinue. 'It's incredible,' he said. 'You'll see a big difference in Richard. He's not at it.'

'What sort of difference?'

'He's very careful about everything,' explained Gaston, 'very hesitant. He carries his script in the Rolls, and looks at it on the way to the studio in the mornings.' This was something he had never done before.

It was, indeed, a very different actor that played Trotsky. Burton was not so good when he was sober. He was too tense, awkward in his movements and hesitant on dialogue. The character did have long speeches but, under normal circumstances, Richard could have coped with them. Sober, he had to break them up and take them bit by bit.

The Burtons were staying in the Grand Hotel in Rome. One evening Spike received a phone call from Elizabeth. 'Just a little warning, Spikey,' she said. 'You know Richard's not working today; well I doubt that he'll be working tomorrow either.'

'Why's that?' asked Spike.

'Well you'd better get back to the Grand Hotel and look in the bar and see for yourself.'

So Spike went straight to the bar of the hotel, a small decorous room, and found Burton and Peter O'Toole, both as drunk as skunks, lying on the floor, fondly embracing one another and singing 'Happy Birthday'. They had been there since lunch time and, had Spike not broken them up, they would doubtless have remained there for the rest of the night too.

Richard was furious at the interruption and had to be carried to his suite, angrily cursing everyone in sight. He was so drunk that Spike was frightened he would not be able to film the following day. Yet, the next morning he gave the best performance and the best day's work he had done in the entire film.

The Assassination of Trotsky received poor reviews, but as usual Burton was two or three films away by then and past caring. Next on the schedule was a film called *Bluebeard*, made in Budapest with a bevy of beautiful women, including Raquel Welch and Nathalie

Delon. Once again Richard's interest was aroused, particularly by an actress called Dora Zakablukowa, who was naked for one of their scenes together. Elizabeth could take only so much. 'There was someone who put too much passion in certain scenes,' she recalled. 'And moreover she was naked. I smacked her face for her pains. And Richard, I don't know how many plates I broke over his head.'

Filming coincided with Elizabeth's fortieth birthday, for which a mammoth extravaganza was organized at the Inter-Continental Hotel where they were staying. Family, friends and colleagues were invited out to Budapest from all over the world, for an all-expenses-paid weekend celebration. The party from England and Wales alone filled a Viscount jet. All the guests had to do was turn up at the airport, everything else had been arranged for them, tickets and visas included, by Marjorie Lee, chief public relations officer at the Dorchester, who had known Elizabeth since she first began staying at the hotel, and was a good friend.

Had a bomb been dropped on Budapest that weekend, a large proportion of the top names in the world of entertainment would have been wiped out in one go: guests included Princess Grace of Monaco, Michael Caine, Victor Spinetti, Joe Losey, Ringo Starr, Raquel Welch, Suzannah York, Frankie Howerd, Emlyn Williams. Poet Stephen Spender was invited. So too was Nevill Coghill. On the family front, Elizabeth's brother Howard, his wife Mara, and four of their children, and all Richard's brothers and sisters, with the exception of Ifor and Gwen, were there.

Everyone arrived in the Hungarian capital on the Friday afternoon and that evening the first of the parties began – cocktails in the Burtons' suite. Elizabeth's birthday fell on the Saturday, and they took over the cellars of the hotel for a sumptuous feast which went on for most of the night. Elizabeth was wearing her present from Richard, a huge, lemon-coloured diamond necklace, which came from the Taj Mahal and had once belonged to an Indian prince. On Sunday a lunch was held in the main dining room, and in the evening guests moved on to another big party in the nightclub area at the top of the building, for which a band had been specially flown in from Paris.

The entire weekend was given over to the most ostentatious display of wealth and over-indulgence, which some people felt was misplaced and insensitive given the political nature of Hungary. Alan Williams, Emlyn's elder son, could be heard quite clearly expressing his disapproval, when there was such poverty in the world. His sentiments were picked up by the press, much to the embarrassment of Emlyn. To deflect further criticism, Richard promised that he would give the same amount of money that he had spent on Elizabeth's diamond to a British children's educational charity, plus the same amount that he had spent on the party to the United Nations Children's Fund.

Since giving the remainder of his money to charity after his divorce from Sybil, over the years he had continued to donate large sums to a variety of causes; many of which were never publicized. He put a number of children through school, for example, including David, son of the late actor, Michael Rennie. Giving away money was one way of reconciling his blatantly capitalist way of life with his innate socialist principles. It was also the result of genuine kindness, and a desire to help people who were less well off. But Richard tended to give without much notion of how much he had to be generous with. He was so prone to handing out money to anyone who asked that Aaron Frosh had to take over, keeping a tight rein on what went out. Occasionally money promised never materialized.

On his return from Budapest, Richard came a step closer to his dream of Burton the academic. Years before, when he was at the Old Vic, Richard had been intrigued by a production of *Dr Faustus* which was playing at the Irving Theatre in St Martin's Lane. The director, Francis Warner, was seventeen years old, and no one in the company was over the age of nineteen. Richard saw the show several times, and became firm friends with Warner. The latter went on to become a poet and playwright, and latterly fellow and tutor in English Literature at St Peter's College, Oxford.

They had been plotting together for some time to find a way of getting Richard back to the university, so that when Francis suggested an honorary fellowship of St Peter's, Richard jumped at the idea. He wanted to take his position seriously, looking with Elizabeth for houses. They found one they thought they might buy in the countryside near Woodstock, where Elizabeth could keep horses; but it went no further. There were too many films to do, and organizing classes around Burton's schedule was impossible.

He spent one week at Oxford, during which time he and Elizabeth stayed at the Hornbys' house in Pusey, but after that his appearances were rare.

The three or four times he did take classes, however, he was very good. He would take a play like *Hamlet*, for instance, and talk about the various ways of treating it, of delivering the speeches, the emphasis and meaning. The students found him fascinating, and Burton's fantasy about becoming a full-time don developed, but he could never have done the job. Talking to the students was second nature, but the administrative side and time-tabling were tasks that Richard could never have begun cope with, and would never have wanted to do so.

What he liked was being surrounded by people who read. He would frequently ring Francis quite out of the blue, sometimes from thirty or forty miles the other side of London, and say, 'What are you doing today? Let's go out.' He would then drive all the way to Oxford, and they could go off and spend the day touring the pubs of Gloucestershire and discussing the literature of England.

Not long after the Jenkins brothers and sisters had recovered from their three-day blow-out in Budapest, Ifor died. Richard was devastated by the news. He had loved his elder brother dearly, and his loss created a gap which could never be filled. He went to pieces and drank himself into oblivion day after day.

Elizabeth took over and coped with everything for him. She organized the funeral, and even wrote back to all the friends who had written letters of condolence. She set their marital problems to one side and saw him through what was one of the most traumatic times of his life.

Their marital problems were too severe to be ignored for long, however, and one more film together about an unhappy marriage, in which they played bickering husband and wife, was the final straw. They had both felt obliged for some time to make a contribution to Harlech Television, and had announced the previous year that they would be making some films for the company. After much wrangling, a change of writer and of location – from England to Europe because of tax difficulties – the result was two films about the break-up of a marriage seen from each partner's viewpoint: *Divorce His* and *Divorce Hers*.

They were appropriately named. There were tales of long, drunken lunches, of the Burtons arriving late for their calls and leaving the set early, of public squabbles, of oft-told stories from the Old Vic and of ugly displays of temper from the leading man. It all ended shortly before Richard's birthday in November, when the production threw a party for him, and Elizabeth gave her husband an original copy of one of Goethe's works.

Early the following year, Burton was making a film for Carlo Ponti in Italy, *Massacre in Rome*, based on a true story of hostages killed as a reprisal during the Second World War. Elizabeth was with him as usual. Then, in May, their roles were reversed for the first time in their relationship. She was working and he was the one who was coming down to the set for lunch every day. This grated, affronting his ego, and becoming intolerable to him. As always, he drowned his sorrow in alcohol. The film was called *Ash Wednesday*, and rather than face up to the real cause of his resentment, he blamed the film. It was about the rich, the jet set, and he complained that they offended him, they represented the worst sort of people, and Elizabeth should never have agreed to take part. Had she been playing Lady Macbeth, he said, he wouldn't have minded in the least.

There were angry scenes, followed by reports of rows in the gossip columns. One story focussed on a quarrel outside a Hollywood discotheque. Elizabeth went to stay with a woman friend for the night. The next day she appeared at the Beverly Hills Hotel, walked up to Richard who was in the Polo Lounge bar, punched him on the nose, then sat down and had a drink with him. Another reported a row when Elizabeth flew to Beverly Hills for two dates with Peter Lawford, while Richard stayed in New York to meet twelve-year-old Maria, who was arriving from Europe. The press had the scent of blood, and were not going to let go.

On 3 July 1973, they got their kill. Elizabeth announced to the world that she and Burton had separated. 'I am convinced it would be a good and constructive idea if Richard and I separated for a while,' she said from her suite at the Regency Hotel in New York. 'Maybe we loved each other too much – I never believed such a thing was possible. But we have been in each other's pockets constantly, never being apart except for matters of life and death, and I believe it has caused a temporary breakdown of communication.

'I believe with all my heart that the separation will ultimately bring us back to where we should be – and that is together.'

She was returning to California, she said, to see her mother and some old and true friends, 'Wish us well, please, during this most difficult time.'

Burton meantime was staying with Aaron Frosh at his home at Quogue on Long Island. The next day he came out to brave the reporters and photographers camped on his doorstep. Elizabeth's statement had been faithfully reported in full in all the newspapers; in many, it was headline news, and even rated editorial comment. The world was agog to hear what the man of the partnership would have to say.

Burton had obviously been drinking when he greeted his audience, and was visibly upset, but he gave a stoic performance. 'There is no question of our love and devotion for each other,' he said. 'I don't even consider Elizabeth and I are separated. It is just that our private and professional interests are keeping us apart. I even have Elizabeth's passport in my possession. Does that look as if she has left me?'

Elizabeth did go to California to see her mother, who had been unwell; that in itself had put a strain on Elizabeth in recent weeks. Another worry was her elder son. Three years earlier Michael had married at the age of seventeen, while the Burtons were in London, and now he was in trouble. He was living in a commune in the Welsh mountains, he had been bust by the police for smoking pot, his 'den mother' was pregnant, and his wife had left him, taking their baby, Elizabeth's first grandchild, with her.

Richard meanwhile stopped drinking, but not for long, and throughout the summer he lurched on and off the wagon. Three weeks after the separation they met briefly in Rome. Burton was finishing off the film about Tito, which had suddenly come to life again after two years, while Elizabeth had come to make *The Driver's Seat*. They spent a week together in isolation at Carlo Ponti and Sophia Loren's heavily guarded villa at Marina; but, despite Richard's protestations that everything was all right between them, it was not.

A week later they instructed Aaron to file papers for divorce in Switzerland; but their disentanglement from one another was no easy matter, either financially or emotionally. Within four months they embarked upon another reunion: Elizabeth had undergone an operation for the removal of an ovarian cyst in Los Angeles, and

Richard came sweeping to her hospital bed. They flew to Gstaad for Christmas in a blaze of love and togetherness. But by April 1974, they were on opposite sides of the world, and the divorce was on. The grounds were 'irreconcilable differences'.

After ten years, the most public, most publicized, most tempestuous and romantic marriage in the world was finally at an end.

7

Under New Management

The marriage was over, but Richard and Elizabeth's emotional involvement with one another never died. Neither had fallen in love with someone else, so there was no third party to make clean the break, as had happened when Richard's marriage to Sybil broke up. They remained inexplicably and inextricably bound. As Richard himself said, 'We are flesh of one flesh, bone of one bone.'

They were also bound to one another financially. Although some of their joint ventures were unravelled and divided up in the divorce, some remained. There was the question of the children, too. Burton was not directly related to any of Elizabeth's family, but he had been their 'father' for thirteen years in all. The boys' real father, Michael Wilding, now a theatrical agent, was very much alive, but as far as the two girls were concerned, Richard was their father. He had officially adopted Maria, who was now thirteen, and when the divorce was granted in the mountain ski resort of Saanen, near Gstaad, Elizabeth specifically requested that Richard be given the right to visit her.

During their last attempt at reconciliation, Burton's drinking had become chronic. When the end came he was making *The Klansman*, a film with Lee Marvin, who is a renowned drinker himself, in Oroville, northern California, about the Ku-Klux-Klan. Richard was drinking heavily from the time he woke up in the morning until he went to bed at night; and whose bed it might be was anybody's guess. His consumption of vodka alone was two to three bottles a day, and he had been living that way for nearly six months. One day Elizabeth quite suddenly walked out. A variety of reasons were given, but as one of the film crew remarked, 'The booze, the broads and the bad weather got to her.' It was a close assessment.

As soon as the film was over, Richard was taken to St John's Hospital in Santa Monica, a special therapy clinic, where he was given the plain facts: if he carried on drinking he would be dead within two weeks. The doctors who examined him said that they feared there was no way they could save him. 'I am not afraid of death,' said Richard. 'I am just amused that you think I can be killed off this easily. Don't forget I come from Welsh mining stock and I am only forty-eight. My father was the greatest boozer in our valley and he lived until he was eighty-three – and then he died not from drink but from a stroke.'

Despite the bravado, their prognosis gave him a serious fright. Over the course of the next four weeks he was gradually weaned off alcohol, but it was a painful and an undignified process, and when he came out he vowed he would never drink again.

Nearly a year later, he described the sensation to David Lewin, and such was Burton's fame that the *Sunday Mirror*, a national newspaper, carried the story on the front page:

> But after those first four days I was taken off drink altogether and that was bad, very bad. I had to be fed through a tube I would shake so much.
>
> People are supposed to see pink snakes and spiders on the ceilings or crawling up the walls when they are being dried out.
>
> I didn't. I just could not sleep. I could get off for forty-five minutes and then I'd have a nightmare – always the same nightmare and I'd be awake again.
>
> I dreamed of my elder brother Ifor who was paralysed in an accident in Switzerland in 1968 and was unable to move until he died in London four years later.
>
> I kept seeing Ifor alive and perfectly fit in my dreams and in my room with me.

After four weeks of hell, Richard went to Puerto Vallarta to recuperate. He had lost nearly three stone in weight, and although he was not drinking anything stronger than soda water, he habitually smoked about sixty cigarettes a day. The clinic had encouraged him to take exercise to increase his pulse rate, but for someone who had taken virtually none for years, he was surprisingly fit. He had given up rugby long ago, because he found there was always someone in the team who went for him, so they could say they had kicked Richard Burton. He was a spectator at cricket, and his only pastimes that were remotely physical were a few gentle lengths of the swimming pool, table tennis, croquet on an English summer afternoon, and walking. It was losing a game of table tennis that had cost Richard a diamond. He and Elizabeth had had a bet; she won, and he bought her the Krupp. Exercise was no pleasure to him. He would far rather sit around and talk, read a book, or play Scrabble.

But the warning had sunk in, and when he came to England in August to appear in *Brief Encounter*, Noel Coward's classic film first made nearly thirty years earlier with Trevor Howard and Celia Johnson, Burton took up cycling. He was also still on the wagon.

He was a last-minute choice for the film. The part of the doctor who has a brief encounter with a housewife on a railway station, was to have been played by Robert Shaw, but he was held up on another film. Sophia Loren, playing the housewife, therefore suggested Burton. They had become close friends. Not only had she co-starred with him in *The Voyage* the year before, shortly after his first separation from Elizabeth; she had also acted as hostess to them both in Marino when they were having the first of their reconciliations.

From *Brief Encounter* Burton went straight into a ninety-minute documentary film about Sir Winston Churchill, which was to be made for both British and American television. Entitled *A Walk With Destiny*, it was a reconstruction of Churchill's career from 1936 to 1940, based on his memoirs. Churchill had specifically requested when he was alive that the actor to portray him should be Richard Burton. He had already impersonated his voice on several occasions, including *The Valiant Years*, which he had made for television back in 1960, but he had never appeared as the great wartime Premier.

Burton was evidently nervous about the part. It was an important series, in which he would be judged not just by the critics, but by the public, to whom Churchill was a household name and, in the majority of households, a hero. He insisted on rehearsing in the sort of clothes Churchill wore and smoking a cigar, to feel his way into the character, which was something he had never done in his career before. Indeed, it was the sort of 'method acting' that he would have derided as pretentious.

He was already well versed on Churchill, for he knew his writings inside out. One of his most treasured possessions was a bust of the man, which he had once lovingly taken down to the Hornbys' house in Oxfordshire so that it wouldn't be stolen from his house in Hampstead while he was out of the country. He and the producer, Jack Le Vien, had been to have tea with Lady Churchill before they began work in August, and Richard had apparently enjoyed the meeting very much. He had also had lunch with Churchill's grandson, Winston Churchill, the Conservative MP, and had been very full of the role he was about to play, and how much he had admired the old man.

Yet days before *A Walk With Destiny* had its first showing, in America at the end of November, an article written by Burton appeared in the *New York Times*, causing a furore on both sides of the Atlantic. It was entitled 'To Play Churchill Is To Hate Him', and went on to say that Winston Churchill was a 'monster', 'a vindictive toy-soldier', and that playing him had made Burton 'realize afresh that I hate Churchill and all his kind. I hate them virulently. They have stalked down the corridors of endless power all through history.' Sir Winston was essentially a coward, he said, and put him on a moral par with Hitler, Stalin and Genghiz Khan.

Everyone who had been involved with the production was mystified. But while they were busy composing telegrams of outrage and disassociation, a second article appeared in the American mass-circulation magazine, *TV Guide*. Far from retracting his assertions, Richard went further:

> He was short, obese, vigorous, pugnacious, something of a vulgarian, power-mad (and for a time, at least, almost insane with power), afraid of nothing either physically or morally – the former by nature, the second by a lack of sensitivity to other people's feelings.
>
> He was intellectually barren, superficially educated, maniacally industrious and of a physical constitution to marvel at. He drank steadily all day long with time off for sleep – champagne, whisky, brandy – and lived for more than ninety years.
>
> His last device to the free world he served so well might well have been to leave us his liver to wonder at.

Playing Alex Leamas in *The Spy Who Came In From The Cold*. 'His performance makes you forgive him for every bad part he has ever played, every good part he has ever messed up and every indiscretion he has ever committed off the screen or on.'

Co-starring with Elizabeth in *The Sandpiper*. Her days as a full-time wife were over

One of Richard's most constant themes was Oxford. He regarded it as his real home, his intellectual and spiritual *alma mater*. One day he would give up acting and become an academic. It was another fantasy. *Above*: His first return in 1966 to play in an OUDS production of *Dr Faustus*. He and Elizabeth frequently entertained the cast; the students were a new audience for Richard's stories. *Below*: In 1972 he came one step closer to his dream of Burton the academic. Francis Warner was instrumental in Richard becoming an Honorary Fellow of St Peter's College

With Elizabeth playing Helen of Troy to Richard's Faustus. The first and last film he directed, in Rome in 1967

'*Faustus* is the one play I don't have to do any work on. I am Faustus.'

Above: *Kalizma*, 279 tons, named after Kate, Liza and Maria. 'You know how it is when Elizabeth wants something.'

Below: Elizabeth, Richard and John Heyman's son, David, aboard the yacht while filming *Boom* in Sardinia, 1967

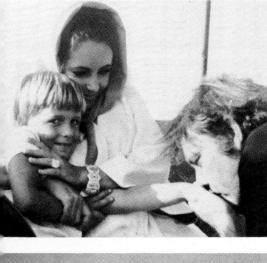

Apart from poetry and Shakespeare, most of his reading was historical – and very thorough

'My wife is known as Lizzie Jenkins.'

Clint Eastwood and Ringo Starr aboard the *Kalizma*, moored in the Thames while working on *Where Eagles Dare*

Sir John Gielgud, another visitor to the yacht

One day Richard would give it all up and become a writer. A portable typewriter travelled everywhere with him

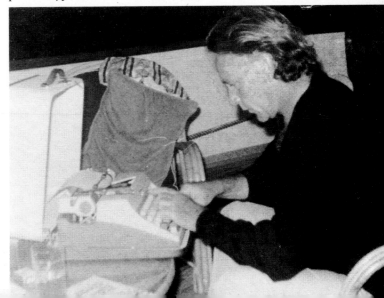

Sheran Cazalet's marriage to
Simon Hornby, 15 June 1968.
The guest list read like a page
from Debrett's Peerage. For
the second time Richard
bought a suit in honour of
Elizabeth's childhood friend

Arriving at the church with
Noel Coward

Sheran, Richard and Princess
Margaret. 'Now, let's get this
right. My sister, who was
Princess Elizabeth, is now the
Queen. My mother is Queen
Elizabeth, The Queen
Mother. And I am Princess
Margaret. Got it?'

Above: Casa Kimberley in Puerto Vallarta, Mexico, with breathtaking views over the Pacific

Right: The New House where Richard went with his typewriter to write each morning

Richard and Elizabeth in a bar in Puerto Vallarta. Burton frequently appeared distracted, as though he were constantly waiting for something, bored, but not just with what was going on around him in the present; it was as if he had an inner boredom, a cosmic desperation

Burton and Rex Harrison as a homosexual couple in *Staircase*, 1969. It was a curious choice of film, for Richard was aggressively anti-homosexual

At the premiere for *Staircase*, Simon Hornby examining Elizabeth's latest acquisition. Her passion for jewels amused Richard

Richard was in Rome when friends, colleagues, fans and strangers turned as one to condemn him. Shaun Sutton, Head of Drama at the BBC, which showed the documentary a week later, said Burton would never work for him again. Correspondents vented their wrath in the letters column of *The Times*. Conservative MP Norman Tebbit said, 'Perhaps his matrimonial troubles have got him confused about life at large. One should really regard this in the light of an actor past his best indulging in a fit of pique, jealousy and ignorant comment.' Fellow MP Neville Trotter was less charitable. 'I don't think Mr Burton is a good advertisement for Britain,' he said. 'His personal conduct leaves a great deal to be desired. If there were more Churchills and fewer Burtons we would be a very much better country.'

Richard remained unmoved. He never explained nor apologized to anyone. Angry letters and telegrams from people like Robert Hardy and Sheran Hornby, expressing their disgust, might as well have never been sent. They were certainly never replied to, and when they next met, he made no reference. He was preoccupied with a new love affair, and he was drinking again. His proclamations on any subject were beginning to sound a little hollow.

His latest love was Princess Elizabeth of Yugoslavia, first cousin to the Duke of Kent, Princess Alexandra and Prince Michael. She was one of Elizabeth Taylor's friends, whom he had first met at a party given by Lord Harlech. She was married to merchant banker and Conservative parliamentary candidate Neil Balfour, and had a four-year-old son by him, plus two daughters from a previous marriage. For the past six years he and Elizabeth had met up with the Princess and Neil when they were in London. Now Richard rang her up when he was again in London filming *A Walk With Destiny*, and three weeks later she had left her home and husband, and was talking about spending the rest of her life with Richard. 'I'm going to marry her,' Burton announced melodramatically. 'I want her to be my wife. I want to be with her for ever and ever and ever . . . . I love her, I truly do. I love her so much, so deeply, it hurts.'

In the end, however, it was Elizabeth, or 'Ellisheba' as he fondly nicknamed her, who was so deeply hurt. Another relationship failed to survive Richard's drinking, another wrecked life was added to the list of casualties.

The affair lasted less than six months. Burton had begun work in the meantime on a film called *Jackpot*, made in Nice in the South of France with Charlotte Rampling and James Coburn, which ran out of money less than halfway through. He played a man who tried to con an insurance company out of millions of pounds, by first faking an accident that crippled him for life, then by claiming a religious miracle cure. But there was no miracle cure for the backers. They filmed on and off from February until early summer, and by July the three stars were taking action in the High Court to have the backers, Irwin Trust Company Limited, wound up. Richard was owed nearly £46,000.

He was drinking intermittently, despite Princess Elizabeth's efforts to persuade him to give it up, and dallying with a black American model and former *Playboy* bunny girl, Jean Bell, whom he had met on the set of *The Klansman* back in the spring. She had a small part in *Jackpot*, and so was on hand in Nice as well. One night Richard became very drunk during a dinner party given by the film's director, Terence Young, where both women were present. Suddenly he left the restaurant alone. Shortly afterwards, his driver came back to the table with a message for Jean to join him, but she refused. The driver came back a second time to try to persuade her to join Richard. Finally Princess Elizabeth went in her place, climbed into the car next to Burton, who slept all the way back to their hotel, and, having been severely snubbed by him the following morning, left for London.

After spending the next few days with Jean, he was filled with remorse and flew to London to try to patch things up with Elizabeth, but the simple cause of the problem was alcohol. Drink turned him into a different man, making him destructive, irrational, belligerent and unpredictable. But, without the clinical environment of the St John's clinic, he seemed incapable of quitting. Elizabeth could finally take the strain no longer and after four desperate, painful months, with her marriage to Neil Balfour in ruins, the romance that she gave it up for, that she thought would last for life, was over.

Richard drowned his sorrows and returned to the open arms of Jean Bell, who spent most of the summer with him and her thirteen-year-old son, Troy, in Switzerland. She worked hard to try to stop Richard drinking, and for a time, at least, succeeded. But although she fell soundly in love with him and he professed to have done likewise, by August he had dropped her for Elizabeth Taylor.

Within weeks of leaving Richard the previous year, Elizabeth had fallen for the charms of a used-car salesman from Los Angeles, Henry Wynberg. Whenever asked about his ex-wife's latest liaison, Richard affected never even to know his name. In recent months she had been filming in Russia and was tiring of Henry. She telephoned Burton, and they spoke frequently. Finally she came to Switzerland and they met up, ejected their resident companions, and announced to the world that they were in love again.

He was buoyant. He rang all his friends and relatives to tell them the news. One of the first people to hear was Sheran Hornby, who was down at Fairlawne in Kent. Her brother called her to the phone and said it was Richard. She could scarcely believe her ears when it turned out to be Richard Burton, who had managed to track her down from a hotel they were staying at in Switzerland to tell her that he and Elizabeth were going to be remarried.

They didn't marry until October 1975, by which time they were in Southern Africa. They had gone to Johannesburg for a tennis tournament the previous month, and Elizabeth had been taken ill. She believed for a while that she had cancer, and there were more bedside vigils, but it turned out to be nothing serious. When she was given the all-clear, they went on a safari holiday to Botswana, and were married in the remote village of Kasane, on the banks of the Chobe River. It was an idyllic setting. The bride wore a green dress trimmed with lace and guinea-fowl feathers. The groom sported a red shirt, red socks and white slacks. And the man who joined the famous pair was the local district commissioner, Ambrose Masalia.

They honeymooned in the bush, but it was now Burton's turn to take to his bed. He became ill with malaria, and a pharmacist, a Chinese American called Chem San, was flown out to treat him. Once again the trouble was exacerbated by drink, and Richard was told that if he didn't stop, he would be dead within six months. So, by the time he was back in London for his fiftieth birthday in November, he was on the wagon.

On their way home, they had spent some time in Johannesburg, where Richard had bought Elizabeth a 72-diamond ring. But before she left the country, she sent the ring back to the jewellers, and asked that the £490,000 be spent instead on setting up a hospital clinic at Kasane. Then from her hotel room, Elizabeth had rung Marjorie Lee at the Dorchester, and asked her to organize a party for Richard. She spent hours on the phone giving her the names of all the people to be invited and, as usual, there was never reference to any sort of budget. Throughout their years at the Dorchester, both together and separately, neither Richard nor Elizabeth ever inquired about the price of anything. But then, neither of them ever directly paid a bill there either. The bills were all sent to their London accountant, James Wishart.

For Burton's fiftieth birthday party, no expense was spared. It was held in the Orchid Rooms and the entire entrance area to the suite was decorated to resemble an East End of London street market, with barrows full of all his favourite food, like fish and chips, and bangers and mash. Richard and Elizabeth were delayed and didn't arrive back in England until the morning of the party, but Liza and Maria were already there and they helped with all the decorations.

Alas, the marriage was doomed to failure. Friends who saw them together knew it could not last. They were the same people that they had been when they divorced, with the same personalities, the same insecurities, the same egos, and the same needs, and neither was prepared to change a thing. They foolishly thought they could survive on the same animal magnetism that had held them to one another the first time around.

Throughout December Richard was in and out of the Wellington Clinic, overlooking Lord's Cricket Ground in North London, with recurrences of his malaria and drink problems, and at the end of the month he and Elizabeth flew to Gstaad for Christmas. He was at a very low ebb. His health was poor, his career was in the doldrums, and his marriage was a disaster.

Someone else with an unhappy marriage in Gstaad that Christmas was Susan Hunt. She was twenty-seven years old, tall, blonde, statuesque and stunningly beautiful, and had been married to world motor-racing champion James Hunt for eighteen months. Their marriage had been a mistake from the start. He was at the peak of his career, twenty-eight years old, world famous, good-looking, wild and neither ready nor prepared to settle down. Suzy wanted nothing more than to be a wife to build a home and to have children.

The result was catastrophic: the harder she tried to please him, the more he tried to shake her off.

They were tax exiles like the Burtons, living in Marbella in Spain, but had gone to stay with friends in Gstaad for Christmas. Immediately afterwards, James had gone to Argentina for the first grand prix race of the season, and left Suzy on her own in Switzerland. It had been a fraught Christmas. James had been in training, so he hadn't been drinking or going out at all, and Suzy's morale was at an all-time low.

Then Richard appeared and swept her off her feet. They first saw one another on the ski slopes. Richard spotted her, but didn't know who she was, so he dispatched Brook to find out. When James came home from South America a couple of weeks later, he was greeted with the news that his wife was leaving him for Richard Burton.

Despite the age difference, Richard and Suzy were a prefect foil for each other, and provided what the other needed. Unlike Elizabeth, Suzy was quite unambitious. She had been a model, and she enjoyed mixing with the fashionable, but she didn't crave fame or fortune. She was warm and gentle and, although not intellectual in any way, she was instinctive. More important, she was desperately keen to have children – as was Burton – and content to devote her life to one man. After thirteen years in competition with Elizabeth, Richard needed someone who would do just that. He, in return, provided her with the husband she could look after, the security she craved, and the glamorous life she enjoyed.

So Richard and Suzy went to New York together, where he was due to start rehearsals for his first stage play since *Faustus* at Oxford ten years before. The play was *Equus*, Peter Shaffer's gruelling drama about a boy who blinds six horses because they were witness to his love-making, and the wretched provincial psychiatrist whose patient he becomes as a result. The play first opened at the Old Vic in London, directed by John Dexter, and since moving to Broadway it had already had two changes of cast. Anthony Perkins who was currently playing the part of Dysart, the psychiatrist, was due to leave the production in February. Since Burton had already been cast to play in the film version, Peter Shaffer, suggested that he should take over for the last three months on the stage.

Dysart is a man without passion, a dry aesthetic character, and

John Dexter thought Burton was quite wrong for the part. But since the film was not his concern, and the play had only three months left to run, he went along with Shaffer's casting. Nevertheless, throughout rehearsals he had a constant struggle to get Richard to keep back his own passion and strength.

Burton was very nervous about appearing on stage after so long. He was nervous about the part, too; worried about whether his vocal chords were up to it, worried whether he could remember his lines in the demanding role, with a lot of long speeches. Officially he was on the wagon, but Brook was seen surreptitiously bringing bottles into the theatre in brown paper parcels for him.

With just over a week to go before Anthony Perkins's last performance, John Dexter suddenly realized that Burton did not know the part at all. Every time he had dropped a line in rehearsals, he would produce a wonderful joke to cover up, and had so charmed everyone that no one really noticed.

'You know you're on a week on Monday, dear?' he asked.

'Yes, yes,' said Richard. 'I know.'

'Well, I think there's only one way to deal with that,' said Dexter, who had known him long enough to treat him as he found him. 'I'm going to put you on on Saturday afternoon when the audience won't be expecting you.'

'I won't be ready on Saturday afternoon,' he thundered.

'You'll be ready on Saturday afternoon, and you'll go out on stage and you'll do it. On Monday night the press will be in and there'll be no excuses. On Saturday, you'll be able to get away with murder.'

Richard grunted; the days passed, and the jokes continued. Dexter came to the end of his patience. He blew him up one day in front of the entire cast.

'Richard,' he said, 'you're disgracing yourself in front of your compatriots. 'You're a lazy, drunken fool.'

Dexter knew that he had to say it in front of the company to make Richard realize he was serious. If he had spoken to him in private, he would have paid no attention. He went to speak to him in his dressing room straight afterwards.

'You're supposed to be leading this company and you're not. They all love you, so you don't need to worry about that, but the public don't yet. They don't know how charming you can be when you don't know your lines. So do something, please. Learn it.'

'Well it's very difficult,' said Richard, 'couldn't we just re-write . . . '.

'No,' said Dexter firmly. 'Peter Shaffer's not here, the play's been running for months, everyone else would have to re-learn. This is the author's text; you may respect it or you may not, but that's all you're getting.'

That Saturday Burton went on for the matinee. It was a disaster. For the first half hour of the play he did not look up from the floor, and he fluffed repeatedly. He looked as though he had never been on stage before. He was like a great wreck floundering. He was shaking, he couldn't remember the lines. The rest of the cast helped him through, by saying things like 'Excuse me, doctor, I think I should tell you that . . . ' and so bring him back to the plot, but he was quite inclined to say, 'Well that's all I have to say to you,' and leave them flummoxed. It was the same tendency that had so unnerved the students in *Faustus* at the Oxford Playhouse.

Richard went back to the Plaza that night and emerged two days later for the Monday night show a new man. He knew the lines and he gave a performance that earned him a standing ovation. Most of the critics raved about him. Walter Kerr in the *New York Times* described it as 'the best work of his life'. John Barber concluded his review in the *Daily Telegraph* with what he described as the finest tribute one can pay an actor: 'He made a fine play seem even finer.'

During those two days in which the transformation took place, Richard was with Elizabeth Taylor. She had recently arrived from Switzerland, where there had been constant press reports that she had been dating a Maltese advertising man, Peter Darmanin. When Richard met her at the airport, he was overhead to say, 'You look like a woman in love.' Then, turning to an airport security guard, he asked, 'Do you want to be her lover this week?' They spent most of the weekend rowing, but by the time he left the hotel for the theatre that Monday, they had reached a truce. And their second marriage was at an end.

When Burton went into his dressing room that night he found she had scrawled a good luck message across his mirror. 'You are fantastic, love.' And one of the first things he did when the applause had died down was to ring Elizabeth to wish her a happy birthday. Nothing had changed, and nothing would change. Richard went óff on the town with Suzy, Elizabeth was soon in the arms of another husband, but there was no dramatic end to an era. The force that bound Richard and Elizabeth to one another was too strong to be broken by divorce. They never tried marriage again, but for the next eight years of his life, they were seldom out of touch for long.

Burton played in *Equus* on Broadway for three months, and during that time he hatched a plot with John Dexter which brought him closer than he had ever come to his dream of playing King Lear. John had recently been appointed resident director of the Metropolitan Theater at the Lincoln Center in New York. Before that he had been at the Old Vic and for years had been trying to persuade Richard to come back, but the National Theatre was so structured at that time that actors needed to make a three-year commitment. Although Burton was tempted, he was never prepared to make the financial sacrifice.

The Met was different. John and Richard discussed two plays which Richard was keen to do: Sartre's *The Devil and the Good Lord*, which he decided he was now too old for; and *Lear*. John wanted to put *Lear* on a plain platform, a production which got away from the ornate sets of the National and concentrated on the acting. But he thought the part too much for any one man to perform eight times a week, so suggested they should alternate with *Romeo and Juliet*. Peter Firth and Roberta Maxwell, both in *Equus*, would play the leads and Burton could play the part of Friar Laurence, which would be the next best thing to a night off. It wouldn't even involve changing out of his clothes; he could just throw a robe on top.

Richard liked the idea, and the plan was to put it into practice the following year. John Dexter was excited by the prospect too. It would be a lot of work, he knew, but he felt that Burton still had just enough ambition left to pull himself together and produce the performance that the public had been waiting for for over twenty years. Unhappily, it was never to be. Alex Cohen thought that America was not yet ready for repertory, and so the idea floundered. Richard never played his *Lear*.

A month after *Equus* closed, Richard learnt the news that Stanley Baker had died of lung cancer. He was shattered. Only weeks before, he had spoken to Stanley on the telephone to find out how he was, and his old friend had made light of his illness. 'Why don't

I ever see you any more?' Richard used to ask, but the truth was that Stanley had the same difficulty everyone else had. For years Richard had been so protected by the people he employed that friends could no longer pick up the phone, dial his home or his hotel room, and speak to him. Letters, too, went unanswered, so there was no way of keeping in touch as they had in the old days. Stanley had been saddened by what had become of his oldest friend.

As soon as Richard heard, he sent a telegram to Ellen, the longest telegram she ever received: 'Can't think, can't sleep, can't speak. I am shattered. Can't get my thoughts together. You must forgive me, I don't know what to say. Devastated. My heart goes out to you and the children. If I can help, if I can help, if I can help. All love, Richard.' Three weeks later, he wrote a tribute to his friend, entitled 'Lament for a Dead Welshman', which appeared in the *Observer*.

That Sunday Ellen was at home in Epsom with the children when the photographer Norman Parkinson and his wife Wendy arrived and asked what she thought of the article. Much to their embarrassment they realized that Ellen hadn't seen it, because the children had been keeping the paper from her. Uttering endless apologies they slipped away. Ellen went off into the garden to sit down under the tree where some of Stanley's ashes had been spread, and read in horror, 'He was tallish, thickish, with a face like a determined fist prepared to take the first blow but not the second and if, for Christ's sake, you hurt certain aspects of his situation like his wife or his children, or even me, you were certain to be savagely destroyed. . . . We smashed windows, broke trains and lusted after the same women. . . . Not that my Stanley liked pianos. He used them as footstools. In fact the lovely old Stanley wasn't exactly cultured. He read minds not books [Ellen had never been able to put a tray down in the house because Stanley's books cluttered every surface], he was harshly unpoetic, he didn't like people very much and made it clear, sometimes painfully, and he hated to lose at anything, and rarely did, but what the hell can you do if you come from such a murderous background?'

'Those low hills, those lowering valleys, the Rhondda fawr, the Rhondda fach, and their concomitant buses and grey roofs and pit-heads and dead grass and crippled miners and cages endlessly falling with your father inside and smashed to bits, and since with a convulsive heave, Stanley shrugged off the mighty mountains and strode across Europe, who or what the devil killed him?'

She read on, ' . . . And once in a bar in Biarritz, there was this impossibly drunken American sunk in a reef of Scotch whisky, blind as an eyeless bull, muttering inanities to himself, and we tried to prop the poor bastard up. . . . And Stanley said, "Good God Rich, he's William Faulkner."' Stanley had never been to Biarritz.

As Ellen read this, she heard Stanley laughing in the tree. 'You know Richard when he's in his cups,' he was saying. 'He suffers from an excess of the verbals.' She smiled, went indoors and asked what was for lunch. But all Stanley's friends were outraged, and the phone rang for the rest of the day with people asking what she was going to do. So she rang the Editor of the *Observer*, Donald Trelford, to find out how the article had come about. Trelford explained that he had recieved a call from Brook Williams saying that Richard had written a piece, did they want it? In the past, he said, when Burton had written for them, they had always been careful to have writers work on it, but this pieces had come over the teleprinter, and when he realized how inflammatory it was, he put eight people to work through the night. 'You should have seen what we cut out of it,' he said. 'Brook had said Richard would like to do this for his best friend. I thought he was doing it for free; but I've had a bill in from his lawyer.'

'Already?' said Ellen.

Two days later, Ellen phoned Sybil, who had already seen the piece. 'Darling, what can I say?' she said. 'The man's mad, you've got to realize that.'

During the remainder of the summer Sybil had all of Ellen's children to stay in turn, to give her friend a chance to adjust. They were grief-stricken by Stanley's death, and bitterly upset by the article. But they could talk to Sybil, who let them talk. They all came back with a better understanding both of their father and of his relationship with Richard.

In the meantime Brook contacted Ellen's lawyer and explained that Richard had written the article for Sally, his goddaughter, and was intending to give all the money he made out of it to her.

'Great,' said Sally, then twenty-three. 'I could do with some. I'll go and see him.' Ellen begged her not to, but she was determined.

Richard had always said that if anything happened to Stanley, he would be a second father to her, but he hadn't been able to cope with Sally's grief, any better than he could cope with his own.

By this time he was married to Susan, and they were staying at the Dorchester. Sally had great difficulty in getting to see him, but finally she was shown into his suite. It was Suzy who took the initiative. 'Richard, will you write a cheque for Sally? How much did you earn from those articles?' In the end Suzy wrote out the cheque herself.

Richard and Suzy were married in August 1976, just as soon as their respective divorces were through. Back in February James Hunt had come to New York to meet the man who had supplanted him, and to discuss the matter with them both. They met two or three times, and he was impressed by Richard's sensitivity. He handled the situation well, and even thanked James for giving him Susan.

They filed for divorce in Port au Prince, the capital of Haiti, where foreigners can be divorced in a day, although it is not universally recognized. Susan's was straightforward, with no settlement. She had been down to Marbella in May to clear her belongings out of their flat, but all their joint possessions, including most of their wedding presents, stayed with James.

Richard's divorce was rather different. Elizabeth kept everything – all the jewels, all the paintings, all the property. A few waspish friends said that the only reason she had married him a second time was because she had failed to get all the jewels in the first divorce, but he didn't begrudge her. All he wanted were the three thousand books in his library in Switzerland, and a new start.

He and Susan were married on 21 August. There were no stunning diamonds: just simple gold bands, exchanged in Arlington, Virginia, one of the three states in America which recognizes Haiti divorce. The service took precisely four minutes, conducted by the man who had ended Henry Kissinger's bachelor days two years before, Judge Frances E. Thomas Jr. Richard enjoyed the Welshness of his name.

Burton was working on a film in New York at the time, *The Heretic – Exorcist II*, and they were living at the Laurent Hotel. When they returned there for the reception, after a round trip of five hundred miles, amongst the telegrams and messages waiting for them was one from Elizabeth Taylor in Vienna, where she was filming *A Little Night Music*: 'May you both enjoy long life and happiness.'

Susan and Elizabeth had met in Switzerland, and there was not much love lost between them. They were two very different women, with very different talents and interests. Susan's father had been a lawyer working in the British colonies for many years, so her childhood had been spent in a number of different countries. She was quiet and unassuming, and did not feel the need to compete with Richard in the way that Elizabeth had. She was happy to sit and listen to him, to laugh at his stories, to appreciate his poetry, and to be the all-attentive, all-adoring audience he craved. She played the piano well, and he enjoyed sitting listening to her play. His life became more placid.

Susan's major feat was to keep Burton sober. She took seriously the sentence had been placed on his life. If they were going to have children, which they planned to do immediately, she wanted to make sure their father would be around to see them. But she had taken on a tougher job than she realized. Richard was an alcoholic by this time, and keeping him off the drink was a fierce, bitter, and twenty-four-hour-a-day battle. But it was essential. If he had one mouthful of spirits, he was instantly insensible.

The following February, they were at the *Evening Standard* Drama Awards luncheon at the Savoy Hotel in London. Burton was presenting the award for the Best Actor of 1976 – the award he had won himself for Henry V twenty-two years before. Throughout the lunch he drank mineral water, until the end when someone put a glass of brandy in front of him. Richard drank it, and his entire demeanour changed: he became quite incoherent and instantly very, very drunk. Suzy, suddenly aware of what had happened, swiftly got him up from the table, took him back to the Dorchester where they were staying, and put him to bed for the rest of the day.

Sharing the table at the Savoy that day was Bette Hill, widow of the former world motor-racing champion Graham Hill, whom Suzy frequently saw when she came to London. Both circuit wives, they had become close friends during the years that Suzy was with James Hunt. During lunch, Richard had written her a note which he passed across the table saying, 'Thank you for saving Suzy for me.' There were times when he was savage with his new wife, as he was with anyone who interfered with his drinking, but he did recognize overall and acknowledge that Suzy had saved him from the brink of self-destruction. But it was a wearing role to play.

Suzy had never had anything to do with the film business before, and was appalled by the number of hangers-on and sycophants that surrounded Richard. She felt they were no good for him at all. They told him what he wanted to hear, and they did nothing to stop his drinking. So she set about weeding the worst of them out. Friends felt they had been weeded out too, but like many a second or third wife, she found it difficult stepping into her predecessor's shoes, particularly when so many people accidentally called her Elizabeth. Even Burton's publicity man, John Springer, had referred to her as Elizabeth when he had talked to the newspapers about their wedding.

Suzy was also taking an interest in Burton's career, not merely for the money – in fact, quite the reverse. When she saw how much Richard hated making *The Heretic – Exorcist II* – another terrible film that was roundly condemned by critics and audiences alike – she declared, 'You must never do anything like that again, not even to get a million dollars.' The film was a sequel to *The Exorcist*, which had made a great deal of money out of the occult, but even the director, John Boorman, admitted this one had been a mistake.

The film of *Equus* followed, made in Canada and directed by Sidney Lumet, for which Burton received another Oscar nomination – but yet again no Oscar. From there he moved to London to record a twenty-six-episode series for BBC radio about the history of the English Crown, called 'Vivat Rex', and a few months later was making a thriller at Pinewood about a man who has the gift of telekinesis, *The Medusa Touch*, directed by Jack Gold. Instead of staying at the Dorchester throughout, Richard and Suzy rented a house in the country near Windsor, and set up home for a while.

They also made the inevitable trip to Wales to introduce Susan to the family. She got on remarkably well with the clan, particularly Richard's sisters who were delighted to welcome anyone who was keeping their brother off the drink. He in turn met Suzy's family, who by this time had settled in a farmhouse near Basingstoke. Richard and his father-in-law, Frederick Miller, became great friends. The latter was a self-made man, very well read, and so they would have great conversations about books and go off for long walks in the countryside together. Suzy's brother, John, lived in Los Angeles, but he met her twin sister, Vivienne Van Dyke. When Vivienne's marriage subsequently broke up, she and her young daughter, Vanessa, went to stay with Richard and Susan, and he and the little girl grew very fond of one another.

Still Richard longed for another child of his own, but the months passed and there was no sign of a pregnancy. Suzy in the meantime had inherited a sizeable family from him, one of whom, Christopher Wilding, was working on Richard's next film, *The Wild Geese*, in South Africa. Richard had come by the part in an unusual way. The producer was Euan Lloyd, fellow rugby enthusiast from the past, who received a phone call from Burton's agent in New York, Robert Lantz. He said he understood Euan had a script that might be interesting for his client. It was increasingly the case that Burton was not first choice for films, and that his agent needed to do rather more work than name the fee.

Lantz met Euan Lloyd at the Connaught in London and took a script straight to Venice, where Richard and Suzy were staying at the Gritti Palace. The next week he rang to say Richard would do it. Euan was very nervous about using him. Much as he liked the man, he couldn't afford to have his film jeopardized by his drinking. Although he was dry at the moment, he was worried about what would happen in the bush. He was so impressed by Suzy, however, and her dedication to Burton, that he decided to take the gamble.

He took a gamble in casting Richard Harris as well, another great drinker who was also on the wagon, but friends assured him that he was unlikely to fall off it. The two Richards were known as RI and RII, and kept one another on the straight and narrow, more or less. Richard Harris did slip from grace on just one occasion, and came to Euan the following morning clutching his head. 'I was a bad boy last night,' he said, 'but it won't happen again, Governor.'

Euan also offered Glyn Baker, Stanley's son, a small part. In interviews Burton would say he had his godson on the film, which irked Glyn. Harry Secombe was his godfather, whom he adored, and he resented the inaccuracy, just as his father had risen so angrily that day on board the *Kalizma* in Naples, when he heard Richard telling a journalist about the one-legged miner, as though he were his own father.

The Wild Geese was a film about mercenaries, filmed on the northern border of South Africa. Richard was anxious on two counts. 'I can't stand mercenaries,' he said. 'I hate them. Why do you want to do a film about them?' Euan explained that the film was based on a real man, Colonel 'Mad' Mike Hoare. 'Meet him,' he implored. And so they did meet, in Johannesburg. The meeting was very brief, and Richard didn't like Hoare at all.

His other concern was the location. 'I hear all sorts of terrible things about South Africa,' he said. 'I was very happy there as a visitor, but I'm worried about working there.'

'Don't worry,' said Euan, 'we're going to be totally integrated.'

'How did you manage that?' said Richard.

'I told the South African Government that if we were going to make the film here I had no intention of having colour barriers. And they said "Fine, you set it up any way you want it".'

As a result, the unit of over two hundred people was a mixture of South Africans and British, black and white, all living and working, eating and drinking together.

Richard was very excited by the set-up. 'Dammit, it works here,' he said.

'Yes, under our control,' said Euan, 'but there are problems elsewhere.'

'Well this is a bloody good start.'

Mike Hoare was technical adviser on the film, and Euan had suggested to him that he treat all the men as soldiers under his command, with the proviso that he didn't upset the stars – the other stars being Roger Moore, and the South African actor, Hardy Kruger.

By the first day he had managed to upset one. A call-sheet had been delivered to Burton which read, 'All artists will report 10.00 hours in the restaurant for a lecture by Colonel Mike Hoare.'

Euan had an urgent message to see Richard.

'Euan, what's all this about?' he said, waving his call-sheet in the air. 'I'm back in the fucking army. What's going on here?'

'Mike thought it would be very useful. . . . '

'I don't give a damn what he thinks. I don't like this, Euan.'

'Well, the others have received the same letter, but if it's a problem, we'll see if we can do it another way.'

Richard grunted and growled as Euan left him. Outside he ran into Roger Moore. 'Good morning, Sir,' said Roger, snapping his heels to attention, and saluting Euan. 'Ten hundred hours, I'll be on parade.' Richard Harris made a similar gesture.

A little later there was a call from Richard. 'I've thought it over,' he said. 'I suppose it's a military picture. Okay.'

The next morning the entire cast of fifty were gathered in the restaurant, and at two minutes to ten the four principals arrived, went through the full military routine of saluting the company, and sat themselves down in the front row. Seconds later Mike Hoare arrived, dressed in full colonel's uniform, carrying a swagger-cane, and stood in front of the charts he had set up for his lecture. Burton, who was playing the part of the colonel in the film, walked forward, saluted Hoare, turned round, addressed the men, who had all stood to attention when he went forward, and said, 'Stand easy, men.'

The lecture was designed to last twenty minutes, but Hoare spoke for two hours. He gave a full picture of the character development of a mercenary officer and his men, with illustrations, which had the four principals sitting in their chairs motionless. At the end of it, Richard came to Euan and said, 'I owe you an apology, you bastard. Now I see what you mean.' From that moment on, Richard watched Hoare's every move, and the character he played in the film was based entirely on Colonel 'Mad' Mike Hoare.

It was a demanding role, physically strenuous, and Richard's back, which had been causing him trouble on and off for years, started to play him up. Without drink to numb the pain, and no real chance to rest it, he began to suffer badly. They were working in temperatures of 120° F in the shade, and he had a punishing schedule, on call almost every day for twelve weeks. He did not complain. 'Damn weather,' he would say to explain away the problem, but Euan became daily more worried as he watched the pain increase so obviously.

The company was insured against this sort of eventuality, but to lose Richard halfway through the film would have been a catastrophe. So Euan set about finding a back specialist who would come up to Tshipise, seven hundred miles north of Johannesburg, to see Richard. It was no mean feat, but eventually he found a man in Pretoria, Professor Kloppers, who was prepared to come. A small aircraft was duly dispatched to collect the professor and bring him to the tiny airstrip at Tschipise. He arrived at noon, and went straight in to see Burton, who was in his trailer, and in such chronic pain that they had been unable to film him that day at all. He was with the patient for an hour, gave him a couple of injections, and at two o'clock, Richard walked out of his trailer a new man. He went straight to work, and suffered virtually no more trouble for the rest of the film.

Despite the improvement to his back, Burton was a shadow of his former self. Every night there would be great drinking parties in the Red Ox, but he steered clear of them. He stayed at home in his rondavel, reading, playing Scrabble, or listening to Suzy playing the piano, and went to bed early, and sober.

Stars would always be asked what creature comforts they required on a location like this, and a piano was one of the things Richard had specifically requested. So, a grand piano was shipped up from Johannesburg for Suzy. He also wanted books, so everything worth reading in that part of the world was gathered together, including all the works of Shakespeare, and made into a library for him. Next was the delicate subject of drink. 'It's hot up there, Richard,' Euan had said. 'What would you like?'

'"Tab",' replied Richard. '"Tab" is my drink.' 'Tab', a non-alcoholic American diet drink, was unavailable in Johannesburg, but they finally found an agent in Cape Town, and shipped a thousand cans north, and made special icing arrangements so that there was always a cold can on hand. Richard drank nothing stronger throughout.

There was just one occasion when he joined the boys for an evening in the Red Ox. The cast included several quite heavy drinkers; Roger Moore was sitting beside him knocking back Martinis. Richard duly bought drinks for everyone, but did not touch a drop himself. Euan joined in the party, inwardly terrified that Richard was going to be tempted, as Richard was evidently only too aware.

The next morning the assistant director came to Euan and said Mr Burton would like a word with him. So, when they broke for lunch he went along to Richard's trailer. He was still dressed in full combat gear, in which he had been filming during the morning, despite the sweltering heat, and had not yet touched his lunch. He was puce in the face and, stamping his foot angrily on the ground, he turned round to look his producer in the eye, and said, 'Don't you do that to me again, ever.'

Puzzled, Euan asked what he was getting at. A paranoiac tirade of abuse followed, in which it became apparent he thought Euan had let him down in front of his friends the night before.

Euan listened in disbelief, but finally could take no more. 'Excuse me, I've got work to do,' he said, and left.

The next day Richard came to his trailer and apologized.

He was prone to vicious outbreaks of temper, for most of which Suzy bore the brunt. One day he invited Christopher and Glyn to dinner. When they arrived, they found Richard sound asleep in the garden, so they crept past him and into the rondavel to find Suzy. All three were happily playing Scrabble, when suddenly Richard burst in. 'How dare you disturb me when I'm reading *Lear*?' he thundered.

'What do you mean, reading *Lear*?' said Christopher, scathingly. 'You were asleep. You were snoring.'

'I can't bear to be with you non-intellectuals,' roared Richard.

'Then I think I'd better leave,' said Glyn.

'No, you're semi-intellectual. You can sit down.'

Burton felt increasingly threatened by youth. Christopher and Glyn were both nineteen years old, blond and beautiful, and he found them hard to take, particularly when they were around Suzy. He was jealous of Kate, too, as she grew older and collected boy-friends. His defiance was to patronize and to pull intellectual rank. 'You're too young to know this sort of thing,' he would say.

Whenever Richard was on the wagon, far from wanting the people around him to abstain too, he would lavish drink on them, pouring devastating cocktails, giant vodkas, and serving good wine. He was knowledgeable about wine, and while he was married to Suzy he taught her what he knew. Yet at the same time he found it difficult not drinking when other people were.

At a dinner party with James Hunt in Spain later that year, he was very obviously uncomfortable. He and Suzy were staying with Lew Hoad, the former Wimbledon tennis champion, a neighbour in Mijas. To defuse the situation, James had also invited Sean Connery, another neighbour. Connery was three years younger than Burton, and yet it was as if Richard were the old man of the party.

He sat at the dinner table like the odd man out and, although Suzy fussed over him, he was clearly hating every minute. A couple of days later he escaped from his wife's vigilance just long enough to drink himself insensible.

In the long term Richard acknowledged that without Suzy he would very probably have died, but on a day-to-day basis, she received little thanks for her labours. The people she had ousted called her 'The Iron Maiden'; those who really cared for Richard said she was 'Florence Nightingale'. Her devotion to him was complete, but it took its toll. While he began to look healthier than he had in years, she began to look drawn. She lost a great deal of weight, and friends became concerned that she was running herself into the ground.

There were high spots too, of course, and when Richard was feeling good, he was his old charismatic self – the mimic, the raconteur, the romantic, the charmer. And life with a high-spending superstar was exciting. The year they were married they had bought a house on the island of Antigua, two years later they bought another in Puerto Vallarta, further up the mountain from Casa Kimberley, which had gone to Elizabeth in the divorce settlement, and there was still Le Pays de Galles in Switzerland that had remained firmly in Richard's grip. But with Richard's filming commitments they were never long in any of them.

After *The Wild Geese*, Burton's next film, *Absolution*, was made at Pinewood and on location in Shropshire. It was written by Anthony Shaffer, brother of Peter who wrote *Equus*, and Burton again played the part of a priest, this time in a Roman Catholic school, who hears the confession of a boy who has committed a murder. From there he went to Germany to work with Andrew McLaglen, who had directed *The Wild Geese*, and with whom he had become particularly friendly. This was a war film called *Breakthrough*, in which he co-starred with Rod Steiger and Robert Mitchum.

Early in 1980, he was working with Tatum O'Neal, Ryan O'Neal's sixteen-year-old daughter, on a film in Toronto, *Circle of Two*. She was his youngest leading lady ever, and it shook him to be playing love scenes with someone thirty-eight years his junior – even younger than his own children. When she went off on the town discoing until the early hours of the morning, he went home for a quiet evening with his books, his wife and their dog, a mongrel called Lupe, which they had found roaming the streets in Guadalupe – it would climb into Richard's lap and he would refer to it as 'our baby'.

These were fallow years for the new, reformed Burton. With not much film work coming his way, he began writing again, and repeating his avowal that his real ambition was to write a book, 'A really fine book. I'd rather do that than play all the Hamlets and all the Lears.' He took more exercise than he had in years. Swimming helped his back, which was still a source of actue pain at times, and he walked and rode a bicycle. At Susan's instigation, he even tried to give up smoking, but became so impossible to live with that she swiftly countermanded the order. Suzy was with him constantly, and when he talked about his marriage being for ever, it seemed a strong possibility.

8

'That Time May Cease, and Midnight Never Come'

At fifty-four, Burton was looking years younger. The bleary, bloodshot eyes and the puffy face were things of the past. His eyes were clear, his face was taut, and he exuded a vitality that hadn't been seen in years. With the new look and the start of a new decade he went back to a part he had first played twenty years before: King Arthur in the Lerner/Loewe musical, *Camelot*.

There had been a film of *Camelot* in the intervening years, which Alan Jay Lerner had originally wanted Burton to make but, because of a disagreement about money with Warner Brothers, in the end the part had gone to Richard Harris. Much as he liked Harris, Alan always felt that Richard Burton was King Arthur, and wanted people to remember him as such. So, for some years he had been suggesting a revival. At one point Richard had said he would do it if Julie Andrew would agree, and Julie considered it for a while, but in the end nothing came of it. Then in 1980, Lerner's friend Mike Merrick, who had formed a production company with Don Gregory, decided to stage a revival of *My Fair Lady* with Rex Harrison. Alan said, 'If you really want to do something, get Richard to come back and do a revival of *Camelot*.' And so they went to work.

It was a long-term commitment, and Richard was nervous about going back to the stage again. They were to rehearse in New York, open in Toronto in June, transfer to Broadway the following month, and then tour the show for a year. It was Suzy who tipped the balance. Finally, over lunch in Switzerland with Don Gregory and Mike Merrick, which he had insisted Lerner attend too, Burton agreed.

Thus in June 1980 he was back at the O'Keefe Centre in Toronto, where he had last been, playing *Hamlet*, at the time of his marriage to Elizabeth, in the midst of the madness when battalions of police had had to guard the doors. The management were obviously also aware of the association. They tactlessly printed special souvenir programmes marking Burton's come-back with a photograph of Elizabeth as Cleopatra inside, pointing out that he had been married to her twice. Suzy was furious, and insisted that the photograph be removed. So the staff at the O'Keefe Centre spent the night before the opening ripping the offending page out of ninety thousand copies.

More serious things were amiss too. A week before they were due to open, Alan Jay Lerner received a frantic call from the show's English director, Frank Dunlop. There was something wrong with Burton's performance, he said. It was terrible. Would Alan fly over from London and have a look? Alan arrived, and agreed that it was very poor, but instantly spotted the cause. His young leading lady, Kathleen McCearney, was quite wrong in the part of Guinevere, and it was affecting Richard's performance. Alan reasoned with Burton, 'Richard, you can't open this way. I feel responsible because I begged you do this, but I'm not going to let you open next Friday night in Toronto with this leading lady.'

That Saturday night Alan and Frank began auditioning, and found a girl who was singing in the revival of *Oklahoma*. Alan rang one of Oscar Hammerstein's two sons, who were staging the musical, and said, 'You've got to help me, I need that girl.' Billy Hammerstein came to his aid, found a replacement for his singer, and on the Sunday morning Christine Ebersole went into rehearsal. Everyone worked round the clock; new costumes and wigs were hastily made for her, and by the end of the week she was word perfect. As a result Burton's performance improved beyond all recognition.

The critics reviewed his return to *Camelot* with mixed enthusiasm. The *New York Times* said, 'He remains every inch the King Arthur of our most majestic storybook dreams.' John Barber, writing in the *Daily Telegraph*, said, 'The magic and danger of his presence – the corrugated skin, the accusing eyes, the devilish humour, above all a voice like a cello in a coalmine – does a lot to explain his reputed fifty thousand dollar a week salary.' Clive Barnes in the *New York Post*, however, described the evening as 'A knight to forget'. Burton, he said, was 'looking wan and seeming little more than a burnt-out dummy. His face is leathery and unanimated, his arms droop to his sides and his hands are flaccid.'

It was not only Burton's acting that was being scrutinized. He had spoken frequently about his fight against alcohol in newspaper, magazine and television interviews, and now that he was in the public view nightly, everyone was watching closely to see whether he had indeed beaten the demon drink.

He very nearly had. He did take the occasional glass of white wine, which his system appeared to tolerate, but he was still not drinking spirits, although it was a constant battle. Two nights before the opening in Toronto, he had had dinner with Alan Jay Lerner and Edna O'Brien. Suzy was elsewhere. The waiter was taking their orders and Richard said, 'I think I'll have a vodka and Martini.' Then he looked over at Alan.

'Richard, don't you look at me,' he said. 'You can have anything you want, because I know you won't let this play down.'

Richard thought for a while, and then he said, 'Well never mind, perhaps I'll have some Perrier.'

A week after the show opened on Broadway, it looked as though he had succumbed. Burton could scarcely walk or talk, staggering and slurring his way through the first ten minutes on stage. Finally he ground to a complete halt halfway through the first act. As they brought the curtain down, there were cries from the audience of 'Give him another drink'. While Suzy took him home and put him to bed, hundreds of people stormed the box office demanding their money back even though his understudy took over. Photographers camped on his hotel doorstep while the papers debated whether or not he was back on the bottle. He strenuously denied he had been drinking. He had taken a mixture of drugs, he claimed, that had made him ill, although he did confess he had had lunch with Richard Harris that day.

The next night he was back on stage, terrified about the reception he would get from the audience. But, as he made his entrance, they gave him a three-and-a-half-minute ovation. 'I just stood there, and I could feel the audience supporting me and the affection and the warmth,' he said. 'It was one of the most extraordinary experiences I have ever had in the theatre.'

He was, indeed, taking drugs. For the entire duration of the run Burton suffered pain, and not just from his back. Soon after the opening in Canada, he developed trouble with the tendons in his right arm and shoulder, which required cortisone treatment and accounted for the drooping arms that Clive Barnes had criticized. Richard could barely lift his right arm at all. A month later specialists diagnosed that, in addition to everything else, he had a pinched nerve in the base of his neck. He was on a constant diet of medication, which Suzy made certain he took. She never left his side during the run. Not only did she act as his nurse, she also took over his make-up from Ron Berkley, and became his dresser too, so that she was in the theatre for every performance in every city of the ten-month tour.

It was a gruelling year for them both. Burton had said he was treating *Camelot* as a try-out for *Lear*, to get in practice for eight per-formances a week, which he realized was the only way he would ever be able to do the play, given Alex Cohen's assertion that America was not yet ready for repertory. But it was obvious that his health would never have stood the strain. He lost thirty pound over the year – he dropped from 172 to 142 pounds – and was physically and mentally exhausted. The metal fatigue was beginning to show.

The last city that they played in was Los Angeles, and shortly after opening in March 1981 Burton collapsed. Suffering from a viral infection and chronic pain in his arms, he was whisked into St John's Hospital in Santa Monica for tests. A top neuro-surgeon, flown in from Florida, diagnosed severe degenerative changes of the cervical spine, which required urgent major surgery. The oper-ation could not take place until he was over the viral infection, and had gained some weight, so it was nearly a month later that a team of four surgeons opened him up and discovered that his entire spinal column was coated with crystallized alcohol, which had to be scraped off before they could rebuild the vertebrae in his neck. It was a dangerous and delicate operation, carrying the inevitable risk of paralysis. Suzy was camped in his room at the hospital and had been there day and night since he was first admitted. His family flew over from Wales. Elizabeth Taylor sent flowers. Everyone was waiting for news.

The news was good. He had come round from the five-hour operation fighting, and two weeks later he was released from hospital. He and Suzy stayed on in Beverly Hills, until he was given permission to fly several weeks later. Even when he went home to Switzerland to recuperate, he was taking a considerable amount of medication to kill the pain, and had a physiotherapist in constant attendance.

His doctors had forbidden him to work for at least four months afterwards, but at the beginning of July he was asked by the BBC to give the commentary on the Royal Wedding of Prince Charles and Lady Diana Spencer for Radio 4. It was an offer he could not refuse, appealing to his sense of history and pageantry. But it was too soon. Although the voice was as magnificent as ever, he was in great pain throughout, and at one point described Lady Diana leaving Clarence House on her journey to St Paul's Cathedral, several minutes before she did any such thing. While the rest of team tried to cover for the embarrassing mistake, the BBC fended off suggestions that he had been drinking, and called it 'a small hiccup in six hours of memorable broadcasting'.

Richard spent the rest of the summer convalescing: he was putting on weight and seemed to be gaining strength. Then suddenly, at the beginning of October, he collapsed again and was rushed back to St John's in Santa Monica for an emergency operation on a perforated ulcer. Suzy once again kept vigil by his bedside, Elizabeth Taylor once again sent flowers. When he was discharged from hospital he was back to square one, but now, because of the ulcer, he was unable to take the painkillers for his back, so he had to cope with even greater discomfort. And Suzy had to cope with an even more difficult husband.

Richard stayed at the Hermitage Hotel in Beverly Hills to convalesce. While he was there English film-maker Tony Palmer sent him a script to read. It was for an ten-hour television biography of Richard Wagner; a prestigious production in which he was being invited to play the title role. The other people so far approached included Sir John Gielgud, Lord Olivier and Sir Ralph Richardson.

Richard was immediately interested, particularly when he heard that the three giants of the British stage were involved. After all the light-weight films he had made, all the rubbish, he wanted a challenge. He wanted to make a film which would bring him some critical acclaim and establish him as a great British actor, and he saw this as the vehicle. This ambition was fuelled to some extent by Suzy. It was she who enthused and encouraged him. So, a week or so later, he sent a telegram to Tony Palmer in London asking him to meet to discuss the project. Tony rang his producer Alan Wright, then in Zurich, and they both flew to Beverly Hills, where Richard and Suzy had recently moved into a new house.

They found Burton rather tastelessly dressed, in ill-fitting trousers, and cream patent shoes, surrounded by research material and books about the composer. 'I am Wagner,' he said. 'I will play Wagner.'

He was very excited by the project. Wagner was a man he was particularly fascinated by, a man not dissimilar to himself in many ways. When the similarities were pointed out, he would always say, 'Wagner was a genius. I am not.' He enjoyed his music, and a couple of summers before had been filming in the West of Ireland *Tristan and Isolt*, the medieval love story on which Wagner's opera was based. He had also once met Peter Hoffman, the world famous Wagnerian singer, and gone out of his way to befriend the man and learn more.

Richard was clearly keen to give the impression that he was a thinking man, that he was firmly on the wagon, and that physically he was on the mend. He didn't want people fussing over him, and found Suzy's constant nursing an irritation. She seldom let him out of her sight. She sat beside him on the sofa, ran her fingers through his hair, and repeatedly asked if he was all right. He was living on a diet of chicken soup and tea, which she dashed out to the kitchen to bring him at regular intervals, and which he frequently ignored.

His health was something Tony Palmer and Alan Wright were worried about. The part was huge: Wagner was in practically every scene of the ten-hour epic. So, before anything could be agreed, they had to ascertain that Richard was insurable.

Next was the question of money. Burton's latest agent-cum-secretary and personal adviser was a tough and fiercely protective American woman, Valerie Douglas, who had previously been employed by one of the big film companies in Hollywood, and had worked with Richard on and off for years. She was devoted to him, and had taken over as his agent, with Susan's blessing, shortly before his second divorce from Elizabeth.

'Richard doesn't do anything,' she began, 'even if it's five minutes in a film, for under a million and a quarter dollars.'

'Well, I'm sorry,' said Alan Wright bluntly, 'but we don't have that sort of money.'

The figure they arrived at was one million dollars which, for seven months' work, was a very good deal. Valerie gave a word of warning. 'Richard is too generous,' she said. 'He will never turn anyone away, and will sign endless cheques if he's asked, so please, be aware and don't let him.'

Burton was thrilled by the prospect of working with Olivier, Richardson and Gielgud, but anxious about Vanessa Redgrave, who was to play the part of Cosima, Wagner's second wife. 'I think she's a marvellous actress,' he said, 'but don't let her bring politics into it.' He was also worried about Gemma Craven, who was playing Minna Planer, Wagner's first wife, because he had never heard of her. Nevertheless he was reassured on both counts, and he and his party arrived in Vienna where they began shooting in January 1982.

Richard had insisted upon having his make-up organized by Ron Berkley, who was put in charge of the whole unit. In place of Bob Wilson came a girl in her mid-thirties as his new personal assistant. Bob, now in his seventies, had retreated to his home on Long Island, where Richard continued to look after him financially. Richard also brought in a physiotherapist by the name of Joe Rossy from St John's. Brook Williams was a member of the party too. Valerie Douglas had said, 'You don't have to hire him, and I would prefer it if you didn't.' Then Brook had telephoned. 'I know that a stand-in for Richard is a waste of time,' he said, 'but he does have to have one; and I'll do anything you like on the set, be a runner for you, wash dishes. You name it, I'll do it.' So Brook came, and proved invaluable.

The only person missing from the roll-call was Susan. Valerie Douglas explained that she had stayed on in Mexico to sort out problems with the house, and would be joining Richard at the end of January. She strenuously denied there was any truth in the rumour beginning to circulate that there were marital problems. Burton offered no explanation. In fact, their marriage was in trouble. Suzy had finally reached the end of her tether and was in a state of exhaustion. He had lashed out at her one time too many, and she had taken him at his word and left him alone. She had not stopped loving him, she had simply found him increasingly difficult to live with. The perpetual fight to keep him sober, the thunderous temper and the abuse had begun to outweigh the pleasures. She was worn out.

The first few weeks of filming in Vienna went well, despite temperatures of minus 14° F. Richard was completely professional: he wasn't drinking and he did just about every shot in one take. The only slight problem was his height. Wagner was a short man, no taller than 5 feet 2 inches, and Burton was 5 feet 9 inches or thereabouts. He had always been conscious of his height: he liked to believe he was 6 feet, but even with the built-up shoes he normally wore, he was never that. It was important to him, however, and he insisted upon having his cobbler make built-up shoes for *Wagner* too.

In other respects he was not a vain man. He was partially colour blind and had no real interest in clothes. He always had 'stills' approval in his contract – the right to select which photographs were used for publicity – but seldom used it. 'I trust you not to show my big bottom,' he would say. And out of all the films he had made, he had only ever watched seven.

Tony Palmer had made his name with highly-acclaimed documentaries. *Wagner* was the first drama which he had directed and he was nervous. He was also nervous about using Burton, having heard the inevitable stories about him. But as the weeks went by and Richard remained sober and hard-working, it was beginning to look as though his fears were unfounded.

He and Alan Wright had got off to a good start with their star. They were both Oxbridge educated, and Burton immediately warmed to them: he felt he was amongst friends and intellectual equals. Out came all the old stories about Oxford – as well as the other favourites – and until the stories began to be repeated over and over again, they all found Richard modest, likeable and thoroughly entertaining.

By the third week, however, Richard began to drink and a very different side of his character suddenly emerged. The Italians on the film, including Vittorio Storaro, the lighting cameraman, invited everyone to a pasta party at their hotel one night. Richard quite quickly became very drunk, and turned on Vittorio. 'You don't know what you're fucking doing,' he said. 'This is a Micky Mouse operation. You can't shoot films like this.'

Ron Berkley had been very scathing about Vittorio, and he wielded a great influence on Richard. The Italian was intense about his craft, in the mould of European film-makers, and liked to use long tracking shots and complicated lighting breaks. Ron wanted him to cut out the artistic bit and get on with the job, and frequently said so.

'No Richard,' said Vittorio, standing his ground, 'let me explain.' He embarked upon his theory about the spiritual meaning of light and shade, when Burton interrupted.

'Don't give me all that intellectual crap,' he said. It was only Vittorio's cool that saved the evening. Word quickly got about, however, that Richard was drinking again, and with six months still to go, the producers began to worry about the future of their film.

Shortly afterwards Olivier, Gielgud and Richardson arrived. It was a momentous occasion: the first time the three great actors would have acted together. Although they had all been in Olivier's film of *Richard III*, they were never in the same scenes. Burton had been looking forward to their arrival with child-like excitement. He had spoken repeatedly about the three men: stories about being directed by Gielgud, about working with Larry, and about the old days when he used to spend weekends with Olivier and his second wife, Vivien Leigh, when 'everyone' was there. Richard believed that one of the reasons, if not the single reason, they all wanted to be in the film was because he was playing Wagner – they were coming to his film, and he felt very honoured. 'Isn't it great? It will be the first time we four have all played together,' he said. At the same time he was nervous about playing with them, aware of the legend that he had to live up to, and frightened of failing in front of the audience he cared most about. In fact, they were all coming for a variety of other reasons, and had agreed to perform before Burton was ever considered for the part.

The trio brought a breath of fresh air to the production. They were hugely engaging together, leavening the gloom that had set in after weeks of hard work, freezing temperatures and strange food. Gielgud and Richardson, aged seventy-seven and eighty respectively, said they would share a dressing room, being the juveniles, and left the star dressing room to 'the senior actor', Olivier, a mere lad at seventy-five.

The first Saturday night that they were all assembled, the producers gave a dinner party for them and invited Burton. The three older actors had not seen him for some time and were looking forward to meeting again. They all said they thought he was a great actor, had hoped for better things, and were unanimously sad that his career had veered off the rails.

Richard was clearly very nervous when he arrived for dinner, and had obviously had a drink or two. After one large glass of white wine as an aperitif, his manners began to deteriorate. As they sat down to dinner, he grew increasingly drunk and more and more objectionable. He began to attack Olivier.

'I remember you once called me a second-rate actor,' he said.

'Oh I'm sure I never said that, Richard,' said Olivier. 'You've always been a marvellous actor. You're the greatest actor in the world, we all acknowledge that.'

'You called me a second-rate actor,' continued Richard, unabashed. 'Do you know the part you're playing in *Wagner*?'

'Well yes,' said Olivier, nearly twenty years Richard's senior. 'It's a minister, a sort of chief of police, isn't it?'

'Yes,' said Richard, 'you're playing a second-class minister, you're playing a second-class role; and I am Wagner. I am the star. Now the tables are turned.'

Everyone was laughing and trying to make light of what was developing into an acutely embarrassing situation. Finally they managed to get Richard away from the table and into his car, but Olivier was very upset by the incident, as was Richardson. When he left Vienna at the end of his filming, ten days later, Olivier gave a dinner party to which he invited Richardson, Gielgud, Tony Palmer and Alan Wright. There was no invitation for Burton.

One invitation that was extended to Richard during the course of his stay in the city, however, was to the Vienna Opera Ball. The guest of honour was the Duke of Edinburgh; Richard was number two. The invitation had come to Alan Wright, who had been told quite bluntly that Richard sold tickets, and that if they pulled out, having agreed to come, they would be expected to pay compensation – something in the region of £12,000.

Richard was delighted, and asked whether he might bring his daughter Maria too. Now twenty-one, she was getting married in New York the Saturday before. Although Richard did not entirely approve of her match, Steve Carson, a model agent, the two of them would be flying into Vienna to see him that week. The organizers readily agreed and everything was fixed. To complete the party Alan had invited Franco Nero, who was also in *Wagner*, to come up from Rome for the weekend.

It was a Friday night towards the end of February, and after eight weeks the company had almost finished shooting in Vienna. Alan Wright and his wife went to Burton's suite to collect him for the ball, and knocked on the door. His secretary appeared, looking very nervous. It soon became apparent why. Burton and Franco Nero sat facing one another across a card table. Franco looked helplessly apologetic. Richard lay slumped, close to oblivion. There was a full Martini glass next to his head. Nearby lay a short telex from Susan that had arrived the night before, telling him that the marriage was over, she wanted a divorce. He had been drinking ever since.

He was in no condition to go anywhere, let alone the Viennese event of the year. But it was impossible to pull out at this stage: nearly two hundred press photographers were waiting for him in the foyer of the Hotel Bristol. The Duke of Edinburgh would be arriving at the Opera House in less than half an hour. As it was they kept him waiting for five minutes; but with everyone's help, including that of Maria and her new husband, whom Richard insisted upon calling by every name but his own, they dressed him, straightened him up, and propelled him the two hundred yards from the hotel to the Opera House, deflecting reporters, microphones and television interviewers at every step.

The first person who heard the news about Susan's telex was Elizabeth. She had separated from her latest husband, the American Republican Senator, John Warner, in December, and she had been in almost daily contact with Richard for weeks. She would telephone him from the States, often at two or three o'clock in the morning, and they would talk for an hour or more, falling in and out of love, fighting, shouting, slamming the phone down, and ringing back to make it all up.

When the news got out that Burton and Suzy were to divorce, there was immediate speculation that he and Elizabeth would get together again for a third marriage. It was fuelled by the discovery that the two would both be in London the following week. This was actually pure coincidence. Before work had ever begun on *Wagner*, Patrick Drumgoole, Controller of Programmes at HTV, had asked whether Burton could be released for one day in January to appear in a charity reading of Dylan Thomas's work, called 'Dylan Thomas – a Celebration', at the Duke of York's Theatre in London. In the event, the date of the reading was postponed until the end of February, by which time Elizabeth was in London to rehearse her Broadway hit *The Little Foxes*. It was with some misgivings that Alan Wright and Tony Palmer had agreed to let Burton go. What they didn't realize was that the weekend also coincided with Elizabeth's fiftieth birthday and, to celebrate, her producer Zev Bufman was giving an extravagant star-studded party at Legends, the Mayfair nightclub.

Richard spent the weekend in an alcoholic haze. The party was on the Saturday night, the day he arrived, and although there had been reports that he had not been invited, he was not only there, and by Elizabeth's side for the entire evening, he brought her to the venue in his car, and took her home afterwards. It was nearly two o'clock in the morning when they arrived at the house she was renting in Chelsea, and Richard went inside with her and stayed there until dawn. The press were darting about like frenzied bees, and when he emerged at six and was driven back to the Dorchester, he invited a group of reporters into his suite and, over several vodkas, rambled for some hours about Elizabeth and Susan and his love for them both, about babies and children and why he wouldn't marry Elizabeth again. Out came the old stories again, the anecdotes, the poetry.

He repeated the performance with more journalists and more vodka on the Sunday, the night of his Dylan Thomas memorial. It had been a difficult evening for him. As the second half was about to begin, with a reading of *Under Milk Wood*, Elizabeth suddenly appeared on stage, walked towards him with her arms outstretched and kissed him. He entirely lost his composure, began to shake, and his reading thereafter was faltering and at times incomprehensible. 'I have got the wrong page,' he said at one point. 'Excuse me, but I am sort of flustered.' Elizabeth returned to the stage for the curtain call, flung her arms around his neck and whispered, so the audience

Above: Elizabeth's fortieth birthday party in Budapest, February 1972. Family, friends and colleagues were invited from all over the world for an all-expenses paid weekend celebration. *Below*: Richard with his brothers and Brook Williams

The party from the Valleys: Richard's brothers and sisters with their wives and husbands at Elizabeth's birthday extravaganza. Their names have been written in by Richard

Richard temporized by spending money on Elizabeth, buying famous and fabulous jewels. They shone like a brand-mark, as if to say that Elizabeth Taylor belonged to Richard Burton

Opposite, above: Burton with Susan and Bette Hill (centre) at the *Evening Standard* drama awards at the Savoy. Despite the age difference Richard and Susan were the perfect foil for each other. During lunch he passed Bette a note, saying, 'Thank you for saving Suzy for me.'

Below: As Richard Wagner. Burton would sit surrounded by research material and books about the composer. 'I am Wagner,' he said, 'I will play Wagner.'

Above: Burton as Winston Churchill with Robert Hardy playing Joachim von Ribbentrop in *A Walk With Destiny*. One of Richard's most treasured possessions was a bust of Churchill; his sudden attack on the man shocked everyone

Drink turned Richard into a different man, making him destructive, irrational, belligerent and unpredictable

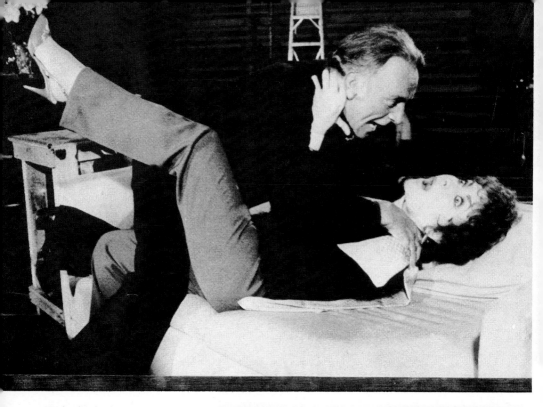

With Elizabeth in *Private Lives*, New York 1983. The scripted fights on stage were a pale imitation of the scenes that went on backstage

'Welsh livers and kidneys seem to be made of some metallic alloy, quite unlike the rest of the human race. One day like aeroplanes, they eventually show metal fatigue.'

Richard with Sally Hay (left) and daughter Kate arriving for a cast party for *Private Lives*. Friends were astonished by the striking resemblance Sally bore to the young Sybil

As the sinister O'Brien in *1984* with John Hurt. Burton accepted second billing; he saw it as the final vehicle for his come-back

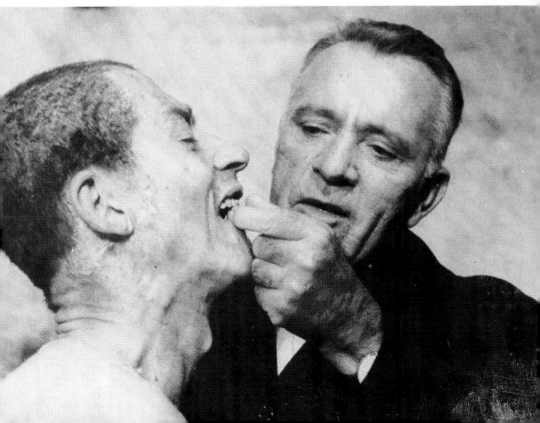

Married for the fifth time, July 1983. With Sally, vestiges of the old Richard were back. His mind was alert again, he was rational and coherent, his eyes were bright, and he was talking with enthusiasm about the future

could hear quite clearly, *'Rwyn dy garu di'*, meaning 'I love you' in Welsh.

They left the theatre together afterwards, with Richard telling reporters, 'We have always been in love.' But later he made his solitary way back to the Dorchester, filling the remainder of the night with the show-business writers of Fleet Street. He was past caring what he told them, and past remembering.

'Elizabeth? She has a husband, I guess. But no one gives a damn about him. Who's heard of him? Is he something to do with Warner Brothers?

'Susan my wife? Taller than a ghost – and just as remote, I may say. She is so English, hopeless, hideously remote.

'Elizabeth, oh so totally different. I might run from her for a thousand years and she from me for a thousand years, and she is still my baby child.'

He was a sad man, physically and emotionally exhausted, lost without a wife, and grateful to have someone to talk to, someone to help fill the lonely hours before dawn.

Ron Berkley broke up the session. He had promised to get Richard back to the set of *Wagner* by the Monday morning for him to begin work again that afternoon. But Richard was in no state to work. They were in Venice by this time, and Alan Wright had a call from one of the production assistants to say Burton was back.

'Oh good,' said Alan, 'I'll come down and see him.'

'You'd better,' she said ominously.

At the Gritti Palace he found Ron, who explained that Richard was sleeping because he had been up all weekend. He would wake him up in a while, he promised. He never managed to wake him. Richard was dead to the world, and remained so for the rest of the day and most of the night. The next morning he appeared on set, head held high.

'Morning, everyone,' he said. 'Terribly sorry about yesterday. I must have got a stomach bug.'

It was a rare show of unprofessionalism. In seven months of shooting, Burton only missed a handful of days. He continued to drink, but he was on the set on time and, for the most part, his acting was good. The presence of so many well-known British actors and actresses in the cast kept up his performance. The only occasions when he dropped below par were in scenes with Hungarian or

German actors whom he didn't feel the need to impress. The two exceptions were the East German actor, Eckhardt Schall, Bertolt Brecht's son, and a young Hungarian actor, Roberto Gulfi, who Gielgud thought was the greatest young actor he had ever seen.

One night at the end of a long session of drinking, Richard and Ron Berkley, who could more than keep pace with his thirst, decided to go to the famous Harry's Bar for a nightcap. They found Eckhardt Schall propping up one end of the bar, severely the worse for wear, with a Martini glass beside him. Burton greeted him with open arms. 'Never before in the history of the universe,' he said, 'have the two greatest actors in the world been seen in the same bar together.' They talked on into the night; and finally Richard asked the German why he was looking so depressed.

'Because I can't remember where I'm staying,' explained Schall, 'and my wife will be going mad.'

'You stay with me and share my apartment for the night,' offered Burton. Thereupon they all moved off in the direction of the Gritti Palace, weaving, shouting, reciting and trying to out-act each other all the way.

'I don't care what you say,' said Richard when they reached the hotel reception desk, 'this man, who is the greatest actor in the world apart from me, doesn't know the name of his hotel so he is staying in my room tonight.'

'But Mr Burton,' began the receptionist.

'Don't give me that,' he interrupted. 'Just because he's Eastern European . . . I pay a lot of money for my suite and he's going to stay in it.'

'Mr Burton,' tried the receptionist again, and was again bidden to silence.

'But, Mr Burton,' he finally managed in desperation, 'Mr Schall lives in the Gritti Palace. He has a room here.'

During their stay in Venice, however, someone else took advantage of Burton's hospitality. An enterprising young woman journalist, Judith Chisholm, found her way up to his suite, found him alone, and within minutes was sharing both his bar and his bed. She stayed with him for five days and five nights and recorded, and subsequently sold, an account of everything that happened, from his dominant love-making to his drunken pillow talk and boasted conquests, including the claim that he had ordered Elizabeth's entourage of homosexuals out of the room, and made love to his ex-wife on the night of her fiftieth birthday party. The sensational account appeared in the *National Enquirer* in the United States and *The News of the World* in Britain, and was picked up by dozens of other newspapers and magazines all over the world.

The production team were on big bonuses to find a way of ejecting Judith Chisholm throughout that week, and Richard's secretary, Judith Goodman, was relieved of her duties for ever having allowed it to happen. Even Richard was shaken by the reverberations. Susan was furious, Elizabeth was furious, so too were all the women he had named. His family were upset, and Cissie gave him a very blunt piece of her mind.

From Italy the unit moved to Hungary, and in Budapest another female journalist found her way to Richard, a woman he had first known there when he was filming *Bluebeard* ten years before. More significant, however, was a relationship that had been developing over the weeks with the film's continuity girl, thirty-four-year-old Sally Hay. Sally had been a production assistant at the BBC and at Thames Television, but had always wanted to work on a major drama. When Alan Wright gave her the job on *Wagner*, she had taken a course in continuity at her own expense. The job involved spending time with Burton every day he was working: giving him his notes, telling him about any script changes, and making sure he was happy. As the months passed, he became increasingly fond of her.

She was unmarried, unsophisticated and not especially attractive, but sweet and enthusiastic and very keen to oblige and, like everyone on the production, she felt sorry for Burton and protective. She was also sympathetic towards his obsession with the bottle, having had a father with the same problem. Although he was worn and debilitated, thin, haggard and virtually unable to raise his hands above his head, he still had huge charm, sex appeal and indisputable magnetism. A shadow of his former self, maybe, but he was still the wild Welshman, the witty wordsmith, the dark, brooding romantic with the thrilling voice. Not least of all, he was still the famous Richard Burton.

It was some time before she realized that Richard's attentions were genuine. It never occurred to her that the star of the film, whose wives were some of the most glamorous and beautiful women in the world, could seriously be interested in her, a run-of-the-mill, flat-sharing girl from Birmingham. But as time passed, it became clear he was, and she was deeply flattered by his affection.

So unlikely was the match that no one on the film tumbled to what was going on for a long time either. By the time they realized, Sally had moved into his hotel, and seemed to be having such a therapeutic effect on him that the producers decided to release her from her contract so she could concentrate on Burton, and to bring in another continuity girl.

When Richard flew to London in June to see Elizabeth in *The Little Foxes*, Sally went with him. By the time the unit had moved to York for the last leg of the filming, he had announced that he would marry her. 'I don't know when my next wedding day will be,' he had said, 'but the bride will be Sally.' It seemed highly unlikely at the time, even to Sally, but she remained by his side. She made the trek down to Pontrhydyfen to meet the family, and when *Wagner* finally came to an end in July she went first to Celigny with him, and then on to America, where Burton was readmitted to the hospital in Santa Monica for a check-up on his back.

Gradually Sally had begun to change. Her make-up, her hair and her clothes all improved beyond recognition as money was clearly lavished upon them. She became conscious of her image – she was a Mrs Burton in the making – and friends were astonished by the striking resemblance she bore to the young Sybil.

Sally and Richard flew to New York to see Kate, now twenty-four, who had opened in her first Broadway play, Noel Coward's *Present Laughter*. Although she was playing a small part, having just graduated from Yale Drama School, it was an excellent beginning. Sybil had been there for the opening night, having flown up from California, where she was now living with Jordan and their daughter, Amy. Burton wasn't able to see the play until August but he was a very proud father. 'She's great,' he said. 'She's my daughter isn't she?'

Meanwhile plans were progressing for Burton to appear in a Coward play on Broadway too – with Elizabeth. It was the thirties comedy *Private Lives*, first performed by Gertrude Lawrence and the Master himself, about a divorced couple who meet by chance while on honeymoon with their new spouses, fall in love with each other all over again, and run off to Paris leaving their puzzled partners in unrumpled beds. There was much talk of art imitating life: 'a revival of their own enduring road show', as one observer put it. It was also an obvious money-spinner, and part of the money financing it was Elizabeth's, for she had formed a production company with Zev Bufman. She and Richard received £42,000 a week, the highest salary any actor or actress had ever been paid on Broadway. Insurance for the show, underwritten at Lloyd's for £2 million, was the highest in theatrical history.

Life did not imitate art however; neither did their performances. The critics were unanimous in their condemnation, and had it not been 'the Liz and Dick Show', as it was widely known, the play would have come off within the first week. 'It was not as bad as the doom-sayers or even advance word of mouth had predicted,' remarked the *New York Post*. 'It even had flashes of mediocrity.' The *New York Times* said, 'We can do little but anticipate the intermissions.' As it was, there was not a seat to be had, and by the first night £2 million had been taken in advance sales.

Burton behaved like a professional throughout: he was sober, he knew the lines, and he kept a low profile, smartly side-stepping the nightly mob that crowded round the doors of the Lunt-Fontanne Theater by arriving and leaving early. The crowds were as huge as those that stormed the theatre back in 1964 with his *Hamlet*. He had just married Elizabeth then, he was thirty-eight, she was thirty-two, and they were at their best: at the height of their beauty and the peak of their passion. He was now fifty-seven, and looked twenty years older than that, she was fifty-one and matronly, and yet their fans still blocked West 46th Street. During previews, a television phone-in revealed that out of 3,500 votes, seventy-three per cent wanted them to marry again.

It was not to be. Elizabeth had a new escort, tipped as her eighth husband, Mexican lawyer Victor Luna, and Sally left no room for her to change course. She was by Burton's side day and night throughout. The play had opened initially in Boston before coming into Broadway in May; and in July, she and Richard slipped quietly away to Las Vegas for the weekend and were married. In the Presidential Suite of the Frontier Hotel, Sally Hay, twenty-two years his junior, became the fifth Mrs Burton. The ceremony was conducted by a Presbyterian minister, the Reverend Phillips, with Brook Williams as best man, and was so secret that the hotel were not even aware it was taking place. The only other person present was Valerie Douglas.

Elizabeth didn't hear about it until after the weekend and, although she put on a brave show of happiness for them both, she went into a decline. She had already been out of the show for a week with a throat infection, and the night she heard the news she nearly collapsed with hyperventilation. Richard wasn't well either; he was still in pain from his back, and was taking medication, keeping an array of pills and vitamin tablets in his dressing room.

But in other ways nothing had changed; Burton and Taylor were still old sparring partners, and the scripted fights on stage were a pale imitation of the scenes that went on back stage. She would come into the theatre every night and say to the doorman, 'Where is he?', go straight up to his dressing room, and they would begin shouting at one another. Strains of 'This is the last time I'm working with you, you cunt', would fill the stairwell. By the next day the slate was wiped clean and they start rowing afresh. It was a constant game of one-upmanship, resorting to such mundane arguments as who had the best dressing room.

As well as his pills, Richard had two photographs in his room, one of Noel Coward, inscribed by the actor/playwright, and the other of himself with Elizabeth and Noel. They had known each other for many years, and had all worked on *Boom* together. Coward would affectionately refer to Burton as 'that silly little Welsh cunt', and told the story of how he had wanted him play in *Conversation Piece* once, but Richard had haggled over the price. 'I told him, "You'll do it,"' said Coward in his inimitable way, '"you'll do it for me and you'll be very, very grateful."'

During the run on Broadway, Sheran and Simon Hornby came to New York and arranged, apprehensively, to have dinner with Richard, Sally and Elizabeth. Elizabeth was several hours late, which was not unusual, but the meeting went off quite amicably. She and Sally were never destined to do more than tolerate one another, but they accomplished that with perfect dignity. It was an entirely new way of life for Sally – rich and glamorous – and she would write long and excitable accounts of what she had been doing to her old friends in England. There were personal letters to former flatmates and open reports for general circulation at Thames Television, the last place she had been working before *Wagner*. She also wrote to Alan Wright thanking him for bringing them together.

Richard's friends all warmed to Sally. She appeared to be nothing but good for him, working hard at rekindling some of the friendships that had fallen by the wayside during his marriage to Susan. When they were in London, she made certain that they telephoned their friends, and when she said she would phone back the next day, they could be certain she would.

The initial curiosity and the massive bookings had made the play look financially secure, but *Private Lives* ran into trouble, and after an unsuccessful tour of Washington and Chicago, it ground to a halt in Los Angeles at the end of the year, with heavy losses. Burton, nevertheless, had made enough money from the ten-month fiasco to be able to buy a house in Haiti, and to do nothing but rest and nurse his health for the next few months. He was still without any strength in his shoulders: the muscles that had been severed in his original operation had refused to heal, and cavorting about on stage with Elizabeth night after night had done nothing to improve matters. He still had Le Pays de Galles, his home in Celigny, his base, but the house in Puerto Vallarta, as well as a million dollars, had gone to Susan in their divorce settlement. So it was to Haiti that he, Sally and Brook went for some sun – the island of voodoo, dictators and instant divorce, which had once banned his film *The Comedians*.

On Haiti his back became worse. Early in 1984 Euan Lloyd, who was in California on a casting visit for his new film, *Wild Geese II*, in which he wanted Burton to star, received a call from Brook. 'Richard sends his love from Haiti,' he said, 'but he's having terrible problems with his back. He's been swimming a lot, but the only man that's ever been able to help it was that professor in South Africa. Can you find him so that our own doctor in Haiti can talk to him to find out what he did that time, because he really is in great discomfort.'

By chance, Euan remembered the man's name was Kloppers, but he didn't have his number, so he rang the South African Embassy in Washington, who looked him up in the Pretoria telephone directory. He rang the Professor and within fifteen minutes Kloppers had spoken to Richard's French doctor in Haiti. Twenty-four hours later, the trans-Atlantic telephonic miracle cure had taken effect.

Burton's back problem was the only thing worrying Euan about using him in *Wild Geese II*. Richard was no longer insurable, and on a ten million pound picture, to have him drop out unexpectedly with no insurance cover would be catastrophic. He decided in the end, however, knowing Burton's professionalism, to take the risk; but he made certain that his role was far less strenuous than the part in the original *Wild Geese* had been. Shooting was scheduled to begin in August following a soap opera to be shot in London that Richard had agreed to appear in with Kate for American television.

In the meantime he and Sally went to Switzerland, where they were joined by Verdun and Hilda and their respective spouses. Verdun had just had an operation on his leg, and Richard insisted he come to recuperate. The next day a limousine was waiting outside the door to take the party to the airport. Richard met them at the other end and gave them all a fistful of Swiss francs to spend while they were there. As usual, everything was paid for – all that their host asked in return was that Verdun's wife, Betty, should make him some real Welsh Cawl – so they never spent their francs. Back home in Wales, they changed the currency into pounds and paid off the gas bill.

Before leaving Haiti, Burton had received a tentative offer to appear in a British film starring John Hurt. He was asked to play the part of O'Brien, the interrogator and torturer in *1984*, based on George Orwell's novel about a police-state in Britain. He had taken the script with him to Switzerland, and within a day of being formally offered the part, accepted. He said that it was the first time in his entire career, except when he had appeared with Elizabeth, that he had accepted second billing in a film. His salary was also less than Hurt's, but it was a British production, a quality script, and once again Richard saw it as a means of re-establishing himself as a serious actor – the final vehicle for his come-back.

He was not the first choice of actor for the part of O'Brien. Initially it was offered to Paul Scofield, but he had broken his leg. Sean Connery was also approached; Marlon Brando was another possibility. By the time they settled upon Burton, they were already six weeks into the film.

Like most directors who knew Richard's reputation, Mike Radford was anxious about using him. He frankly did not like what he had seen of his work in films, and did not want the character of O'Brien simply to be Richard Burton, he wanted something different. So, on the first day of filming, he tried to suppress his performance. As a result, and because Burton kept forgetting his lines, the first small scene had to be filmed twenty-nine times before he got it right. A scene with John Hurt followed, which he did in one take. The cameras turned to Richard again, and he did his second piece in thirty-five takes.

Mike was almost in despair. This, he thought, is Richard Burton. But, slightly shame-faced at having made him do so many takes, he wrote Richard a note of apology. It was an important scene, he explained, and until he saw the rushes, he was nervous about how it would look. Burton called him to his caravan. 'Listen,' he said, 'I've been waiting twenty years to do a film without the "Richard Burton" voice, and I can see this is going to be the one.'

Mike confessed it was music to his ears, and that he had been trying to tell him as much all day. Richard was delighted. Thereafter, whenever he felt he was over-acting, he would say, 'I'm doing a Burton,' and was amused when second assistant John Dodds made him up a deck-chair with the name Jenkins on the back.

He had felt out of it when he first arrived on the set: an old man suddenly thrown into a team of very young, enthusiastic film-makers, who had all been together for weeks and were obviously having great fun. He was clearly nervous, but much comforted when he discovered he was amongst three Oxford men, and a former head boy at Eton. Very quickly he settled into the old routine. Out tumbled the stories, the memories, the anecdotes, the poetry, and day after day he would sit on the set – not retreat to his caravan as everyone had expected he would – and hold forth. As usual, a lot of the stories were very funny, and a lot were very boring. They were the same stories he had been telling all his life, but to new ears; tales about Victor Mature, Lana Turner, Humphrey Bogart and the old days of Hollywood, from the horse's mouth, were spellbinding.

One day they were in the middle of a scene with John Hurt, who played the part of Winston Smith, lying strapped to a torture table, when Burton began to tell a story about Stratford. He was playing in *Henry IV Part 2* with Michael Redgrave. It was St David's Day (on which in all future contracts he made a point not to work) and he had been celebrating with his brothers and become very drunk. His brothers came to see the show; and suddenly, right there on stage, in the middle of a scene with Michael Redgrave, he felt an uncontrollable urge to urinate. 'Luckily the old fellow was pointing upwards,' he said, 'and the costume was pretty heavy, so none of it leaked out. It was all swilling about inside.' He proceeded to demonstrate the expression on Michael Redgrave's face, who was blissfully unaware of what had happened, and his own strangled cries as the relief rendered him speechless. Richard held them in fits of laughter for fifteen minutes while he embroidered his tale, and it was only a desperate squawk from John Hurt, still lying pinned to the torture table, that brought them back to 1984.

Some time later, Mike Radford went to see a house that was for sale, and began talking to the vendor, who happened to be an actor. Mike mentioned he had been working with Burton. 'The nearest I ever got to Burton,' said the actor, 'was at drama school. We did *Henry IV Part 2*, and I wore the very costume that Burton had worn.'

'Was there anything funny about it?' asked Mike, convinced that Burton's story had been codswallop.

'As a matter of fact – yes. It was stained yellow.'

The jokes and the stories were often a delaying tactic, a means of excusing the fact that he did not know his lines, and were quite often about other actors who could not remember their lines. 'His head is so full of stories there's no room in it for my script,' said Mike in exasperation one day, as Burton dried for the umpteenth time. Mike also suspected on occasions, because his psychological analysis of the sinister tyrant, O'Brien, was so far off the mark, that he had never read the book. Others on the set doubted that he understood much of what he was saying.

It did not appear to matter. Directing Burton was like fixing the regulo setting on an oven. Radford would simply give him an adjective, like 'more charming', or 'quieter', and his performance would adjust accordingly.

But Richard had never been interested in psychological analysis of any character he played, and for years had not even been interested in other people very much. His life had grown in on itself. He was living in the past, on memories and achievements long gone. 'They offered me a knighthood if I would come back and play at the Old Vic for five years,' he boasted. 'But I worked it out, and I couldn't afford the tax.' Even everyday conversations came back to himself.

'How's Norma today?' he asked, referring to Mike's girlfriend. 'Nice girl. Is she in the business?'

'No, no.'

'Very wise. I used to be married to someone in the business. It can be very difficult, very competitive. I remember when Elizabeth was earning a million dollars and I was earning a million and a half. She used to get very beady.'

Burton was not drinking throughout the filming, which was made easier by working with another reformed alcoholic, John Hurt. He kept to Diet Pepsi, which Brook would bring on to the set already opened. For a while Mike was convinced the cans were spiked with vodka, and his suspicion, although unvoiced, obviously communicated itself to Richard. He began offering him a swig before he drank himself.

Apart from Brook, all that remained of the old entourage was Ron Berkley, who was drinking heavily because of problems at home. Two days into the filming he disappeared. Richard was very upset, and swore he would never use him again. The old temper was still there, and although he was playing the role of one of the boys on set, he still expected to be treated like the star. Any change of plans had to come from the director, and had to be formally broached. 'Do you mind if we shoot late tonight, Richard,' would always be greeted with, 'Of course, dear boy, there's no need to ask,' but at the same time, it was very clear that there was every need to ask. The little charade was an essential part of oiling the wheels.

Richard wore a neck brace for much of the time. With his head shaven for the part and pale make-up, he looked an ill man, thin and drawn and many years older than his age. He still had the old charisma when he turned it on for the camera, but in repose he was like a wild beast who had lost the will to live. The fire had gone out. He no longer seemed to have any enthusiasm for life. Yet he continued to fantasize about the future. He talked about playing *Lear* at last, but feared his neck might make it impossible now, because he wouldn't be able to carry Cordelia at the end of the play. But he would go back to Shakespeare. 'That little Warwickshire bastard spoils you for anything else.' He would play *Othello*, or Prospero in *The Tempest*, and he hatched a plot to perform in *Richard III* with John Hurt, the two of them alternating the parts of the King and Buckingham.

Instead, it was a soap opera that beckoned. Although it may not have been culture, it did provide an opportunity for Burton to work with his daughter Kate for the first time. *Ellis Island* was about immigrants in New York at the beginning of the century. Burton played an unscrupulous US senator, Kate played his daughter; and the setting, curiously enough, was the old Billingsgate Thames-side fish market in London, and Shepperton Studios.

The result was poor. Richard was sober, but the years of excess had taken their toll, 'sogged the brain' as he once said of alcohol, and he was but a shadow of the man he had been.

He and Sally lived at the Dorchester throughout and caught up with friends. A message was sent via one to John Dexter, 'Ask that Derbyshire git when he's going to employ me again.' Gone were the days of the big parties and the mid-eighteenth-century court. They gave small lunch and dinner parties for six or eight at favourite restaurants like the White Elephant. Richard drank white wine or mineral water and ordered excellent claret for his companions. Friends, who had despaired that he was a lost soul, all agreed that vestiges of the old Burton were back. His mind was alert again, he was rational and coherent, his eyes were bright, he was talking with enthusiasm about his next film, *Wild Geese II*. His stories were the old ones, but he was less repetitive. He seemed happy with Sally. They were planning to have a baby – to try for the boy he so yearned for – and he appeared set for a worthwhile future after all.

At the end of July he flew to Celigny for a few days' rest before flying on to Berlin for the new film. He told friends he would be back again in September. The film was a sequel to *The Wild Geese*: the mercenaries under his command have been hired to rescue the Nazi war criminal, Rudolph Hess, from Spandau Prison. The part of Hess was to be played by Laurence Olivier.

Richard never made it. Four days before he was due on set, on Sunday, 5 August he was rushed to hospital with a cerebral haemor-rhage. That morning Sally had woken in bed to find him in a deep coma beside her. She quickly called a doctor and he was taken to the Cantonal Hospital in Geneva, where he went straight into an emergency operation. It was too late. At 1.15 p.m. the man whom Emlyn Williams had once described as looking 'imperishable' was pronounced dead. Suddenly, without warning, he was struck down at the age of fifty-eight; ironically, four days before appearing with the actor he had once seemed so certain to succeed.

Sally was quite overcome with grief. She had felt so optimistic about the future. At the age of thirty-four, just as she was beginning to think she would never marry and have children, she had found everything she wanted. She had a man she adored, two luxurious homes, a famous name, financial security and an exciting life. Suddenly, after just two years, it had all been snatched away.

Distraught though she was, she managed to ring and break the news to some of the other people she knew would be heartbroken. She rang Kate, who was still in London, she telephoned Elizabeth at her home in Los Angeles, and Richard's brother Graham in Hampshire, who said he would let the rest of the family know. Sybil heard the news from Kate, and immediately asked her daughter to go to see Gwen up in Squires Mount to make sure she was all right. She still had great affection for Ifor's elderly widow and knew how bitterly upset she would be.

Friends, relatives and colleagues were shocked and saddened. Valerie Douglas flew into Geneva to be with Sally, and to help with the funeral arrangements. Brook was by her side too, although deeply upset. John Hurt stepped into the breach. He had been staying in Switzerland while making a film there, and had dined with Richard and Sally on the Friday night. He was a great comfort, having suffered a bereavement himself not long before, when his girlfriend of many years had been killed in a horse-riding accident.

Richard's death was headline news on the front page of every national newspaper in Britain. In some it was the only news carried on the front page that day. 'Burton,' said the *Daily Star*. 'Legend dies at 58', and, quoting from a previous interview with him, '"I smoked too much, drank too much and made love too much." Superstar's own epitaph.' 'Burton the Great,' said the *Daily Express*. 'He threw away greatness like it was a soiled sock.' 'Immense promise not fullfilled,' said the *Daily Telegraph*, and *The Times* called it 'Career madly thrown away.'

Pages were given over to his potential, his early promise, his decline, his drinking, his marriages and his infidelities. As his relatives, both by blood and by marriage, tussled over burial and memorial arrangements, it seemed that even in death he could hold the centre stage and wreak havoc around him.

The family wanted him to be buried next to his parents in Pontrhydyfen, where they claimed he had always said he would like to be. Sally, on the other hand, wanted him to be buried in Switzerland, where for tax reasons he had bought a plot. Despite considerable acrimony, it was in the tiny, overgrown cemetery of the little Protestant church in Celigny that he was finally laid to rest the following Thursday. It was a humble church, with coconut matting and a coke-burning stove in the aisle, where Kate and Jessica had both been baptised over twenty-five years before, by the Reverend Arnold Mobbs, who came out of retirement to conduct Richard's funeral.

Burton went in a way he would have liked: with music, poetry, a touch of irreverence, and an audience of millions, who watched the ceremony on television sets all over the world. There were rousing Welsh hymns, readings in English and Welsh, and prayers in French. Kate read movingly from Dylan Thomas, with the haunting line, 'Rage, rage against the dying of the light', a poem he had written when his own father was dying. And in the graveyard Brook read from another Thomas poem, 'And Death Shall Have No Dominion'.

He was buried as he had lived – a Welshman. He was dressed from top to toe in red, his national colour. His coffin carried a large wreath in the shape of the Welsh dragon; and as it sat on the hillside about to be lowered into the ground, with a copy of Dylan Thomas's selected verse placed there by Kate, and a sealed letter from Sally, his family suddenly burst into song with the bawdy Welsh rugby anthem, *Sospan Fach*.

The one person missing from the graveside was Elizabeth. She was said to be too distraught to make the journey from California, and sent instead a single red rose with no message. She had, in fact, stayed away out of deference to Sally. From the moment the news of Burton's death was released, the media had focussed their attention on Elizabeth. It was as though he had never been married to anyone else.

She tactfully stayed away from the memorial service held in Pontrhydfen two days later as well. There the Welsh was undiluted. There was neither a sombre dress nor a dry eye in the chapel. This was the place that had bred Richard Burton: this was where he found his passion for poetry, for music, for language and for life. There was no holy hush that attends services elsewhere. The congregation chattered cheerfully, and waved to one another. A little boy, with his legs swinging from a pew, buried his nose in an Agatha Christie novel. Then the silver-haired organist started to play, and the service began. They opened their mouths and sang as only the Welsh know how, loud-speakers carrying the sound far into the surrounding hills. The little village was a seething mass of humanity, the green fields around, and the roads as far as the eye could see, were jammed with parked cars. His body may have been laid to rest in Switzerland, but his spirit was home.

Someone who did go to the memorial in Pontrhydyfen was Euan Lloyd. Not only had Burton's death meant the loss of a good friend, it had been a professional tragedy too. His £10 million picture had lost its star, and he had had four days in which to find a replacement. His mind in turmoil, he had left his wife in Berlin and gone home to London alone to try to think. For three days and three sleepless nights he worked at finding another actor and was desperate. Then, on the Wednesday morning he was walking in Hyde Park when the last conversation he had had with Richard came into his head. Over dinner at the White Elephant, two weeks before, they had been talking about rugby, when Richard suddenly changed the subject, and asked Euan if he had seen the television series *Edward and Mrs Simpson*. A friend in Switzerland had recently lent him a video of it, he said, and he thought Edward Fox, who had played Edward VIII, had been brilliant. Euan instantly realized that Edward Fox was the perfect man for the part in *Wild Geese II*, and was convinced that Burton had been guiding him. He went straight home, rang Fox's agent to discover that the actor was available, and by Thursday the matter was signed and sealed.

Elizabeth made her pilgrimage a week later. She went first to visit Richard's grave at Celigny and then see his family at Pontrhydyfen. Both visits attracted a mass of publicity and invited scepticism from even the most faithful of her fans. She spent the night with Hilda in her little terraced house, and stood on the doorstep the next morning, flanked by Richard's brothers and sisters, and declared, 'I feel as if I am home.' For all the theatricality, Elizabeth was profoundly shattered by his death.

So was Susan. During the years since their divorce, Suzy had been building a new life for herself in California, and was on the verge of marrying again. She was in London the day she heard that Richard had died. Her boyfriend, a Virginian property developer, had left her in England while he went to Italy on business, and on the Sunday of Richard's death she was with Bette Hill, Graham's widow, watching their son Damian motor-racing. She was completely overcome when she heard about Richard, and in no state to be left alone, so Bette took her to Alan Jay Lerner and his wife Liz in Chelsea. The next day, when she had composed herself sufficiently, she rang Sally in Switzerland, and Sally was quite comforted to hear from her.

She and Sally were both at the memorial service held at the Wilshire Theater in Los Angeles for Burton on 24 August. It was a fitting tribute from the city that had given him two of his three ambitions: to be the richest and the most famous actor in the world. Eulogies was provided by stars like Frank Sinatra, George Segal and John Huston. Richard Harris broke down in the middle of his – a passage from *Richard II*, 'Let us sit upon the ground and tell sad stories of the death of kings.' While he wiped the tears from his eyes and left the stage for a moment, a Welsh choir sang 'We'll Keep a Welcome in the Hillsides'. 'If Richard had seen me a moment ago,' said Harris, 'he would have been howling with laughter.'

He would doubtless have had a gentle chuckle if he had seen his memorial service in London too. It was like the grand finale to a tragic comedy that he had been writing since he fled from the drapery department of the Co-op in Port Talbot more than forty years before.

On 30 August, the streets around St Martin-in-the-Fields were jammed solid as hundreds of sightseers packed into Trafalgar Square for what they were hoping might be the drama of the decade – Richard Burton's four glamorous wives under one roof for the first time ever. Sybil did not come, but they were not disappointed by the rest.

Elizabeth arrived first and was showed to a seat with Richard's family. The church was packed to its capacity of twelve hundred, thronged with stars and people who wanted to see the stars. The number of true friends amongst them could be counted on the fingers of two hands. Susan arrived second, late because she had been caught in the traffic, and took the organizers entirely by surprise. She had told Sally she was coming, but no one else seemed to be expecting her, so they had hurriedly to find her a seat. Last came Sally, looking a match for the other two, and took her seat beside

Brook at the front of the church. Brook sat in the place normally reserved for the widow.

Emlyn Williams, now seventy-eight, aware that he had a tight-rope to walk with his address, failed to mention Sybil or Susan at all, gave Sally the most cursory mention, and spoke as if Elizabeth had been Richard's only wife.

Lord Olivier, possibly still smarting from his last encounter with Burton in Vienna, chose not to give a reading, and did not even attend. Kate read passages from Shakespeare, as did Paul Scofield. John Gielgud had virtually been given up for lost when he finally came gliding into the church to read from *Hamlet*. He had been found motoring up Shaftesbury Avenue in the wrong direction, apparently heading for a different church altogether.

Richard would have laughed. He might not have told it quite as it happened, he might have borrowed the odd character from some-one else's memorial service, thrown in a new godchild, or had Elizabeth, Susan and Sally wrestling one another in the vestry, but you can be sure that whatever he said, it would have made a damn good story.

Epilogue

The obituary writers dwelt on Richard Burton's failures: his squandered talent, his lost opportunities, the giant that might have been. It was only half of the story. Burton undoubtedly did have great talent that he failed to utilize, but only in terms of the theatre, and the theatre was never something to which he was as committed as other people were on his behalf. He achieved what he chose from life. When he told Alan Jay Lerner that he wanted to be 'the richest, the most famous and the best actor in the world', he knew that he could not be all three. What he had gone for were the two that excited him most: the fame and fortune. And his talent for making money was something nobody could accuse him of squandering.

He made money and he gave it away with remarkable generosity, which should not be forgotten. His innumerable donations to charity were made public at the time, and some details of individual gifts came to light after his death when auditors examined the books of his London company, Bushel Investments Limited. It was run by his accountant, James Wishart, and set up purely to provide loans and presents for relatives and friends who were in need of money. There were loans of up to £6,000, some of which had never been repaid. A great many more will remain undocumented.

The £3.6 million he left in his will was a measure of how little he kept for himself, considering the colossal sums he had earned and the low tax he had paid. His estate was divided amongst his four surviving brothers and three sisters, his daughters Kate, Jessica and Maria, and his widow, Sally. There was also money for the man who made it all possible: Philip Burton.

The tragedy in Richard's story was twofold: the destructive element in his nature; and his failure to come to terms with himself. He died a lonely man, having destroyed himself as surely as he destroyed those around him. Astrologists would put it down to his birth sign, the scorpion, with the pincers and the poisonous sting in the tail. Sir John Gielgud attributed it to 'a dark Welsh streak of pessimism and carelessness'.

The more he destroyed, the less he liked himself, so that his life became one long story of escape – escape from people, from places, from relationships, from tragedy, from pain, even from his own sexuality. What he could never escape was his deep sense of morality, his working-class, Welsh, Chapel heritage that disapproved of every step along the way.

Ironically, after such difficult beginnings, life became too easy. He did not have to work for anything, his charm saw him through. Women doted on him, men doted on him. Burton went straight to the top in the theatre, and began at the top in films; and he became desperately bored. There were no risks in his life, no uncertainties to stimulate his mind, not even the pleasure of wanting.

After the war his ambition had been to collect all thousand Everyman books. When Frank Hauser bumped into him twenty-five years later he asked if he had ever got his collection. 'Oh yes,' said Richard. 'Elizabeth gave them to me for my last birthday. Leather bound.'

The little boy who once had to queue to warm his bottom against the fire in Caradoc Street had achieved his goal. But at what cost?

Sybil was once asked how she would write the final paragraph to Richard's story. 'In the final analysis only he has suffered,' she said. 'He has given an awful lot of pleasure to a lot of people but he hasn't been able to find that pleasure for himself.' That was Richard Burton's tragedy.

Index